THE GOLDEN AGE OF
FLYING BOATS

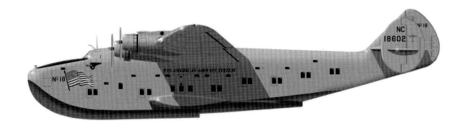

Burnt Ash Publishing

Dedicated to everyone who has had anything to do with flying boats, those who designed and built them, who flew them, maintained them, flew in them, or who are just interested in them.

First published in Great Britain by Burnt Ash Publishing in 2020

Burnt Ash Publishing
86-90 Paul Street
London
EC2A 4NE

Copyright © 2020 by Peter Pigott
Printed by Swallowtail Print
Typeset in Bookman Old Style, titles in Impact, captions in Acumin

ISBN 978-1-9162161-8-1

A CIP Catalogue for this book is available from the British Library

Contents

Acknowledgements

In researching this book, I was faced with an unprecedented challenge: there were no primary sources available. All who knew flying boats were dead and, because of the virus, their journals, letters, and diaries were inaccessible. So too were most secondary sources including libraries, aeronautical collections and heritage centers and my enquiries as to research assistance were met with apologies for the temporary suspension of services. I thus relied on online resources, the digitized archives from newspapers, magazines and airlines, chief of them: *Cleared to Land: The Records of the Pan American World Airways, Inc.* from the University of Miami Digital Collection.[1] I am grateful too for the information culled from the Foynes Flying Boat & Maritime Museum, Ireland and, in Canada, the Botwood Heritage Park and Museum, Newfoundland and the archives of government of New Brunswick, especially the town of Shediac where its Flying Boats Brewing company keeps the memories alive, brewing S-55 Pale Ale and a *Dixie Clipper* IPA. Invaluable too was the Solent Sky Museum, Southampton, and the Poole Flying Boats Celebration with its public access online archive. In Australia, the Museum of Sydney, provided research on Rose Bay and the Double Sunrise flights. One day I hope to visit the Museum of Transport and Technology in Auckland, New Zealand and drool at the Solent and Sunderland on display. I thank them all for allowing me to reconstruct the world of flying boats, bringing to life significant characters in their evolution, placing them in the historical significance of their time.

Of the few books I was able to purchase before the local postal service (and even Amazon) became overwhelmed, I owe

---

1   www.panam.org/about-pahf/pan-am-collections

a debt to Phillip E. Sims for his *Adventurous Empires: The Story of the Short Empire Flying Boats,* to James Trautman for his *Pan American Clippers: The Golden Age of Flying Boats* and to Graham Coster for: *Corsairville: The Lost Domain of the Flying Boat.* Years ago, I was given books by two men who have since died. R. E. G. Davies at the National Air and Space Museum, Washington, DC, not only signed his, *British Airways: An Airline and Its Aircraft,* for me but gave me some advice on being an aviation author I have since followed. My late father-in-law, George Stafford O'Neill, served during the war in 205 Squadron RAF and flew a Sunderland from Britain out to Koggala, Ceylon (now Sri Lanka). In 1986, when he heard I was being posted to Hong Kong with the Canadian government, he handed me a copy of Alexander Frater's enchanting *Beyond the Blue Horizon.* I know now that it is where all of this began.

This book would not have happened had Malcolm Turner, another aviation storyteller, not seen something in me. Finally, I owe everything to my wife, Donna Hudson, who, like most people knew nothing of flying boats, but was my sounding board, even while successfully battling Stage Two breast cancer.

Peter Pigott
Ottawa
Ontario

Introduction

Too young to have known flying boats and living as far inland as Ottawa, Canada, I did not expect to see one. With my dad in the airlines, I had grown up with Lockheed Constellations, Vickers Viscounts and "Daks" (Dakotas) — he had served in the Royal Air Force during the Second World War and refused to call them DC-3s.

In their search for the lost world that flying boats had been part of, the authors Alexander Frater and Graham Coster had, like archaeologists, sought out their old haunts, uncovering artifacts and interviewing former captains. But with the world convulsed in a pandemic, airlines, archives, museums, and libraries were closed. There were no reminders of these extinct half-boat half-planes around me... or so I thought.

Knowing of my interest in aviation, elderly neighbors had once told me that as children they saw a flying boat crash in our lake. Intrigued, I discovered that it was a "Canso" (the Canadian version of the Catalina) flying boat belonging to the Royal Canadian Air Force's 162 Squadron. Although a home defense unit, in January 1944, the squadron had been posted to Reykjavik, Iceland, and later Wick, Scotland. Tasked to cover the North Atlantic where German submarines were expected to break through and attack the D-Day invasion fleet, the squadron sank five U-boats, shared in the destruction of a sixth and damaged a seventh. An unforgiving Atlantic and die-hard enemy exacted their toll and in desperate battles against both, forty-two personnel had been killed. Because of what had occurred in one of these engagements, Flight Lieutenant D. E. Hornell was posthumously awarded the Victoria Cross in July 1944 — he is buried in Lerwick Cemetery, Shetland Islands and the inscription on his tombstone is a quote from the poet Milton which, as a former high school teacher, he would have appreciated. Nine of the squadron's flying boats were lost, three to enemy activity, five to accidents, and one disappeared without trace.

With VE Day, the crews flew home in June 1945. If burdened with a sense of loss at those comrades who were buried in Iceland and Scotland — and the seventeen who have no known grave, like millions worldwide, the airmen's relief at making it back alive must have been enormous. For just over the horizon, they glimpsed hometown victory parades, proud parents, impatient fiancées, and "civvy street" jobs — the future they had been fighting for.

There was to be a final mission before 162 Squadron was disbanded. One of the crews was ordered on a photographic survey of Baffin Island and they flew to Ottawa for the Canso to be outfitted. It was when they were practicing landings on our lake on 23 July that Death's scythe reached out to them. The Canso stalled on take-off and its wing tipped into the water to tear away. Onlookers watched in horror as the aircraft then flipped over and sank. It went to the lake bottom within minutes, trapping the crew inside. By the time locals (that included the children's fathers) got to the scene, it was marked by floating logbooks, oil slicks — and bodies. Five of the crew had been killed and two injured. What was left of the Canso was dragged up onto the beach that my family and I now walk on. There was no record of an inquiry and in the euphoria of VJ Day in August, the crash slipped between the cracks.

This was my introduction to flying boats and the men who flew them. In memory of what occurred on our lake, I had Veterans Affairs Canada put up a plaque at the local sailing club.

Peter Pigott
Ottawa
Ontario

1   The man who invented flying boats

I sn't it astonishing that all these secrets have been preserved for so many years" wrote Orville Wright "just so that we could discover them." With a 12-second flight on December 17, 1903 he and brother Wilbur changed our world forever. The dawn of the 20th century was a time when men with imagination, tenacity and courage could soar into the heavens, hoping like Icarus they wouldn't fall to an untimely death. To fly higher, faster, longer was an obsession of these first aviators and those who succeeded are the fathers of aviation today. As with the computer start-ups Google and Apple a century later, their beginnings were humble — tinkering in a bicycle repair shop. The bicycle craze of the day afforded these entrepreneurs the materials required to build a flying machine — wooden spars, fabric, glue, ropes and chains. The sustained belief in themselves was limited only by their finances.

That two self-taught American bicycle mechanics working in isolation had just developed the first aircraft was beyond comprehension. The brother's penchant for secrecy until 1908 meant that few knew of or believed them. The French, who, since the Montgolfier brothers, held that all things aeronautical were part of their national patrimony, did not. To most people, attempting to emulate nature whether in balloons, airships, gliders or hydroplanes was vaguely sacrilegious, and led nowhere. After all, none of the giants of aeronautical flight, including Sir George Cayley, Otto Lilienthal, Hiram Maxim and Octave Chanute, had solved the complexities of defying gravity. So how did small-town unsophisticated bicycle mechanics do it?

Lake Keuka is one of the Finger Lakes scratched by glaciers into the hills of upstate New York. Keuka means "Canoe

Landing" in the Iroquois language and the lake is long and thin, freezing in the winter. At its southern end is the town of Hammondsport with its Civil War monument, many churches and steamboats. Glenn Hammond Curtis was born here on May 21, 1878, four years after the railroad arrived. His father had a harness shop on Pulteney Street and for Curtiss it must have been a Huck Finn childhood on the lake. Those who knew him remembered that he had an intensity to improve — himself and machines. Although he excelled in mathematics, Curtiss had little use for school and left to care for a widowed mother and deaf sister. The biggest employer locally was Eastman Kodak in Rochester and initially Curtiss worked for them, until returning home he took over the harness goods shop, expanding it to bicycle repair. In 1901, he motorized a bicycle and then expanded to begin his own motorcycle business at Hammondsport. To publicize his motorcycles like the V8 Hercules, Curtiss raced them, covering a mile at the speed of 136.3 miles per hour in 1907. The newspapers called him "The Fastest Man on Earth". As the Wrights had discovered, because of the inherent instability of bicycles Curtiss found he had a natural feel for aerodynamics, and it was only a matter of time before his lightweight engines were powering airships and, later, aircraft.

Such was the fame of Hammondsport's favorite son that he was invited by Alexander Graham Bell to join the Aerial Experiment Association (AEA) at Baddeck, Nova Scotia along with T. Selfridge, J.A.D. McCurdy and F.W. Baldwin. Financed by Bell's wife, the Association set out "'to get into the air' by the construction of a practical 'aerodrome' (as Bell called 'aircraft') driven by its own motive power and carrying a man." To foster competition, Bell had each of the four young men design his own aircraft for a documented controllable flight. On March 12, 1908 Selfridge's "Red Wing" biplane took off on runners from frozen Lake Keuka and actually flew 319 feet! Because of the Wright's secrecy, this was the first public demonstration of a powered aircraft flight in the United States. But on March 17, tilted by the wind, the "Red Wing" was demolished in a crash, the members realized it needed better lateral stability.

They put rudimentary ailerons as small flaps on the wings of the next plane, Baldwin's "White Wing". On May 13 McCurdy flew it from an old nearby racetrack to a height of 20 feet and distance of 200 yards before it crashed. In June, Baldwin flew Curtiss's "June Bug" named after the flying beetles then banging on screens in the warm summer evenings, from the same track. It did so well that on the Fourth of July Curtiss himself would fly it a distance of 5,000 feet, winning the coveted *Scientific American* trophy and $2,500.

He also saw the opportunity of being the first person to perfect an aircraft capable of lifting off water. The Wrights carried a canoe for flotation in case they came down in water. Why not make the water the aircraft's natural habitat? Surrounded by lakes and rivers, Curtiss realized that such a "flying boat" would not only be safer but would dispense with airfields — such as they were — giving every Hammondsport in the world its own air service.

In December re-configuring the "Red Wing" (now renamed "Loon") with canoe-like floats, Curtiss first attempted to become airborne on the icy lake. This time it refused to leave the water — the suction created by the lake surface anchoring it down. He and McCurdy rebuilt the machine in the winter darkness but when a float was holed accidentally, it sank at the dock — at which point they wired Bell: "Submarine test most successful." Getting airborne on smooth ice was easier and returning to Baddeck, Curtiss witnessed McCurdy's "Silver Dart" take-off from a frozen lake surface on February 23, 1909 to perform the first sustained controlled flight in the British Empire. Having accomplished its mission of powered flight, the AEA then disbanded.

Once the monopoly of the Wrights, the aviation field was now crowded. At the 1909 flying meet at Rheims, France where Curtiss won the Bennett Trophy on August 29, there were 23 different aircraft which broke the Wright's speed and altitude records. The brothers had refused to enter the competition on the grounds that they didn't compete with imitators. The truth was that their aircraft, with its wing-warping controls,

Glenn Curtiss, at the controls of his "June Bug" (above) and the "Loon" (below)
which had canoe-like floats added, but failed to get airborne from water.

was obsolete. By continually innovating, Curtiss was now in the lead.

Unlike the Wrights, Curtiss relished hometown publicity and knowing the value of public opinion encouraged spectators. "Flying was such a novelty at that time," he would later write, "that nine-tenths of the people who came to watch the preparations were skeptical while others declared: 'that thing won't fly, so what's the use of waiting around?'" Instead, the Wrights put their energies into the courts, suing other aviation pioneers, the litigation destroying their business and reputations.

Growing up on Lake Keuka, Curtiss would have been familiar with the locomotion of insects and birds on water and how they overcame the surface tension to create a hydrodynamic lift and get airborne. His only other competition was Henri Fabre, a French marine engineer experimenting with hydroplanes. On

In 1910 Henri Fabre designed, built and successfully flew the world's first floatplane at Martigues, France.

March 28, 1910 Fabre would succeed in taking off from Etang de Berre, Martigues, near Marseilles, becoming the inventor of the floatplane. When $10,000 was offered for the first aircraft to fly from Albany NY to Manhattan, Curtiss saw his chance to build an actual flying boat. Much of the flight would be over the Hudson River where he could land if necessary. His "Albany Flier" the world's first practical flying boat had metal tanks as pontoons and a long tubular flotation device made of fabric and filled with cork for buoyancy.

Tests on Lake Keuka went well and May 29, 1910 he took off from an island in the Hudson River near Albany and with two fuel stops set down in New York City harbor in an actual flight time for the 143 miles of 2 hours and 51 minutes. The tubular flotation device proved unnecessary as whatever the reason, each time the flying boat left the river's surface easily.

When his motorcycle company went into receivership in the fall, hoping to attract the attention of the United States Navy, Curtiss moved to the warmer waters of North Island, San Diego for the winter months. The United States Army had just bought the Wright's Model A and with his experience of waterborne aviation he hoped the Navy would be interested. As an incentive, he offered to instruct a naval officer without charge in the construction and operation of a Curtiss hydro-airplane. Lieutenant T.G. "Spuds" Ellyson was an engineer with the skills that Curtiss lacked. The pair worked on the problem of getting airborne from the water and on January 26, 1911, one of their float configurations allowed the aircraft to rise a short distance and land. To break the suction, a longer waterplane surface and the upturned lip on the main float got the aircraft to bounce into the air. The Navy was impressed enough to order two Curtiss machines designated A-1s to be made in Hammondsport which with the naval personnel being instructed there had become an unofficial naval facility. It was the beginning of naval aviation in the United States.

Other aircraft designers like the Benoist Company of St. Louis, Missouri emulated Curtiss and designed their own hydroplanes. Even the Wright brothers who had by now lost

Sailors pull a Curtiss A-1 floatplane out of the water during trials in California (National Naval Aviation Museum, Pensacola, FL.).

their lead, built an "Aeroboat", hoping to interest the Navy with it. Through the winter of 1911–12, Curtiss concentrated on designing an actual flying boat. He envisioned a large flat-bottomed hull to which a lower wing would be attached, and the tail assembly held by an outrigger framework. A 60 hp engine that drove two tractor type propellers by means of a chain drive would be enough to get it in the air. Built at Hammondsport, the flying boat was shipped across the country to North Island for tests. But it refused to take-off, the suction keeping it glued to surface. Returning to Hammondsport with the machine, Curtiss moved the engine up between the wings, changing its center of gravity. But the aircraft still wouldn't be persuaded into the air. Something was eluding him. Then, from a motorboat running alongside the aircraft at full power, he noted the water flow around the hull. Back on shore, he made a rough sketch of his solution and asked his workmen to fasten two wooden wedges to the flat bottom. This broke the lines along the hull, reduced drag and allowed the flying boat to lift into the air. To overcome hydrostatic friction (the suction-like force that keeps flying boat hulls from breaking free of the water), Curtiss had invented the "step" — the angled break that enable the flying boat to rise off the water. Later, the F-Boat as it would be called, was given a streamlined bow and a V bottom, ending the suction problem. From that day, every flying boat built would employ the "step" principle to escape the suction. Curtiss would patent this in 1915 and hundreds of F-Boats would be built with Curtiss selling them to Russia and Japan. The first practical flying boat, it would join the 1905 Wright Flyer, the Douglas DC-3 and the Boeing 747 in changing the world.

In April 1913 the British newspaper publisher Lord Northcliffe offered the sum of £10,000 or $50,000 to the first person or persons who could successfully fly across the Atlantic Ocean in seventy-two consecutive hours without changing planes. To commemorate the peace and friendship between the United States and Great Britain, department store owner Rodman Wanamaker agreed to finance the building of such a machine with Curtiss and gave him $25,000. Working with British

The Curtiss F-Boat was the world's first practical flying boat and hundreds would be built for customers as far afield as Russia and Japan.

flying boat pioneer Lieutenant John Cyril Porte of the Royal Navy, Curtiss designed the "Curtiss-Wanamaker Transatlantic Flyer". Its upper wing was 72 feet, the lower 46 feet. It was 32 feet in length and 4 feet across at its widest. The hull was constructed of a quarter inch-thick planking attached to a wooden frame; its V bottom had a double layer of planking and the entire hull was made watertight with two layers of fabric saturated in marine glue. Curtiss's chief designer Emmitt Clayton Bedell is credited with designing the "step" built into the hull that would allow the flying boat to break clear of the water. Two pusher type 90 horsepower Curtiss OX-5 engines between the wings were to power it across the Atlantic.

In an innovation that would not be seen again until the Consolidated Commodore flying boats in 1931, the Flyer's cockpit was completely enclosed with celluloid windows for visibility. Instrumentation in the cockpit was elementary — a sextant, a magnetic compass, an anemometer and the pilot's own watches. Wanamaker had selected Porte and an American, George Hallett, for the flight. The two pilots were to be seated side by side — to symbolize the American-British partnership. Behind them were three huge tanks to hold 300 gallons of fuel. The "Transatlantic Flyer" would take-off from St. John's, Newfoundland, make for the Azores and then to Vigo, Spain, ending its flight in Plymouth, England. Today, the innocence of such an ambition boggles the mind. Without support ships en route, weather forecasts, life jackets or radio — or rescue if the aircraft came down in the Atlantic, the chances of Porte and Hallett surviving were nil. Roland Garros had barely made it across the 500 miles of the Mediterranean Sea on September 23, 1913.

Just as the Flyer was being readied that summer, Curtiss's past asserted itself. The U.S. Court of Appeals upheld the Wrights' patent suit, ruling that all other aircraft manufacturers had infringed upon the brothers' invention. Curtiss could have been closed down with disastrous results in the coming war. But Wilbur Wright had died of typhoid fever in 1912 and Orville did nothing. Vindicated, he retired from their company three years later and returned to tinkering.

In June 1914, the "Curtiss-Wanamaker Transatlantic Flyer" rechristened "America" was wheeled down to the lake, ready for its test flight. In bright red — in case it went down in the ocean — *America* was painted in white on each side of the bow and that became its name. On June 22, the newsreels recorded that all of Hammondsport came out to watch its launch. It was hard to believe that six years before everyone had marveled at the tiny "June Bug" flying 5,000 feet to capture the *Scientific American* prize. Launched with a bottle of locally grown champagne by Katherine Masson, a young woman whose father had contributed to it, the "America" slid off its cradle into the water. Taxiing trials the next day went well. The trouble began when it was loaded with 5,000 lbs. the amount of fuel it would need to reach the Azores. Now it was too heavy to leave the water. When Curtiss added a third engine over the wing (which would be shut down after take-off) it reluctantly lifted off. But the drag of the third engine with the extra fuel meant the range of the "America" would have been severely depleted and the aircraft would have come down somewhere in the ocean. The U.S. Navy would have to provide a chain of ships across the Atlantic so the "America" could leapfrog from one to another. Before this could be arranged, on June 28, the news came to Hammondsport that Archduke Franz Ferdinand, heir to the throne of Austria-Hungary had been assassinated in far-off Sarajevo. Porte was recalled to naval service in England and the flight was put on hold.

The First World War proved a bonus for flying boat designers like Glenn Curtiss, John Cyril Porte and the Short brothers Eustace and Oswald of Rochester, Kent. Submarine warfare made control of the air over the country's shoreline and fleets as vital as over the Front and flying boat patrols countered the threat effectively. As the world's pre-eminent designer, Curtiss was flooded with orders from Europe, the British alone ordering 62 "Americas" (now designated H-4s) from Hammondsport. By 1916, the contracts totaled 11 million dollars and Curtiss had to expand out of his hometown. Without the capital to do so, he cabled the British Admiralty for an advance of 75,000, leaving

A replica of the Curtiss "America" flying boat at the Glenn H Curtiss Museum
in Hammondsport, NY.

out the word "dollars" to save the cost of the extra letters,
thinking the British would understand his meaning. They did
not and sent him a draft for £75,000. With that, he was able
to convince investors to finance a factory in Buffalo, NY where
with the JN-4 trainers, the four engine triplane flying boat
the "Curtiss Model T" (commissioned by Wannamaker to fly
the Atlantic after the war) was born. Hammondsport was now
too small, and Curtiss would move his design team to Garden
City, Long Island.

The Model T was shipped to England and reconfigured by Porte
at the Seaplane Experimental Station at Felixstowe, Suffolk
with a new hull for better buoyancy. The result was Felixstowe
F series, built by the Short Brothers, the final model the F.3
laboring on through the 1920s.[1] When unrestricted submarine
warfare prompted the United States to enter the war, the U.S.
Navy required 864 Curtiss H-16 flying boats and contracts were

1 In 1920, a Felixstowe F.3 would make it as far inland as the middle of Canada when
the Canadian Air Board would sponsor the first Trans Canada flight for a future
airmail service. Using rivers and lakes along the way, the leg from Riviere du Loup
on the South shore of the St. Lawrence river, Quebec to Winnipeg was flown by
Lieutenant Colonel Leckie and Major Hobbs in a Felixstowe F.3.

spread around other manufacturers including Boeing. By war's end Curtiss's flying boats had patrolled hundreds of miles of the ocean, escorted convoys and sunk U-boats.

His ambition of conquering the Atlantic came true in 1919. With the Armistice, Lord Northcliffe renewed his £10,000 offer and contenders for crossing the Atlantic appeared. Using landplanes, three British teams, Harry Hawker and Lieut. Cmdr. K.F. Mackenzie-Grieve, Capt. John Alcock and Lt. Arthur Whitten Brown, as well as Admiral Mark Kerr, had arrived in Newfoundland to attempt transatlantic flights. Commander John Towers proposed that the U.S. Navy use the competition as an opportunity demonstrate the capabilities of its latest flying boats. The NCs for "Navy Curtiss" were to be Curtiss's swansong and he minutely scrutinized their assembly. Powered by four Liberty engines, with a wingspan of 68 feet, the hull 10 feet wide, 45 feet long, with watertight doors and primitive radio direction-finding equipment, the NCs (called "Nancies" by the media) would demonstrate the pre-eminence of American aviation technology and emerging military strength of the United States in the post-war world. As this was for national honor, the crews were forbidden to accept the prize money if they won.

Nothing was left to chance. Sixty-eight destroyers were stationed at fifty-mile positions across the Atlantic. When notified by radio, each would fire star shells until the planes passed overhead and then a searchlight would be turned on to indicate surface wind direction. A young naval officer Lieut. Richard E. Byrd designed bubble sextants for the aerial navigation.

On May 8, three NCs (NC-2 would be cannibalized for spare parts) flown by naval pilots some of them Curtiss-trained, took off from the Naval Air Station at Rockaway, NY. They flew to Halifax, Nova Scotia and then to Trepassey Bay, Newfoundland to wait out the fog over the Atlantic. A break in the fog and the news that Harry Hawker and McKenzie-Grieve were about to take-off caused them to make for the Azores on May 16. The slowest, NC-1 was lost in fog and came down in the Atlantic, the crew rescued but the aircraft sank. Towers, flying NC-3, would take the wrong bearing and, soon low on fuel, would put down in the ocean. The flying boat would taxi for 200 miles and arrive in the Azores 2 days later, weather-beaten and balanced by the crew sitting on the wings.

After fifteen hours in the air, the NC-4 commanded by Lt. A.C. Read reached Horta in the Azores on May 17th. It took off on May 20 for Portugal, but mechanical trouble forced it to return. The flying boat would touch down in Lisbon harbor at 9 pm on the 27th to be greeted by crowds on the waterfront. They would leave two days later and stopping at Figueira and Ferrol along the way, arrive at Plymouth on the 31st - the total flying time from Rockaway was 57 hours and 16 minutes. Here too, huge crowds welcomed them, with one newspaper calling Read the Christopher Columbus of the twentieth century. An aircraft had conquered the Atlantic — and it was a flying boat. Every Clipper that would cross an ocean in years to come, owed a debt to the NC-4 and the man who had designed and built it.

(Below) The Curtiss NC-4, the aircraft that conquered the Atlantic in 1919, is preserved at the National Naval Aviation Museum at Pensacola, FL.
(Opposite) Glenn Curtiss in 1909.

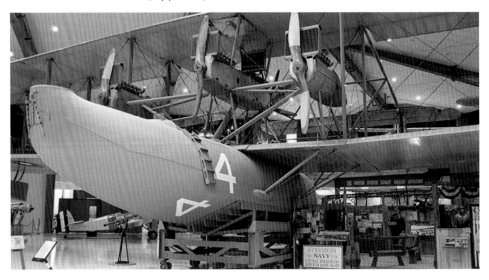

Glenn Curtiss died on July 23, 1930 at the age of 52. He had moved to Florida by then and retired from his company which had merged with his archenemies to become the Curtiss-Wright Corporation. His funeral service was held in the Episcopal Church in Hammondsport that he knew well, and he is buried in the family plot in Pleasant Valley cemetery, not far from where the "June Bug" was launched. Except for the Glenn H. Curtiss Aviation Museum, Lake Keuka and Hammondsport

returned to complete obscurity, though.[2]

The "America" was never to cross the Atlantic, but its descendants have. Every flying boat from the Pan American Boeing 314, the Short Empire Class, the PBY Catalinas and Howard Hughes' "Spruce Goose" can trace their bloodlines to this single aircraft. Curtiss's life was a Horatio Alger story in which a boy from a small town, through energy and purpose, fulfills his ambition to make the flying boat a reality.

2 I used to help run the annual Ottawa Air Show and one year met an American Airlines pilot James Harlan "Jim" Poel. He and his wife Lovada took me up in their Seabee. Jim was a pilot's pilot and his passion for seaplanes led him to the birthplace of seaplane aviation at Hammondsport. As chief pilot for the Glenn H. Curtiss Museum, Jim helped restore and fly some of the most famous machines in seaplane history. This included the 1910 Curtiss Albany, the Hudson Flyer and the 1911 Curtiss A-1 Triad. Together with his friend and co-pilot, Lee Sackett, Jim flew the 1914 flying boat *America* over Keuka Lake in Hammondsport in 2008 and in 2009. Poel died January 29, 2011 and is honored at the Smithsonian.

A viation is usually about the technical possibilities and promise of the future, except for flying boats, which are steeped in history, romance and nostalgia. To fully appreciate why they evolved as they did in Britain, one has to trace the 15-year progression of Imperial Airways from cross-Channel hops by former Handley Page bombers in 1924, to Short C-Class flying boats landing at Durban, South Africa, Port Washington, New York and Sydney, Australia in 1939.

One of the very few benefits of World War 1, in which millions died, were the advances in aviation. In a reworking of the sword to ploughshares theme, aircraft built to bomb civilians a hundred miles from the Front, were now transformed into "argosies of the air". And unlike the unemployed ex-soldiers, with their military training, pilots could earn a living flying them. Aircraft manufacturers, their pipeline of government orders turned off by the Armistice, expediently modified military designs to attract airline entrepreneurs.

Even before the guns fell silent, in August 1918, Curtiss's pre-war colleague John Cyril Porte, now a Lieutenant Commander, had engineered the largest flying boat ever built, the Felixstowe Fury. But as Howard Hughes would discover with his "Spruce Goose" in 1945, the war's end meant that there was little interest in the "Porte Super Baby". The window of opportunity to publicize the aircraft closed quickly, and as he had attempted at Hammondsport, Porte seized on the race across the Atlantic. But in May 1919, as the Fury was being prepared for shipment to Cape Broyle, Newfoundland to enter, the news came that Curtiss's NC-4 had won. In what seems like a desperate cry for attention, the five engine triplane was then readied for an 8,000 mile odyssey around Africa, from Plymouth to Cape

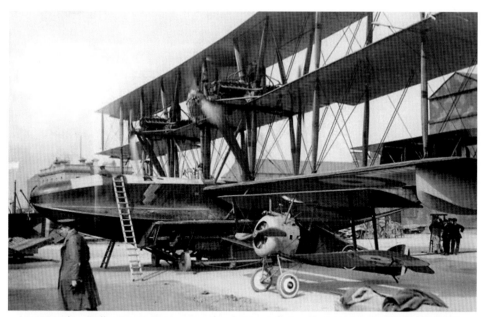

In 1918 the Felixstowe Fury was the largest flying boat ever built. A Sopwith Camel is parked in the foreground to show the scale of the Fury. The prototype later crashed into Felixstowe harbor with one fatality.

Town. Unfortunately, on a trial flight on August 11, 1919, the behemoth stalled and collapsed into Felixstowe harbor, killing one of its seven-person crew. The unfulfilled potential of the Fury was a blow to more than Porte who died of tuberculosis two months later. Had it been developed further it might have put the British aviation industry in the forefront of flying boat design. The United States would retain the lead in transatlantic flying boat technology followed by the Germans, Italians and French. It would be almost two decades before another British flying boat would attempt the Atlantic.

In May 1919, when commercial aviation was no longer forbidden in Britain, Thomas Cook began to advertise aerial sightseeing trips over London and southeast England, publicizing flying in their brochure "Aerial Travel for Business or Pleasure". In optimism (or desperation) with the glut of surplus warplanes and unemployed pilots, manufacturers began flights from London to Paris, Amsterdam and Brussels. At about 200 miles away, the European capitals were within reach and pilots navigated by "the iron compass" i.e. following railway lines — with place names painted on the station roofs — and rivers. The only hazard that they encountered was 40 miles of Channel between Lympne, Kent and Saint Inglevert, north of Boulogne, France.

An aviation visionary, George Holt Thomas was first off the mark. He had founded AIRCO to build light bombers during the war, hiring a young Geoffrey de Havilland as a designer. As early as 1916, Holt Thomas began Aircraft Transport & Travel Ltd (AT&T) at the RAF training camp at Hounslow Heath but had to wait until the Armistice before flights could begin. His first customers were businessmen. Department store owner Harry Gordon Selfridge (who in 1909 had displayed Louis Bleriot's aircraft at his store), on an unknown day in June 1919, hired an AIRCO D.H.9 from AT&T to fly from Hendon to Dublin, before his rivals could, to buy the Brown Thomas store on Grafton Street. With a refueling stop at Chester, Selfridge and pilot arrived at RAF Baldonnell in 3 hours, 15 minutes.

W.H. Pilkington of the St. Helen's glass firm who had read that commercial flights were now allowed, telephoned AIRCO on July 14, 1919, requesting a flight to Paris the next day. A D.H.9A, barely converted from its bombing purpose (both Pilkington and the pilot Captain H. "Jerry" Shaw ex-RAF sat in open cockpits) took him from Hounslow Heath to Paris in 2 hours 45 minutes. It cost Pilkington £50 and he returned home by air the next day, so well satisfied by this new form of transport that in years to come he would fly to Australia by Imperial Airways and during the war on Pan American flying boat from Lisbon to the United States. The first scheduled daily service to Paris began on August 25, when E.H. "Bill" Lawford (said to be a burly amiable man who loved Wagner) flew a AT&T D.H.4A to Le Bourget in two-hours, 20 minutes. The aircraft carried newspapers, grouse, several jars of Devonshire cream and a single passenger, George Stevenson-Reece, of the *Evening Standard.* The return flight was bumpy and on landing at Hounslow, Mr. Stevenson-Reece was sick in his hat.

To bomb Berlin (as London had been as recently as May 20, 1918 by Zeppelin-Staaken R.VIs), Frederick Handley Page built the four-engine 0/1500, the largest airplane of the war. The Armistice prevented its use as a bomber but on December 13, 1918 the 0/1500 would be used to fly to Karachi via Malta, Cairo and Baghdad, the first aircraft to do so. Using the smaller twin engine 0/400s, Handley Page Transport began a passenger service on September 2, 1919 from its Cricklewood plant to Paris. Brussels and Amsterdam were added in 1920 and Basle and Zürich in 1923. With their 100 foot wingspan, the 0/400s impressed passengers, their twin Rolls-Royce Eagle engines promising safety, especially over the Channel. In the cockpit, the pilot sat on the right, the flight engineer on his left. With the front gun taken out, two unfortunate passengers could be fitted into the gunner's cockpit, wearing helmets and goggles. Within, seated on wicker chairs separated by a single aisle, 7 and later 14 passengers enjoyed panoramic views from the 0/400's large windows. Handley Page Transport would also provide a lunch from baskets (the first meals ever in an aircraft) and the later model W.8 would be the first airliner to have a lavatory.

Capitalizing on the fame of the Vickers Vimy (as used by Alcock and Brown to cross the Atlantic and later the brothers Ross and Keith MacPherson Smith to Australia), in October 1919, the shipping company S. Instone & Co. Ltd operated Vickers "Commercials" from Birmingham and Cardiff to Paris, Brussels and Cologne. Marketed as "Vickers Vimy Rolls-Royce Limousines", they had "a well-ventilated cabin fitted with mahogany beams, upholstered armchairs and sliding triplex glass windows." In 1922, with its maritime experience, Instone would introduce blue serge uniforms with brass buttons for pilots and staff — a first in commercial aviation.

The only flying boat airline in Britain was British Marine Air Navigation (BMAN) which on September 28, 1919 would begin operating from the Supermarine works at Woolston, Southampton to St. Peter Port in the Channel Islands. Designed by R.J. Mitchell of future Spitfire fame, the Supermarine Sea Eagle amphibian used was powered by a Rolls-Royce 360 horsepower engine in pusher configuration and its 6 passengers

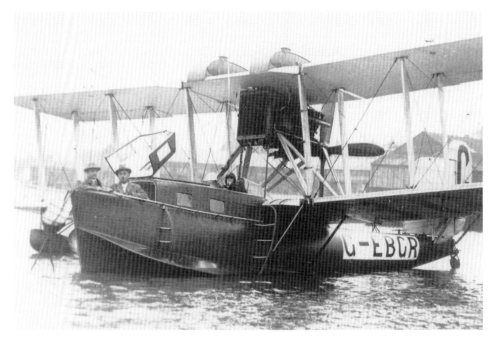

Supermarine Sea Eagles of British Marine Air Navigation operated Europe's first scheduled flying boat services.

sat in an enclosed cabin. The first scheduled passenger service by a flying boat in Europe, the hope was that BMAN would connect with the ocean liners at Cherbourg, but this never materialized.

There was an ambivalence to fixed wing commercial aviation in post Great War Britain. Aircraft were too slow, cramped, unsafe, and they were limited by nightfall and poor weather. Travel by plane in 1919 was for masochists – and affluent ones at that. The country had an extensive rail and ferry network and only the adventuresome flew. As much as airlines attempted to seduce them in the press, flying did not appeal to the public whose ideals were based upon the comforts of ocean liners and train travel. A more practical alternative were airships, especially over long distances like the Atlantic Ocean. The British airship R.34 proved this was possible when it made the first east-west crossing of the Atlantic on July 6, 1919, returning home successfully on July 13. Organized aerial excursions by airships had begun in Germany as early as November

16, 1909 with the birth of the world's first airline DELAG.[1] Its two airships, the *Viktoria Luise*, in 489 flights carried 2,995 fare-paying passengers in total, and the *Sachsen*, which carried 2,465 passengers before being handed over for military purposes. In 1911, the Thomas Cook travel company made an agreement with a Lucerne-based company of hoteliers to sell tickets for airship travel round the lake. To politicians and the public alike, until 1930, much was expected from airships, but less from aircraft, their immature cousins.

What impressed everyone, especially the man in the street who couldn't afford to fly to Paris, was airmail — the internet of the day. All four airlines vied for the Post Office contracts — mail bags were much less of a nuisance than passengers — and the first public overseas airmail service from London to Paris began on November 11, 1919. The service quickly extended to The Netherlands, Belgium and connected with the French airlines to Morocco the following year. For those who actually ventured as passengers in an aircraft, it was a slow, cold and deafening experience fraught with fear of the wings folding or engine failing. Contrary to popular belief, passengers were not issued with parachutes.

The airlines suggested that they wear "fur-lined coats, lined combination suits, mackintosh combination suits, fur-lined helmets plain helmets and a pair of goggles."[2] Pilots thus flew under the weather — if the cloud cover was 200 feet, they flew at 150 feet. The air sickness brought on by low altitude turbulence — which would always plague flying boat passengers — delayed the introduction of meals onboard. "Instead, the British," Carol Wright wrote in *Tables In The Sky*: "with somewhat Victorian sensibility, prided themselves on the provision of lavatories. They also provided aluminum cuspidors for sickness while the Germans gave cardboard cartons and the French handed out paper bags."[3]

1 Deutsche Luftschiffahrts-Aktiengesellschaft German Airship Transportation Corporation Ltd.

2 Cabin heating derived from air circulated around the hot engine exhausts (the basic idea still in use today) and began when the three-engine W.8f G-EBIX built in 1924 for Imperial Airways was equipped with this.

3 Carol Wright, *Tables In The Sky*, London: W.H. Allen & Co. 1985, P. 1–11.

Waddon, a former Royal Flying Corps (RFC) airfield in Croydon, South London became the city's first airport — the location chosen so that aircraft from the Continent no longer flew over the city. The 4,000 foot grass runways between Plough Lane and the Waddon Water Works, clipped by a horse-drawn mower, were extended. In 1921, the world's first "Aerodrome Control Tower" was built at Croydon.[4] With nothing to compare it to, the unknown architects gave the Tower a balcony, large windows in all four walls, and a wind vane on the roof with a "geared-down indicator" inside that would allow the control officer to "read changes of wind". There were three clocks on the airfield side of the Tower balcony so pilots could synchronize their own aircraft clocks for the correct time. A high speed pneumatic vacuum tube communication system connected the air traffic controllers in the Tower with the Meteorological Office and the Commandant's office. The Pyrotechnic Store where the rockets were kept for the Duty Officer to fire on foggy nights was mounted on the terminal's roof. As Plough Lane separated the maintenance hangars from the passenger terminal, a one-armed official carrying a red flag at a level crossing, (the missing arm had been amputated by a mahogany propeller) controlled traffic. A radio mast and "Radio Position Fixing" from the Control Tower would be approved by the Air Ministry in 1922. Croydon opened on March 29, 1920 and the first aircraft to land was a Compagnie des Grands Express Aeriens (CGEA) Farman Goliath from Le Bourget, a portent that the British taxpayer was paying for aerodrome facilities that soon would be used exclusively by foreign airlines.

The British airlines not only competed with each other for traffic to the same destinations but also with their government-subsidized French, Dutch and German counterparts. Fearful of a revived Germany, from the start, the French supported their airlines as auxiliaries to their air force. Without colonies and forbidden to build military aircraft, the Germans focused instead on technical achievements and as early as June 1919,

---

4 The Swiss architect Henri Lossier would design the world's first airport terminal building at Le Bourget in 1922, the reinforced concrete structure still evident today.

Junkers had built the historic all metal, cantilever wing "F-13" for its own airline, Junkers Luftverkehr AG. The British government's *laissez faire* attitude to commercial aviation was limited to the provision of aerodromes like Croydon and nothing more. Winston Churchill the first Secretary of State for the Air (1919–1921) spoke for many when he stated that airlines in Britain should "stand on their own feet."[5] The government had not supported other means of transport and this would set an expensive precedent, especially with much of the country's merchant fleet sunk during the war. But, nevertheless, Churchill was persuaded to endorse the recommended subsidies.

Thus, within a year of operation, commercial aviation in Britain was in a sorry state. Traffic was too seasonal — in 1920 of the 6,716 passengers flown between Britain and Continental Europe, 3,106 were carried in the third quarter (July, August, September). Operating an air company meant balancing expenses against profitability: there was a limit as to how much fuel could be loaded without decreasing space for revenue-earning mails, passengers and luggage. Not only were the British airlines competing with foreign fare cutting but they were also being bankrupted by their own ex-military aircraft. The more passengers that aircraft could carry, the cheaper they were to operate. The ex-military planes like a D.H.4A (4 passengers) were uneconomical to operate, their costs so high that even with a one hundred percent load — and that was rare — they still lost money.[6]

Never meant for prolonged use, the intricately rigged Handley Page 0/400s were dangerously unreliable, hence

---

5 His lack of enthusiasm for civil flight may have been because of an accident in the summer of 1919 in which he crashed while piloting an airplane during a flying lesson. While Churchill escaped with bruising, his instructor broke both legs, and Churchill thenceforth gave up piloting airplanes, that is until January 1942 when he famously took control of the Boeing 314 "Berwick" on the way home from meeting President Roosevelt.

6 "The total operating costs of the private operating companies between August 1919 and March 1924 averaged around 110 pence per capacity ton-mile, against a revenue of 56.0 pence per ton-mile." Peter G. Masefield, *Some Economic Factors in Air Transport Operation*, Journal of the Institute of Transport, March 1951.

the nine emergency landing sites en route to Le Bourget. Wing Commander R.H. McIntosh who flew the 0/400 on the London-Paris run soon found out that flying in peacetime was much harder work than military flying. Wrestling with the uneven controls all the way to Le Bourget was exhausting and engine failure was so frequent that the pilots always carried chewing gum, insulation tape, and a small botte of ether. If the oil gauge showed the engine had overheated: "We would land in the nearest field, switch off the motor, find the leak, and then stick chewing gum over the hole and bind it with insulation tape. Then we would scrounge some water from a house and fill the radiator. Now the problem was to start the engine again, especially in the winter. So, what we used to do was take out a couple of plugs, put in a teaspoonful of ether, put the plugs back, then churn round and wait for the bang. It was quite successful."[7] Captain Gordon Olley reported that on a flight to Paris, he once had to make 17 landings to pump petrol into the tank.

To avoid the weather (or at least the worst of it), pilots crossed the Channel at no more than 40 feet above the water. There was no meteorological information available and consequently not knowing the winds, they ran out of fuel frequently and had to find a beach to put down. Forced landings were quite common, McIntosh wrote. "I remember on one occasion we had Charlie Chaplin aboard, and owing to bad weather, we landed on Boulogne sands. He was immaculately dressed in a blue suit and a blue Melton coat and crowds gathered round, with quite a lot of children. Eventually it got out who he was, and he was amused at the people, who were running up and down doing his famous walk."[8]

When on December 14, 1920 a 0/400 hit a tree in the London suburb of Golders Green, killing four passengers, as the first recorded airliner crash in history, commercial aviation

7 Kenneth Hudson & Julian Pettifer, *Diamonds in The Sky. A Social History of Air Travel*, The Bodley Head, 1979. P.16.
8 Ibid P.17. Wing Commander R.H. McIntosh, DFC. AFC known as 'All-Weather Mac', died on April 9, 1983 aged 88. His flying career beginning with the RFC and then Imperial Airways and BOAC spanned 54 years between 1917 and 1971.

received much adverse publicity. Three days later, Handley Page ceased operations, Instone did so in February 1921 and AT&T would be purchased by Daimler Airways in 1922. The prospect that soon, Britain, a nation that considered itself the strongest military power in the world, would be completely dependent on foreign airlines to carry its citizens and the Royal Mail, was humiliating. National prestige (to say nothing of a systematic approach to commercial aviation) was at stake and government subsidies (in the form of airmail contracts) were grudgingly given in March 1921 so the airlines could resume flying. This did little to prevent the former military aircraft from continuing to fall out of the sky, especially the Handley Pages. On December 30, 1921 a 0/400 (G-EATM) crashed at Berck-sur-Mer, France without causalities but on 14 January 1922 on approach to Le Bourget another (G-EATN), crashed, killing all 5 onboard.

From the very birth of commercial aviation, the clientele appealed to were wealthy — they had to be. For one thing, on scheduled flights, airlines did not then insure against liabilities like air crashes (which were frequent) and the passengers had to insure themselves for very large sums of money, depending on their wealth. Not until the Air Navigation (Consolidation) Order 1923 which defined strict licensing requirements for aircraft and personnel came into effect, would the British Aviation Insurance Group be established and, even then, the premiums for flying at night or over the Channel were exorbitant.

Daimler Airways, AT&T's new owner, targeted those who crossed the Atlantic on the great ocean liners of the day and entrained to the French Riviera on *Le Train Bleu.* Owned by the luxury car firm of Daimler, it would buy new nine-seater de Havilland 34s to fly them to Paris. Made aware that through its cars, the airline had royal patronage, (even carrying "By Appointment" on its timetable) Daimler Airways' passengers were chauffeured to Croydon from the Hotel Victoria, London (all others were put on a charabanc) and at Le Bourget, were met by more chauffeur-driven Daimler limousines to begin a tour of Europe.

To help their privileged charges ignore the aircraft's headache-inducing roar, nauseating fuel fumes and bumpy ride, Daimler Airways would employ slightly built teenage "cabin boys" like 14-year-old Jack Sanderson to look after them. Trained at the Savoy Hotel, London, they wore page boy uniforms – tight trousers and monkey jackets and before take-off distributed pre-packed lunch boxes filled with a selection of fruit and sandwiches. As with the passengers, the boys were weighed before the flight and, if over seven stone, were fined. It was thought they were more for decoration than any real service — Daimler using the same psychology as when young women were hired as stewardesses in later years — to help the travelers stay calm. Sadly, five days after its first flight to Paris, on April 7, 1922 a Daimler Airways aircraft collided in the mist with a CGEA Farman Goliath and among the six killed was Sanderson, the first flight attendant to die in a plane crash. After that, the service was discontinued.

Commercial aviation in Britain between the wars was shaped for better or worse by men of their time — Edwardian dreamers — aviation enthusiasts unschooled in revenue management or aeronautics and self-serving politicians. Described as an air travel "propagandist", Sir Sefton Branckner a director on the AT&T board was appointed Director General of Civil Aviation in 1922. He evangelized that Britain's future, "lay in the air, just as our past has come from the sea." Britain was a nation of seamen, Brancker would write, and to keep its place in the world it had to become a nation of airmen. Anglo-Saxons were particularly well suited for the work of pilots; in fact, he thought that they were superior to any other race in this.[9]

Sir Samuel Hoare, Secretary of State for Air (1922-1929) was passionate about both military and commercial aviation and fighting for the independence of the Royal Air Force, he would send it on publicity flights to the ends of the Empire. In his autobiography, Hoare wrote that his interest lay in imperial possibilities: "brought up in the days of Rudyard Kipling, Joseph

9 *Wings versus The Trident : Famous Authority Says Britain's Future Greatness Lies In the Air,* MacLean's Magazine, Sept 1, 1925. p.12

32

Chamberlain and Milner, I saw in the creation of air routes the chance of uniting the scattered countries of the Empire and the Commonwealth." But as with many of his generation, it was his belief in the practicalities of airships over aircraft — their abilities to fly continuously day and night over great distances without refueling — that led to the government investing in the Imperial Airship Scheme and building two airship prototypes, the R-100 and R-101. Once in operation, Hoare promised they would foster Imperial unity. By their very size and majestic movement, airships were the dreadnoughts of the air — awe-inspiring and memorable — whereas sputtering, crashing aircraft were just dangerous. The Burney Airship Scheme had captured the collective imagination of those who governed the Empire. As a result, public money spent on airships diverted funds from aircraft development, especially from the designing of aircraft capable of flying long-distance routes.

Sir Philip Sassoon, Parliamentary Under-Secretary of State for Air, (1924–29 and 1931–37) cast a long shadow over civil aviation in Britain. Having inherited wealth with a baronetcy, beginning in 1919, he flew a series of his own aircraft, using them, it is said, in a way that poorer people used their motor cars. A cousin of the poet Siegfried Sassoon, he was influential and politically ambitious, achieving the zenith of his power when Neville Chamberlain became prime minister. Twice Under-Secretary of State for Air, Sassoon was an early advocate of Imperial's ambitions, especially to India where his family had made their fortune — even donating two DH Gypsy Moths to the Bombay Flying Club. Although he affected the role of a self-depreciating effete aesthete, Sassoon would pilot his own aircraft to Sudan, Persia and India to scout out routes for Imperial Airways. His book, *The Third Route,* about the flights is half travelogue, half pilot's manual. Trent Park, one of his London houses had its own airfield and was used by another pilot, HRH The Prince of Wales.[10] When Sassoon died in 1939, aged 50, of complications from the flu, his ashes were scattered by plane over his airfield.

---

10 During the Second World War, Trent Park was requisitioned by the government and high-ranking German prisoners of war were incarcerated there. Their rooms were "bugged" and German Jews were tasked with secretly recording and transcribing their conversations.

As to the Band-Aid mail subsidies keeping the struggling airlines in the air, Hoare appointed a Civil Air Transport Committee under the chairmanship of Sir Herbert Hambling to make recommendations on the future of commercial aviation in Britain. On February 15, 1923 the Committee reported back that a commercial organization be created out of the faltering airlines which would "show the flag" and operate on business principles. A subsidy of £1,000,000 would be given it for start-up costs, to be paid in diminishing terms over a ten years period by which time it would be self-supporting.

After a summer of bitter wrangling with the four airlines (who saw it as a shotgun marriage) the Air Ministry merged them under the Imperial Air Transport Co. Ltd Act. The company was initially called British Air Transport Service (BATS), until George Woods Humphery, given the onerous task as its general manager, realised that Imperial Air Transport Ltd sounded better. Not quite the state airline that its European rivals Lufthansa and Air France would one day be, Imperial Airways (as it became on March 31, 1924) was a private monopoly subsidized by the government that would pay an annual dividend to shareholders. There were two stipulations: that only British pilots be hired and that they would be part of the Royal Air Force Reserve, and British aircraft and engines be used exclusively. Secondly, because only on long distances could aircraft compete with surface transport, the government's "chosen instrument" was now to pioneer routes throughout the Empire — South Africa, India and Australia for a future airmail service. The British were late in this as the French, with more fortunate geography, were already subsidizing scheduled air services to Morocco, Tunisia and Algeria in addition to European countries. From now on, whatever party was in power, the limited funds allocated to commercial aviation by a suspicious Treasury would be spent in Imperial establishing distant routes far away from European and American competition.

Imperial Airways began life with a pilots' strike, a motley collection of weary ex-warplanes unsuited to commercial aviation and an air crash on the edge of the airfield. The company's nineteen pilots were status-conscious, ex-RFC individualists, who could have stepped out of the *Boy's Own Paper*. If some gave out signed photos of themselves like movie stars, a few were true air aces like Walter Raymond Hinchcliffe[11] and Albert E. Woodbridge, who was credited with wounding the "Red Baron" Manfred von Richthofen in 1917.[12] Imperial had not offered them contracts, just a small retainer and promise of payment of miles flown. No longer adored by the public as dashing 'Knights of the Air', the pilots complained that they were being treated like common engine drivers. There was some truth to that — the company chairman, Sir Eric Geddes, acknowledged that he knew nothing about commercial aviation (who did?) but had managed railways in the United States, India and Britain.

---

11 Known as "Hinch", Hinchcliffe had lost an eye during the war. He would disappear over the Atlantic with Elsie MacKay in 1928 trying to set an east-west record.

12 One of the four Albatross D.V.s that he and Donald Cunnell claimed, on July 6, 1917, was piloted by Manfred von Richthofen the " Red Baron." Still suffering from the head wound, Richthofen returned to flying and was shot down either by Australian gunners or Roy Brown on April 21, 1918.

Alan Cobham's DH.50 floatplane in India in 1926, en route to Australia
(RAF Museum).

Alan Cobham lands his DH.50 floatplane beside Parliament, having completed a 26,000-mile round trip to Australia. A million people lined the banks and bridges to greet him (RAF Museum).

Their profession was so new in a class-conscious Britain that no one knew where the pilots "fitted". When Woods Humphery saw one lounging around the terminal, he threw him out — only to discover that it was a passenger waiting for a delayed flight.

The strike was soon settled — the pilots realizing that Imperial Airways was the sole employer of civil pilots in Britain, and the first flight left Croydon for Le Bourget on April 26. A Brussels-Cologne service began on May 3, and a Manchester-Amsterdam-Hanover-Berlin service, in conjunction with Deutsche Aero-Lloyd AG, on June 2. The company's first air crash occurred on December 24 that year, a mile and a half from Croydon, near Purley, when a DH.34 (G-EBBX) nosedived into the ground, overturned and burst into flame, the fireball killing the pilot and seven passengers.

Now mandated to link the distant parts of the Empire together by air, Imperial was fortunate to have Alan Cobham as its pathfinder. A larger than life personality, Cobhman and his "flying circus" had already inspired hundreds of boys to become pilots. Six months after the inaugural flights, on November 10, using a D.H.50, he would fly 18,000 miles to India, taking Sir Sefton Branckner with him.[13] On June 16, 1925 he would reconnoitre a future Imperial Airways route from Cairo to Cape Town, South Africa, in a DH.50 floatplane. By June 30, 1926, Cobham had flown from the Medway to Australia, in an epic journey of 47 days, reaching Melbourne on August 15. On return to England, he would dramatically alight on the Thames opposite the Houses of Parliament on October 1, to deliver a petition about the benefits and importance of civil aviation to the nation. The next day Hoare would announce that King George V had conferred a knighthood on Cobham.

The ultimate goal was an air service to India, Australia and South Africa (Canada was to be reached by airship) and a first step towards this was to cross Europe, the Mediterranean and the Arabian desert. Each segment of the route presented Imperial with major problems such as refueling stations, traffic rights and the need for more reliable aircraft engines that could cope with desert temperatures. As a subsidized airline, it would be scrutinized by the gnomes of the Treasury, and throughout its history, only allowed to buy the minimum number of aircraft needed. In 1925, the Air Ministry would order for Imperial two tri-motor aircraft directly off the drawing board from different manufacturers — the De Havilland DH.66 Hercules and the Armstrong Whitworth Argosy, both of which were to be used in the Middle East and Africa.

---

13 An indication of the penury that commercial aviation faced was Branckner's flight. Initially, the Air Ministry instructed him to travel by sea because, *Flight* magazine reported, "A very 'Scotch' Treasury failed to see any obligation" to finance his journey by air. Cobham went to see Hoare, who was sympathetic but could offer only to donate the cost of the sea voyage towards an air journey. Cobham then set out to raise the balance himself from the private sector. Fortunately, he was able to do so.

Designed to carry 20 passengers and thereby break even, the Argosy made commercial aviation almost profitable. Initially put on the high-density European routes, its first flight from Croydon to Le Bourget was on July 16, 1926. The pilot still sat above the cabin in an open cockpit — it was his profession's choice — and while the passengers could slide the windows open, with the Jaguar radial engine and propeller mere feet away, this was ill-advised. To compete against the "Golden Arrow" service on Continental Railways, beginning May 1927, Imperial Airways would employ its first stewards for a luxury service marketed as 'Silver Wing' between Croydon and Le Bourget. Charles Lindbergh had landed at the French airport that month, giving Le Bourget a social cachet that (although Amy Johnson would fly to Australia from Croydon in 1930), the London airport would never achieve.

The Great War had demonstrated the power of propaganda and to "put bums on seats", the airlines ensured that the public's attention was drawn away from the cold and crashes and towards their passengers — or at least to their titles, notoriety or current celluloid status. If flying was good enough for royalty, matinee idols and millionaires, it had to be good enough for plebeians. Paris in the 1920s was jazz, Coco Chanel, Cole Porter and Salvador Dali, a 'moveable feast' to quote Ernest Hemingway, one of its residents, and rather than enduring four hours by train and ferry, flying there was artistically appropriate. Equivalent in snob appeal to flights on the British Airways Concorde five decades later, regular 'Silver Wing' passengers were Douglas Fairbanks, the Mountbattens, Charlie Chaplin, Fred Astaire, King Faisal of Iraq, the King and Queen of Belgium and authors like Freeman Willis Croft and Agatha Christie who would write one of her short stories *Death In The Clouds* in flight — (the murder would take place on the return flight to Croydon).

Then as now, the ultimate in celebrity status was royalty and Handley Page would even name their W.8s after the King's children Princess Mary, Prince Henry and Prince George. Although His Majesty had initially forbidden his sons from entering an aircraft (which only made them defy him), the princes patronized Imperial from the start — and the company's monthly bulletin made sure everyone knew. The first member of the royal family to fly commercially was HRH Prince George who traveled incognito in 1927 as a passenger for shopping trip to Paris.[14] He would make up for his reticence in 1931 when he and HRH The Prince of Wales concluded their tour of South America.[15] The pair rewarded themselves with a brief sojourn in Paris and flew home from Le Bourget on April 29 on the Imperial Airways Argosy *City of Glasgow.* Escorted by five RAF Siskin fighter planes, the airliner landed at Windsor Park ("a stone's throw from Windsor Castle" the Airways bulletin ensured the newspapers), where Their Majesties, the Duke of York and members of the Royal Household were on hand to greet them as they alighted.

Until the artist Theyre Lee-Elliott designed the modernist "Speedbird" in 1932 for Imperial Airways (the original is in the Victoria & Albert Museum), the airline's original logo was the "Silver Wing". It was printed on menus, postcards, writing paper and envelopes, all available to passengers from the steward.

A warm lunch, the first time a cooked meal had ever been served in a plane, was included in the Silver Wing return fare of 11 Guineas (£11.55, equivalent to about £700 today). Typical fare was a cold salmon salad and Chablis served on the way to Paris and on return French cream cakes and tea. Having bought the ingredients on the way to Croydon, the stewards made it in the airport's kitchens before departure. With two seats removed in the cabin a bar was set up and alcohol served without charge. As in all aircraft then, cooking

---

14 As with Princes William and Harry today, the princes were very much aviation-minded. Prince George earned a pilot's license in 1929 and was made Air Commodore in the RAF at the beginning of the war. He would be killed on August 25, 1942 when the Short Sunderland flying boat he was in, hit a hillside in Scotland. Prince Henry would be romantically linked with the aviator Beryl Markham the first person to fly the Atlantic Ocean east to west.

15 The Prince of Wales had his own Fox Moth (G-ACDD) sent out to South America and piloted it for much of the tour. The aircraft was kept for years in a private collection outside Ottawa as C-FYPM.

and smoking were forbidden.[16] In the first discount, no frills service in aviation history, Imperial Airways also offered for £7.10 what was called "second class travel" to Paris on the lumbering Handley Page W.8s. The flight was twenty minutes longer and sandwich boxes were available for 1/3d. Besides the cross-Channel flights, the company also advertised Silver Wing "Take A Tea Flight Over London" excursions "as the perfect antidote for a hard week" for £2.2d.

At a time when all onboard were uncomfortably aware that they shared the cabin with the aircraft's fuel tanks — (they were between the pilot and the engine), 'Silver Wing' passengers were assured that there was a fireproof bulkhead behind the Argosy's middle engine and that petrol was stored in tanks under the plane. As all London-Continental Europe flights were over the English Channel, passengers were made aware of the "emergency flotation devices'" onboard and how to deplane in case of ditching — this was the origin of those ubiquitous safety cards which then (as now) were probably ignored by all. If some of the instructions would still be familiar to us today: "Do not inflate the life vest until after you have left the cabin", others would not, like: "Emergency exits are provided in the roofs of all our aircraft and clearly marked. In the event of trouble, these must be opened by the steward only — and not by the passengers". When the Imperial Airways Handley Page W.10 (G-EBMS) lost power from its starboard engine on October 21, 1926 and came down in the Channel, obeying the safety instructions, the 2 crew and 10 passengers did climb out onto the aircraft's roof. When the aircraft began sinking at the nose, they moved up to the tail. Happily, two fishing smacks arrived in time to rescue all and the mail bags too, the only casualty was a Pomeranian dog belonging to one of the passengers. Less fortunate were the passengers (one of them was Canadian) of the Imperial Airways Handley Page W.10 (G-EBMT) "City of Ottawa" which on June 17, 1929 landed in the Channel off Dungeness also because of engine failure. The seven passengers seated in the front of the aircraft were

---

16 Passengers caught ignoring the smoking ban on Imperial Airways flights were fined £200 and could be sentenced to six months in prison.

thrown from their seats and died — the other 4 and the 2 crew in the open cockpit made their way onto the roof and were rescued. Among the recommendations from the Accident Investigationboard was that from now on all passengers be provided with seat belts.

Given the standards of luxury available in the 1920s on a train or Cunard liner, it is a wonder that the wealthy chose to fly at all. If they did so, they had to be as resilient as they were rich. According to a contemporary guide (written by an American) about what one should expect about flying in Europe): "Two cabins were recommended; seasick persons being placed in one cabin... a spacious washroom is desirable where a special vomiting basin should be provided... disinfectants should be carried as the smell of airsickness may induce this malady in persons otherwise immune. Disinfectants are particularly desirable when the results of sickness are on the floor of the cabin. Thanks to the lack of cabin pressurization and sound-proofing (ear plugs were necessary to withstand the noise of the engines), and the primitive heating and ventilation equipment (if a passenger opened the window he or she was likely to be poisoned by the exhaust fumes from the central engine on tri-motored aircraft), many passengers staggered off the plane at their destination, pale-faced and nauseous."[17]

At the 1921 Cairo Conference, the delegates called for a British air link from Cairo to Basra, Iraq, to deliver the mail onward to India. Churchill, now Secretary of State for the Colonies, was said to be outraged that a letter from London to Baghdad took 28 days to be delivered. An airmail service through the desert was calculated to reduce this to under nine days. Ordered to do so, the RAF struggled to deliver the mail fortnightly, operating their Vickers Vernons in pairs as the Bedouin tended to fire at them and also because of forced landings — their water-cooled Napier engines were unsuited to the climate.

The navigational problems of flying over a vast, featureless desert of some 470 miles between the refueling stations at

---

17 *Safety and Accommodation in European Passenger Planes*, No. 3, New York, Daniel Guggenheim Fund for the Promotion of Aeronautics Inc., 1928, P. 29-30.

Ziza, south of Amman, and Ramadi, north of Baghdad were challenging. With few landmarks in the desert, a pilot could get disoriented as there were no radio directional beacons and radio range was limited. But as this was the generation of pilots who navigated by following railway lines, in 1922 to serve as a line-of-sight navigational aid, the RAF had a 6.5 foot wide oil-based furrow ploughed through 300 miles of desert.[18] Every 25 miles the plowing crews (protected from marauding tribes by Crossley armored cars), demarcated emergency landing fields, each prominently numbered for identification from the air and marked with arrows indicating direction of approach. Fuel was made available at two of them, protected from theft by a heavy bronze dome. The RAF pilots (one of whom was Arthur Harris better known as "Bomber Harris" in the following war) would refer to it as flying "FTF": Follow the Furrow.[19]

Now relegated to delivering the post rather than jousting with the Hun, one of the RAF pilots penned this rather acerbic ballad:

> *And for ninepence you can purchase if you are wise,*
> *The same efficient service of the man who yesterday*
> *Chased the black-crossed Birds of War from out your skies.*
> *The letters that they carry from Cairo to the East*
> *Bear little slips of papery coloured blue,*
> *And the loss of crew and pilot doesn't matter in the least,*
> *If the Mail Bags see the Desert journey through.*

Branckner wanted the mail flown to Istanbul and then overland to Baghdad but in 1926, Hoare took the Desert Air Route away from the RAF (who were pleased to give it up as they thought it was making their pilots lazy) and handed it to Imperial

---

18 It was an undertaking worthy of a movie. One convoy went eastward from Amman, the other westward from Ramadi. Each struck out on a roughly predetermined course assisted by Arab guides and, wherever possible, followed traditional Arab caravan tracks. At night, the parties which included surveyors, meteorologists, motor transport experts and radio operators, fixed their position by the stars. The correct time was obtained from a portable radio set. Maps were prepared for the pilots of the aircraft accompanying the two convoys.

19 Alan McGregor, *Flying the Furrow*, Saudi Aramco World, March/April 2001, P. 24–31.

Airways as the first sector of the route to India. A government subsidy of £93,600 was granted to build new aerodromes and accommodation. On January 7, 1927 Imperial began flying their sturdy DH.66 Hercules aircraft from Heliopolis, then a garden suburb of Cairo, to Gaza-Amman-Rutbah Wells-Baghdad-Basrah.[20] With the Hercules' three radial engines, up-to-date navigational equipment and radio, the Imperial pilots didn't really need to follow the Furrow, but they did so for the emergency fuel dumps. As they had been with the RAF, the fuel dumps were the subject of a long running battle between Imperial and the desert nomads who plundered them at will. They had no use for the petrol which they poured out but made the cans into knives, cups, mirrors and water bottles. Imperial buried the dumps and locked them, but the nomads dug them out and shot the locks off. Then the company came up with bullet-proof locks with special keys, but the pilots would forget to carry them. Finally, the fuel dump key was combined with the key the pilots used to open their aircraft doors in the morning.

Air India's founder, J.R.D. Tata who flew to Croydon by Gypsy Moth in 1930, returned to India on Imperial Airways. "As we droned across the Iraqi desert," he recalled, "the captain sat reading the *Illustrated London News* with such intense concentration that he flew right past Rutbah Wells without even noticing... he clearly did not wish to be interrupted. He only looked up when the plane began to run out of fuel and, quite calmly, landed on the sand, broke into one of the RAF's emergency dumps and stole enough petrol to get us back to Rutbah in time for dinner."[21]

If in later years Imperial's passengers would overnight at some of the world's great hotels such as Raffles (Singapore) and the Peninsula (Hong Kong), none could have matched the romance of the rest house at Rutbah Wells, halfway between

---

20 A competition in *Meccano Magazine* for boys called for a name and a Mr. E.F. Hope-Jones of Eton College won with his suggestion of *Hercules*.

21 This and many other quotes are from Alexander Frater's *Beyond the Blue Horizon* (Penguin Books, 1987). Frater who died on January 1, 2020, almost the day I began writing this book, was the essence of a true travel writer. His love affair with flying boats began at nine years old.

Damascus and Baghdad. The airline overnighted passengers in a purpose-built fort which was defended against hostile tribes by armed infantry. The silent movie version of *Beau Geste,* the Percival Christopher Wren novel (starring Roland Coleman) had just come out and with its Foreign Legion architecture, the Airways rest house could have been part of the Hollywood set.

When approaching Rutbah Wells, Imperial's pilots were warned that the surrounding high ground was sometimes obscured by low, heavy cloud and that the "irregular shaped" landing area had a gravel surface. If the aircraft was late arriving from Amman, "goose-necked" flares would be lit for night landings. There was a windsock attached to the fort and on the roof a radio and observation tower whose beacon was visible to aircraft for 80 miles around. One passenger wrote of the "unforgettable experience of arriving at the most desolate and extraordinary hostelry in the world", while another remarked on "the absurdity of coming down (in the morning) to an English ham and egg breakfast in the middle of the desert". A common complaint in winter was the cold, for the local builders had, unaccountably, made no provision for fireplaces or chimneys. "It is often bitterly cold in December; we dined in overcoats," a disgruntled passenger reported, "and had a very shivery night." One compensation, whereby passengers might momentarily forget the temperature, was after their dinner of pilaf and barbecued chicken, an armed sentry would lead them up a circular stone staircase to the Fort's flat roof. "Breathtaking, millions of stars sparkling in the clear desert air," one said. If few travelers praised the rest house meals as first-class, all agreed that lounge, bedrooms and other conveniences were "clean, comfortable and well arranged."[22]

In Baghdad, passengers originally overnighted at the Nairn Motor Transport Company's hotel. Gerald and Norman Nairn were two New Zealanders who operated a weekly bus service through the Syrian desert between Beirut and Haifa, and some of their passengers were Agatha Christie, Freya Stark,

---

22 Ibid, Frater, P. 183.

Gertrude Bell and the explorer H. St. John Philby. Mail carried by the Nairns to Baghdad was not only quicker than the RAF's fortnightly run but cheaper than the surcharge set by the General Post Office. The Nairns (who also operated the only other hotel at Rutbah Wells) understood the passengers' needs better than Imperial and advertised that their guests could not only enjoy hot baths but "tipple" and dine on fried fish, Yorkshire pudding, roast beef and custard!

Later, Imperial Airways would move its passengers to the Maude Hotel on al-Rashid Street, the first street in Baghdad to be lit. According to its brochure, the Maude Hotel had electric lights and toilets in every room and shared baths on each floor. The hotel had been named for Lieutenant General Sir Stanley Maude who captured the city from the Turks in 1917 and then promptly died of cholera from drinking the local unboiled milk.[23] As hotel guests, the passengers had the use of the town's three main clubs. In descending order of status, these were the 'British', the 'Railway' and the 'Alwiyah'. The first was exclusively male and was used mainly by "city gents". The other two clubs had a mixed membership and offered facilities for swimming, tennis, squash, polo, pig-sticking and shooting game. One of the "transit" passengers attended a cabaret in a city nightclub. There, among Arab gigolos, he spotted buttoned-up, "Englishmen trying to appear indiscreet". [24]

Basrah, then known as the "Venice of the East", where the Tigris and Euphrates meet, was a short flight from Baghdad. Pilots were warned not to fly too low over the banks of the Euphrates. Attempting to avoid a dust storm, Cobham had done so and his radio operator, Arthur Elliott, had been fatally shot by a Marsh Arab hunting for gazelles. Passengers were first put up at the Iraqi Railway Rest House — the railway was under British civilian administration — with its "...well-fur-

---

23 While his equestrian statue in Baghdad has long been toppled and his grave defiled, Maude is remembered by a mountain named after him in the Canadian Cascade Range. A Canadian medical corps (with female nurses) had served in the capture of Baghdad, setting up a hospital for typhus patients in a former harem.
24 *Daily Express*, 17 September 1929, P. 8.

nished dining room, lounge and billiard room." Later, Imperial Airways used the sprawling riverside Shatt al Arab Hotel which had fifty bedrooms, a swimming pool and tennis court. It also had its own airfield with night landing facilities for flying boats which included a revolving flashing beacon which was much appreciated by the pilots of the Empire boats later on. In the Iraq war of 2003, the "Shatt" would house a British Army battle group — the hotel's chandeliered entrances, high-ceiling corridors and (now scum-filled) swimming pool hinting at the luxury that Imperial's passengers had enjoyed. The hotel's airfield was just large enough for the military's Lynx and Merlin helicopters.

It wasn't only the high air fares that deterred everyone except the wealthy from flying. The middle class wisely refused to waste their limited vacation time on slow, cramped, daylight-only flights that stopped frequently for refueling. Mass tourism was five decades away but it was Hoare's intention as Minister of State for Air to demonstrate to the disbelieving taxpayer that flying to India was not only for the sake of national prestige but would soon be routine. In December 26, 1927, an Imperial Airways D.H. Hercules G-EBMX left Croydon for India on a survey flight. It carried Hoare, his wife Lady Maud (who wished to show that the adventure of flying was not only for men), Branckner and Woods Humphery. The Minister of Health Neville Chamberlain (who had not yet been in an aircraft) begged Hoare not to go.

The flight proved anything but routine, but did foreshadow air travel to come. As sensible travelers, the Hoares made their wills before departure and sent their main luggage ahead by sea. Without her maid and a minimal wardrobe (i.e. only carry-on baggage) and anticipating the varied climates and diplomatic functions to be suffered en route, Lady Maud decanted her toiletries from their cut glass crystal bottles into lighter aluminum containers. There were some compensations to status however (she was after all, the daughter of an Earl) as when the Hercules flew over her brother's villa at Cannes, the entire family came out to wave. Once over the Mediterranean,

(Above) Supermarine Southampton flying boats of the RAF. Between 1927 and 1929 four Southamptons were flown to the Far East and on to Australia. (Below) Attempts to rescue Alan Cobham's flying boat during a gale in Malta.

a chain of Royal Navy destroyers bobbed below them, sent by Hoare's chum William Bridgeman, the First Lord of the Admiralty to "keep an eye on things."

Several adventures/inconveniences later, on January 8, 1928 the Minister of State for Air arrived at Delhi's new Willingdon Airfield, named for the new Viceroy and Governor General. When asked about the danger and discomfort she had encountered en route, the indominable Lady Hoare would only say "We were much too interested to be frightened."[25]

The return flight left Delhi on February 1,1928 and arrived at Heliopolis, Cairo on February 7 from where the Hoares returned home by ship. The flying time from Croydon to Delhi had been 62 hours, 27 minutes and Delhi to Heliopolis 32 hours 50 minutes. Hoare's initiative inaugurated a weekly Imperial Airways service to India beginning March 30, 1929. The seven day trip (compared with three weeks by ship) cost £130 — said to be half a year's wages for the average working man.

The controversy over the use of landplanes versus flying boats to South Africa, India and Australia received a boost from the long-distance flights by the RAF and Cobham - and especially the Schneider Trophy races. Most major cities had been built near water – whether river, lake, or seacoast – and with flying boat services, the expense of constructing an aerodrome would be unnecessary. In November 1927, Cobham (now Sir Alan) and his co-pilot Capt. Henry Worrall began a circumnavigation of Africa in a Short Singapore flying boat which because of the absence of airports in Africa could not have been accomplished in a landplane. He would far sooner be in a flying boat flying over land Cobham said, than in an airplane flying over the sea. Between October 1927 and January 1929, the RAF flew four Supermarine Southampton flying boats to Singapore and onto Hong Kong and Australia. But thanks to Woods Humphery, Imperial Airways would play it safe with a mix of land and seaplanes on its routes.

---

25 For this feat Lady Hoare was appointed Dame Commander of the Order of the British Empire. She was the first woman ever to fly so many miles.

To get to India meant flying through Persia, refueling as the Hoares had done at Bushir, Lingen and Jask before arriving at Karachi. In 1925, the RAF had prevented Junkers from establishing an air service between Baghdad and Teheran. Operating a flying school in Teheran, German influence soured any British negotiations with the Persian government and overflights rights were withdrawn in January 1927, the Hoares doing so without permission. In 1929, Teheran had a change of heart and allowed Imperial to refuel at Jask once more. The Hoares had overnighted in this desolate town with an Anglo-Indian, a Mr. Janes, the representative of the Indo-European Telegraph company who told them that it grew so hot there in the summer that flies died on the wing and dropped lifeless from the sky.

It was at Jask on December 6, 1929 that Imperial's D.H. Hercules G-EBMZ crashed. Attempting a night landing, Captain Woodbridge (who had wounded the Red Baron) misjudged the altitude, stalled the plane and, like the flies, it had dropped out of the sky. Magnesium flares fitted to an aircraft's wing tips were the only night landing aids available and Woodbridge had ignited them on approach. Unfortunately, when the aircraft hit the ground, the flares set off what remained in the fuel tanks. Woodbridge, a mechanic and passenger died, but the wireless operator and flight engineer survived.

The end of the decade saw Imperial Airways preparing to embark on an expansion befitting its name. Except for Paris, the airline had been relinquishing its European routes as early as 1925, generously giving them either to the Danes, Deutsche Aero-Lloyd AG or KLM (which was even allowed to carry passengers between Hull and Liverpool). For the British, the East began now not at Calais but at Croydon. The Airport was enlarged in 1928 with a new terminal building opened by Lady Hoare on May 2.[26] Accommodation for pilots and

---

26 The new airport suffered its first crash on July 13, 1928 when the Vickers Vulcan G-EBLB on a test flight and filled with Imperial Airways employees (i.e. a joy ride) would crash, killing four of the six occupants. Imperial would then ban employees from taking joy rides during test flights.

passengers was at the nearby Croydon Aerodrome Hotel which had just been built. Once a staple at airports in the 1950s, the airport terminal had a rooftop viewing gallery allowing onlookers to marvel at the aircraft below — KLM's Fokkers, Farman's boxy Goliaths, Junkers of the newly formed Luft Hansa A.G. (whose manager after 1936 would bid his aircraft farewell with an extravagant Nazi salute) and SABENA's little Westland Wessex.[27] Within the Administration Building was the passenger check-in area known as the Booking Hall. Now a standard airport design, it had six check-in desks for Imperial and its rivals. Passengers disembarking from the London bus were met by the station superintendent in white gloves and blue uniform and conducted into the *art deco* Hall. It featured a large two-story atrium surrounded by a first-floor balustrade with geometric patterned railings. Atop the atrium was a magnificent steel-framed glass dome, flooding the area with light. The Booking Hall led through to Immigration and Customs checks before passengers exited through the world's first departure gate to the south side of the Control Tower. The Arrivals gate was on the north side of the Control Tower. Today the terminal building and tower are a museum, but the Croydon Aerodrome Hotel is still in use.

Political issues dogged the airline's expansion which was not uncommon in the era. As Clement M. Keys (1876–1952), the American head of the Curtiss Airplane and Motor Company, once said: ten percent of aviation is in the air, and ninety percent is on the ground. "Freedoms of the Air" and the Chicago Convention were decades away and countries guarded the air above them as jealously as they did their coastlines. In 1911, the British Aerial Navigation Act declared that all of Britain's airspace, including that of her colonies and dominions, was sovereign territory and therefore inviolable. This would prevent French, German and Italian attempts to begin flights over all British territory which at the time was much of the planet. German airships, for example, were forbidden to fly over whatever was red on the globe, especially Egypt with its

---

27 Societé Anonyme Belge d'Exploitation de la Navigation Aérienne (SABENA) and Koninklijke Luchtvaart Maatschappij N.V. (KLM).

military installations on the Suez Canal. Lufthansa would similarly be prevented from crossing India and KLM, Imperial Airway's closest competitor in the East, was delayed from doing so until the British had their own airmail system in place.

With the planned all-air route to India, the British were hoist by their own petard, and had to negotiate with the Italian and Greek governments in the Mediterranean, the Persian government and Trucial States (now the United Arab Emirates) in the Middle East and, once in Karachi, the Indian government. When London refused to trade with Mussolini, who wanted landing rights in Gibraltar for those in Italy and Tobruk, North Africa (then an Italian protectorate), the airline had to pay £5,000 per year for use of Genoa, Rome (Ostia), Naples and Corfu as temporary refueling bases. Italian and later Persian intransigence would dictate Imperial's routes through the 1930s, and on getting off the Argosy at Le Bourget, passengers bound for the Levant and India were first bused to the Hotel Ambassadors in Paris for dinner and then delivered to the Gare de Lyon where they were put on a wagon-lits either to Genoa in 1929, or in 1931 to Brindisi, on the southern tip of Italy where the Apian Way ends.

At Brindisi's Piazzale Crispi station, (sometimes the flying boat captain was there to greet them), a bus took them to the waterfront where, after customs formalities, an Imperial Airways pinnace transferred them to the flying boat.

3   Out in the midday sun

Derived from the Short Singapore that served Cobham, the Short S.8 Calcutta was Imperial Airway's first flying boat. Bought for crossing the eastern Mediterranean from Italy to Egypt, on February 28, 1929 the first was put on the Genoa-Alexandria route.

The five Calcuttas (each, like the Argosies, named for cities that the airline served, or hoped one day to) had a stressed skin and metal hull and could seat 12 passengers. Its three Bristol Jupiter IX nine-cylinder, air-cooled radials of 540 horsepower, were mounted in monocoque nacelles between the mainplanes, driving four-blade wooden airscrews. To the passengers' relief fuel was not carried in the hull — a precedent that became standard with S.23 Empire flying boats — but in thickened sections of the upper mainplane with gravity feed to the engines.

The Captain and First Officer sat side-by-side in an open cockpit with dual controls. The Radio Officer had a workstation on the starboard side immediately aft of the cockpit. Passengers entered by a hatchway on the port side forward, with the hat and coat storage immediately opposite. The single cabin, with fifteen seats, was 17' 6", long by 6' 6", wide by 6' 3". high, and trimmed in blue leather up to dado level, changing to buff-colored felt to the ceiling — to help absorb engine and airscrew noise. The seating, also upholstered in blue leather, was arranged in four rows of three seats with the aisle offset to port, between the single seat on that side, and the double seat on the starboard side. An extra double seat was installed in the coat storage area and a single seat at the rear of the cabin. The toilet, pantry and steward's seat were aft. Some of the windows could be opened for ventilation and four of them served as emergency exits.

The all-metal Short S.8 Calcutta was Imperial Airways' first flying boat.
Each of the five aircraft was named after a city.

When Italian permission to use Genoa and Brindisi was withdrawn in September 1929, Imperial's passengers flew by Argosy to Paris and then endured a long train journey to Salonika, Greece. Imperial even attempted to avoid Italy altogether by flying an all-air route north of the Alps via Cologne-Nuremberg-Vienna-Budapest-Belgrade-Skopje-Salonika and Athens, but the mountains between Skopje and Salonika were too high and after two flights, this was ended.

The flying boats landed at Piraeus, the historic port of Athens from where the Athenian fleet had sailed for the Trojan War. The passengers would overnight at the Hotel Grande Bretagne on Syntagma Square before continuing on to Alexandria. From their balconies they could see the Parthenon, the parliament buildings and the changing of the Evzone guards. The hotel had its beginnings in 1872 when a Russian-born Greek chef Stathis "Eustace" Lampsa bought a large house on the Square and made it a hotel. Everyone famous has stayed at the Grande Bretagne — from the Rockefellers, the Kennedys and Krupps to Indira Gandhi, Yasser Arafat and Mary Pickford. Like the Chateau Laurier in Ottawa, much of the country's history was made within its four walls. Early in the Second World War the hotel was British Army headquarters for General Sir Archibald Wavell. When the Axis advance forced him to escape in 1941, Wavell left the hotel for the flying boat base at Scaramanga, now the site of a huge refugee camp, to fly to Alexandria.[1] When the Germans set up headquarters in the hotel, Hitler, Göring and even Himmler were the Grande Bretagne's guests. On Christmas Day 1944, just after the Wehrmacht withdrawal, the hotel — once more British military headquarters — narrowly escaped being blown up by the Greek resistance who were ready to set off dynamite in its sewers. Only the arrival of Churchill, who feared the Russians would take over Greece, and his aides Anthony Eden and Harold Macmillan prevented it.

As adventuresome as it was, a journey by aircraft to India was a sideshow when compared with a trip on the airships R-100 and R-101, both preparing in 1930 to make their first flights to Canada and India respectively. On a hot August night in 1930, the R-100 floated over Montreal (as windows were open, everyone was awakened by its engines) and docked at the mooring mast at St. Hubert airfield, having completed a flawless Atlantic crossing. It wasn't the first airship to cross the Atlantic Ocean, but it was a diversion from the economic misery of the Depression and its sheer majesty inspired imperial dreams throughout the Dominion. After Montreal, the R-100 floated over Ottawa and then Toronto where a city newspaper exaggerated "Airship Darkens the Skies Over Toronto". There, traffic downtown ground to a halt, schools and offices closed as thousands flooded into the streets, some

---

1 To read, on the flight to Alexandria, Wavell took with him Shakespeare's *Anthony and Cleopatra* — not for the amorous information but for how Mark Anthony had handled his retreat.

climbing roof tops and trees. This was exactly what Hoare and his generation of statesmen had hoped for, the pride in being part of the British Empire.[2]

The Imperial Conference was to be held in Delhi that year and the launch of the R-101 was a perfect opportunity to demonstrate the government's ambitions for an Empire Airship Network. Mooring towers at Ismailia, Egypt and Karachi, India were ready to be used — as was the great airship hangar there. Hoare had been replaced by Lord Thomson who wanted to make his own mark in commercial aviation and invited Branckner who had misgivings about the airship, to join him on the inaugural flight of the R-101 to India. The R-101 left Cardington on October 4 overloaded and under ballasted, and it struggled to maintain height over the Channel. That night a storm caused it to settle into a low hill at Beauvais outside Paris. The impact was gentle and probably survivable, but inflated with hydrogen, the airship burst into flame, possibly from the magnesium flares in the cockpit. The fire incinerated 46 persons onboard, including Major George Scott who had commanded the R.34 across the Atlantic in 1919 and poor Branckner. After the disaster, the R-100 was dismantled. This didn't end the hopes of the airship lobby which formed the British Zeppelin Syndicate and as late as 1937, lobbied the Air Ministry to purchase two Zeppelins from the Nazi government to use on the Montreal and Karachi routes where the masts in those cities were still standing. But when the *Hindenburg* was also destroyed by its hydrogen igniting at Lakehurst, New Jersey, Britain abandoned the airship competition to Germany. The future belonged to aircraft — and Imperial Airways.

The demise of airships for the long-distance routes to Canada, South Africa and Australia was a watershed moment for Imperial Airways. The difference between the beginning

---

2 The R-100's Canada journey, the engineer/author Nevil Shute (who was onboard) wrote, was 'dictated by political motives alone.' Like the R-100 flight to come, it was rushed by Britain's desire to outdo German airship developments.

of commercial aviation in the United States and Europe is what aircraft carried in 1919. In Europe, the guinea pigs were people, and in the United States, rather than heavier, prone-to-complain passengers, it was airmail. Against the lobbying of a powerful rail lobby, in 1918, the United States Post Office Department appropriated $100,000 for an experimental airmail route. Harking back to the days of the Pony Express, the mail was flown from New York to San Francisco by DH.4s, this soon progressing to night flights. By 1925, (having killed 19 of the 40 original pilots), the Department contracted airmail carriage to private air companies, thus beginning the commercial aviation industry in the United States. Within a decade, diversifying into passenger service, the US airlines had freed themselves from reliance on mail subsidies.

In Britain it was the opposite — the high fares charged to passengers were expected to subsidize the airmail. From the earliest days of aviation, what to charge for airmail had always been an issue for the post office clerk behind the counter, as not only did the sender pay the surface charge for a foreign letter but the air conveyance as well. This varied depending on the country in Europe according to distance as well as weight. In 1930, a general postage rate for all of Europe was introduced and surface and airmail postage rates were merged (Imperial Airways always held this to be unfair). As Woods Humphery explained, the airline assumed the entire commercial risk while the Post Office fixed the rates. Mail was carried at a pre-arranged bulk contract rate but without guarantee of minimum loads. The letter writing public were also to blame. Despite the Post Office's publicity, even until 1939, they continued to time the mailing of letters to Asia and Africa on days when the Union Castle or P&O ships left — not the Imperial Airways flights throughout the week. As a result, the weight of airmail on Thursdays and Fridays swamped even the Empire flying boat's capacity, preventing any passengers from flying that day.

The larger the aircraft, the more profitable it would be to transport mail and passengers to the farthest ends of the globe and within a year of the R-101 disaster, two such aircraft came online, the Short S.17 Kent flying boat and the Handley Page HP.42/45, both heavier and more luxurious than their predecessors but neither faster. As if in a twilight of the gods, on October 30, 1930 the last of the Handley Page W.8s (G-EBIX) on approach to Le Bourget, stalled and crashed at Neufchatel. Three of the passengers died, the pilot

The Imperial Airways Short S.17 Kent, *Scipio*, at Alexandria in the early 1930s. The S.17 Kent was the true ancestor of the great Short *Empire* flying boats that would follow.

J.J. "Paddy" Flynn injured his spine and had to have his left leg amputated.[3]

The eastern Mediterranean "water jump" between Greece and Egypt was of vital concern to Imperial Airways as the Calcutta barely had the range needed. In response to an Imperial requirement for a flying boat that would, in October 1930, Short Brothers began building the S.17. First flown on

---

3 That did not prevent Flynn from flying and, once out of hospital, the only one-legged pilot in England began his own flying club.

February 24, 1931, the Short S.17 Kent flying boat (known in Imperial Airways service as the *Scipio* Class) was the true ancestor of the great Empire flying boats to come. But just as they became available, the Italians relented and from October 1931 Imperial Airways was once more allowed to operate through Genoa and Brindisi.

The *Scipios* were enlarged versions of the Calcutta, with the same passenger-carrying capacity but an increased payload for mail. An extra Bristol Jupiter engine was added for increased

Crew members relax in the sumptuous forward cabin of an Imperial Airways *Scipio* class flying boat.

LONDON–EGYPT
IN 57 HOURS BY
IMPERIAL AIRWAYS
THE BRITISH AIR LINE

reliability, all four engines were, thanks to the long exhaust pipes and collector rings, quieter. The two pilots were now in an enclosed cockpit, with the radio operator/navigator in a cabin in the rear. The wider cabin allowed sixteen passengers to sit in Pullman style — facing each other in pairs on both sides of an aisle with a table between. A publicity photograph shows the tables laid for luncheon complete with linen serviettes, daffodils in cut glass vases and cruets. A steward's "pantry", a toilet and washroom was aft. The steward's first duty, once the flying boat had lifted off, was to uncork the clarets so they could breathe unhurriedly before lunch. As a measure of the times, the twin-burner oil stove in the galley was available for a gentleman's valet or lady's "travelling companion" to serve their employers their usual fare.

Only three *Scipios* were built, the first Imperial flying boats to be christened (no doubt by the generation of Imperial's directors educated in the classics) with names from antiquity *Scipio, Sylvanus* and *Satyrus*. The last would be in the royal spotlight in August 1932 when both their Royal Highnesses the Prince of Wales and Prince George rejoined the Mediterranean Fleet at Corfu from Brindisi. Three years later on November 9 while being refueled at Brindisi, the *Satyrus* would be set on fire by an arsonist who had fascist sympathies.

The *Scipio's* range would enable them to fly from Athens, refuel at Mirabella, Crete then onto Castelrossso (Karistos) on the Greek island of Euboea to refuel once more under the old Venetian fortress where Air Orient also had a flying boat base. From here it continued on to Lake Tiberius on the Sea of Galilee, Palestine where passengers were transferred to a landplane for India. Making the longer flight from Athens to Alexandria for the Cairo-Cape Town route was also supposed to be viable, but just barely, as on March 4, 1933, running out of fuel, Captain V.G. Wilson was forced to put *Satyrus* down, 20 miles short of Pireaus, Greece.

At Mirabella, to act as the radio and meteorological station (and transfer passengers ashore for lunch), the company kept the motor yacht-depot ship M.V. *Imperia* captained by Francis Grant Poole. The building where the passengers ate is today a listed one, in poor condition and alleged to be where Churchill and Mahatma Gandhi spent the night (not together, the guidebook

Cabin service on an Imperial Airways flying boat.

emphasizes) while passing through. A remnant of Imperial Airways will always be on the island. The original *Scipio*, G-ABFA after a heavy landing in a downdraft on 22 August 1936, would crash into Mirabella Bay, killing two of the seven passengers, both of whom are buried at Agia Triada cemetery overlooking Elounda, the site of the crash.

When the war began, the M.V. *Imperia* was moved to Port Said[4] but Captain Poole, fluent in the Cretan dialect, remained, helping to smuggle stranded Commonwealth troops from the island.[5] Poole was awarded the Distinguished Service Order and Distinguished Service Cross and became the British Consul in

---

4 It served in Akaba and Djerba during the war only to be found one day in 1946, like the *Marie Celeste*, drifting in the Mediterranean with no one aboard.
5 During the German occupation of Crete in 1941, Middle East Command learned that some 800 British, Australian and New Zealand troops were sheltering in the island caves. Lt. Cdr. Poole was landed by submarine. Disguised as a peasant selling oranges, he contacted the troops and, with the help of an abbot of a monastery, got them away.

Volas where he died in 1947. He is buried at the Commonwealth War Graves cemetery at Phaleron Bay, Piraeus within sight of where the Imperial flying boats had landed.

Like Mirabella, Tobruk would be the scene of savage fighting twelve years later but in 1929 it was a mud-hutted village without a hotel. The airline's auditor, a Mr T. D. Goord and Bill Bailey, the pilot, did an exploratory flight to Tobruk from Alexandria with a *Calcutta* flying boat. The pair managed to find a single bed in the local hospital where they spent a hot and uncomfortable night. In the morning Bailey suggested a swim in the lagoon and they walked down to the beach. Hardly had they got there when a startling sight greeted their eyes. Rattling over the hills in Model T Fords, a number of Arabs appeared, bearing some gruesome trophies. Human heads, apparently still dripping blood, were festooned over their decrepit cars. Both men piled into the plane's dinghy on the beach and made for the flying boat. It turned out that the tribesmen were more curious than menacing, only wanting to show off their trophies. Once in the air, the pair flew over three Italian naval vessels rushing to Tobruk, no doubt to deal with the locals. Imperial's passengers would have to press on to Alexandria from Crete and then by rail to Cairo for a night's sleep.[6]

As well as expanding east, Imperial Airways was also mandated to operate south to Africa. In 1918, the Baird Committee, reporting to Lloyd George, had advocated the inauguration of a weekly Cairo to Cape Town air service. The continent of Africa, most of it British — either as a Dominion, colony or protectorate, with its rivers, lakes and long coastline — was ideally suited to flying boats. The first section of the route, from Cairo to Khartoum, was opened in 1931 using an Argosy, and on January 20, 1932 to Kisumu by a Calcutta flying boat. The Nile was easy to follow from Cairo to Kisumu on Lake Victoria, and arrival times at refueling stops en route could conveniently be afternoons and evenings. During the rains of June to October, most of the landing grounds in south

6 The first hotel to be built in Tobruk opened in 1937 and became General Erwin Rommel's headquarters during the siege.

Sudan were too sodden for landing. As they could put down on any convenient body of water, using flying boats between Khartoum and Kisumu eliminated the need to hire workers and expensive construction equipment to clear landing strips. "We were," Wing Commander William Sholto Douglas wrote of a floatplane tour of Sudan in 1929, "taking our aerodrome along with us; and if things got too bad, we could always flop down on to the water, throw out the anchor... and wait for better times". But having known only the Medway, the flying boat designers at Short's were unaware that their thin aluminum hulls were liable to puncture on African rivers and lakes from rocks, floating debris of all sorts and, sometimes, hippos and crocodiles.

After enjoying the comforts of legendary Shepheard's Hotel in Cairo, Imperial's charges overnighted in accommodation less than salubrious — at Wadi Halfa, Khartoum, Juba, Nairobi, Mbeya, Salisbury, and finally Johannesburg. Having read their G.A. Henty (who wrote about Gordon holding Khartoum against the Madhi's hordes), the passengers would have been conscious of the history they were flying over. The battle at Omdurman had taken place only 30 years before — within their lifetimes — and the Maxim guns and chain mail armor now at the Khartoum museum was a 'must' on their itinerary.

After Khartoum, the flying boat stopped at Malakal for refueling; the place where Grace Chile wrote, in *Skyways to a Jungle Laboratory: An African Adventure*: "The passengers (were) invited into a cool, screened tent for lunch. Here tables were spread and delicious Nile fish, veal, potatoes, beans, a compote of mixed canned fruit and coffee were served on pretty Airways china. This is England-off at the end of nowhere. Other passengers would often wander off to see the sites there or to gawk at the residents of nearby villages or photograph crocodiles."

The paddle steamer took twelve days to travel from Khartoum to Juba; but by 1932, this was covered in a single day with passengers arriving at the Juba Hotel for teatime on its veranda. As to locals, wrote travel writer Alan Moorehead,

Imperial Airways Short S.17 Kent flying boat *Satyrus* in Palestine.

the Sudanese, especially the Dinka and Shelluk tribes, were dismissive about the miracle of the flying boats alighting on the White Nile: "It is one of the mad things that white men do." Women were forbidden to fly solo by the RAF south of Cairo, the fears well portrayed in Evelyn Waugh's *Black Mischief* published in 1932. Aviatrix Beryl Markham who did fly over the Nile from her home in Kenya was more fortunate. "If you can visualize twelve thousand square miles of swamp," she wrote in her memoir, *West With The Night*, "that seethes and crawls like a prehistoric crucible of half-formed life, you have a conception of the Sudd. It is an example of the less attractive by-products of the Nile River, and one place in this world worthy of the word 'sinister'."

The RAF had already established bases in Sudan to police the area. Squadron commanding officers hearing of the wadi dug for the Desert Airmail in Jordan laid down strips of white calico cloth cut as arrows to guide pilots to their destination. This proved a boon for local dressmakers who appropriated the cloth arrows at night.

Sadly, after decades of famine and civil war, some of the places that Imperial's guests slept in no longer exist — the old city of Wadi Halfa with its pleasant railway hotel was submerged after the Aswan High Dam was built in 1964 and

Raja, where the flying boats landed for Juba, is an empty shell.[1] The complete journey from London to Cape Town took eleven days, 72 hours in the air, four changes of aircraft, two railway connections and 30 stops.

At Kisumu the passengers transferred to a Hercules for Cape Town. As to the use of landplanes, the colonial governments in Uganda, Kenya, Tanganyika and Northern Rhodesia, eager to connected with the mother country, would build and maintain the necessary airstrips. Cecil Rhodes' dream of a Cape Town to Cairo all-red route, by air as opposed to rail, had been fulfilled — but not quite. In 1934, the Afrikaner government refused to renew Imperial's airmail contract and demanded that it terminate its service in Southern Rhodesia. From here, the newly formed South African Airways (which was quick to buy Junkers aircraft) would carry the mail to the Cape. A compromise was arrived at and Imperial would fly as far as Johannesburg.

To cope with the temperatures, altitudes and the rough landing fields in Africa, the company replaced the Hercules with Armstrong Whitworth A.W. XV Atalantas. A High wing monoplane with four Armstrong Siddeley Double Mongoose engines, it was a sturdy little aircraft that, besides the African routes, would also be used by Indian Trans-Continental Airways to carry the mail from Karachi to Singapore.

The long range Scipios had arrived none too soon, allowing the Calcuttas to be put on the Cairo to Cape Town route in 1932. But after the destruction of the *Sylvanus* at Brindisi, two of the veteran Calcuttas were returned to the Athens-Alexandria route. One of the reassigned was the Calcutta G-AASJ *City of Khartoum* flown again by Captain Wilson on December 31, 1935. On approach to Alexandria at nightfall, the aircraft ran out of fuel and its three engines stopped simultaneously. The aircraft then fell 600 feet to the water and its hull split open. The flare path had been lit in the harbor and an audience in a New Year's Eve party mood on the waterfront saw the plane

1 When I was researching material for my book *Canada in Sudan: War without Borders*, Juba, now the capital of South Sudan, was deserted except for desperate refugees — even the Red Cross had fled.

Imperial Airways passengers passing through Alexandria were given afternoon tea at the famous Cecil Hotel.

suddenly vanish. The Imperial launch had no radio to contact the pilot and was too small to leave the harbor. Nine passengers and three crew were killed either by the aircraft's impact to the water or drowning, and by the time the duty destroyer HMS *Brilliant* arrived on the scene at dawn, Wilson was the only survivor, having spent 5 hours in the water. A mechanic had adjusted the carburetor jets to produce 10 percent more fuel and the Inspector of Accidents accepted that Wilson had been unaware of this.

Alexandria and Cairo were the "Clapham Junctions" of Imperial Airways for the exchange of mail, especially when the Empire Airmail Scheme began in 1934.[2] The flying boats would land in Alexandria's East Harbor where a bus would take the passengers arriving from Athens to the Cecil Hotel for afternoon tea before they were put on a train at Ramleh

2 Further drawing the Empire together, it aimed to carry all first class mail throughout the British Empire at the rate of one and half pence per half ounce and one penny for post cards.

66

Station for Cairo. Here too the passengers from Cairo would be picked up to overnight at the Cecil. Named after the Cecil hotel in London that its owner Albert Metzger admired, the Cecil had just opened when Imperial Airways overnighted its passengers and crew there in 1929. Its Moorish architecture, elegant revolving door, *art deco* elevators and high ceilings were soon all to be immortalized in Laurence Durrell's *Alexandria Quartet.* The author, who was the press attaché at the British Embassy in Alexandria, would have been familiar with the flying boats when in Corfu.[3] Now he would see them dock beside the Yacht Club on the eastern end of the Corniche. The obelisk mistakenly called Cleopatra's Needle had once been stored there until 1878 when it was transported to London and erected on the Thames Embankment. Across the harbor from the hotel, King Farouk summered at his palace, refusing to turn its lights out during the war, even when the city was being bombed. Within walking distance of the slums with their hashish houses, cabarets and brothels, the Cecil attracted the famous including W. Somerset Maughan, Al Capone and Noel Coward. During the war the British Secret Service had an office on the Cecil's first floor — something that Maughan, who had worked for them in the previous conflict, would have appreciated.

There were those passengers who, in another era, would be called "sex tourists". It was desirable, remembered Ian Scott-Hill who was one of Imperial Airway's managers in Egypt in the 1930s, that the traffic staff would know the going rate for a lady of pleasure and what time the night clubs closed and what was the price of a gin and tonic. So many of Imperial's charges patronized the more notorious clubs that the company was obliged to alter the route of its early morning bus service to include a pick-up point in the red-light district. Imperial issued currency coupons in 2s.6d and 5s. units which, at any port of call, could be traded for local money. But in Alexandria they were frequently used to obtain certain essential services,

---

3   Durrell was living with his family at Kalamata, Greece in 1941 and escaped to Crete in a caique — fortuitously, as the Sunderland flying boat sent to evacuate the British would crash in Kalamata Bay.

The six-engined Dornier Do X, (above) which first flew in 1929, was then the world's largest, heaviest, and most powerful flying boat. The Latécoère 521 (below) which first flew in 1935, was one of the first large passenger aircraft to be capable of flying trans-Atlantic routes.

and the Imperial staff grew accustomed to the madam of a popular whorehouse calling at the office with bundles of coupons which she wanted cashed for piastres.[4]

Rather like Rick's nightclub in the movie *Casablanca*, during the war the Cecil bar teemed with spies (Axis and Allied), refugees, corrupt government officials and members of Alexandria's Jewish community trying to get out of the city before Rommel entered. It must have been especially frightening for them in June 1942 when his Panzers were barely 68 miles from the hotel, and they watched the British move their navy to Beirut for safekeeping. All BOAC staff were evacuated from Alexandria and Cairo to Khartoum. After the Battle of El Alamein, the bar was renamed The Monty in gratitude to General Bernard Montgomery who, although a strict teetotaler, is supposed to have visited it. The Cecil was nationalized in 1952 (but spared the fate of Shepheard's Hotel

---

4 Frater, ibid, P.67

The lavishly appointed dining room of a Dornier Do X flying boat which was powerful enough to carry sufficient fuel for an Atlantic crossing.

in Cairo which was burned down that year) and the Metzger family finally got it back in 2007.

By the beginning of the 1930s, flying boats were powerful enough to cross the Atlantic carrying the necessary fuel to do so: the German Do X monstrosity in 1932, General Balboa's 24 Savoia-Marchetti warplanes in 1933 and the French Latécoère 521 *Lieutenant de Vaisseau Paris* in 1935. In his correspondence with Pan American's president Juan Trippe, Woods Humphery was aware that with the Sikorsky S-42, Trippe at last had a flying boat that (with the proper refueling stations), could fly the Atlantic. In a gentlemen's agreement, Trippe and Woods Humphery promised that neither company would fly the Atlantic until the other was able to do so.

In 1929 Imperial Airways placed an order with Handley Page to build a four-engine biplane that was "large, roomy, luxurious and above all slow". With the history of Handley Page crashes, it is mystifying that such an order be given at all but more so that it came not from the Air Ministry but from Imperial itself. No longer competing with the Americans, French and especially the Germans on technological advances, Imperial Airways could now concentrate on improving the reputation of its services. Targeting the clientele who frequented the great ships of the day including the SS *Normandie* and SS *Europa* (the RMS *Queen Mary* was even then being built for the same purpose), and with its experience designing outsize aircraft like the 0/400 and W.8, Handley Page was happy to oblige. The manufacturer saw it as a four-engine sesquiplane with the cabin more forward of the wings than behind and a fixed undercarriage. The aircraft weighed 14 tons, its metal fuselage was monocoque in the front and metal tube construction in the rear. The four Jupiter engines were placed two on the upper wing and two on either side of the fuselage on the lower wing. Rather ungratefully, Handley Page would later blame Imperial for the HP.42 and HP.45's built-in obsolescence, saying that, "the basic requirements specified by the operators as to performance, and in particular speed, did not take into account the aerodynamic advantages which could have been obtained had a higher speed been asked for."

Eight were built in two versions — four short range HP.45W (*Hercules* Class) which seated 38 passengers for the money-making Paris route and four HP.42E (*Hannibal* Class) for the Cairo to Karachi route which seated 18-24 passengers and had more space for mail. Their fuselages were divided into two cabins, both with large windows and curtains, separated by the bar, toilets and luggage and mail compartments. The cabin décor was wood paneling, with large chintz-covered armchairs, a carpeted floor, soft lighting and flowers on the table before every seat. The aft saloon was curtained and carpeted in pink with tables and chairs a silvery blue, the latter upholstered in flowered yellow chintz. The forward salon had a sky blue carpet and curtains and wood laminate bulkheads inlaid with classical designs. At each cabin entrance next to the clock and altimeter was the commander's name in brass plate. During the flight, the captain, who wore white gloves, left the piloting to his first officer and would stroll through the cabin, chatting with passengers and autographing the menus.

With its gecko-like upturned nose, the aircraft's enclosed cockpit was 21 feet above the ground, the pilots sat side by side with the wireless operator on the port side. It must have been as if on the bridge of a sailing ship for them as they wrestled with a joystick that had a 20-inch diameter wheel fixed to it and a complicated system of wires, pulleys and chains to operate all other controls. On taxiing, the Royal Mail pennant and Civil Air Ensign fluttered from a mast on the aircraft's roof — and if the first officer forgot to lower and retrieve the flags before take-off, the Tower would frantically warn him that the pennants were about to foul up the huge four bladed propellers. Air and ground crew thought the HP.42s a very stable, sturdy aircraft. When the first HP.42 *Hannibal* G-AAGX had its wing torn off by wind on Lake Tiberias on November 17, 1932, the aircraft was dismantled, put on flatbed cars (with the wings packed in crates and the great tires used as padding) and sent by rail to Cairo where it was reassembled, "hammered back into shape" at Heliopolis and returned to service.

Named after Roman emperors, Carthaginian heroes and legendary conquerors of Britain, beginning on June 11, 1931 the HP.42/45s gradually entered service on the London-Paris and Cairo-Karachi routes.[5] Edward Samson Alcock, (the younger brother of the late Sir John Alcock who had flown the Atlantic) would fly the first HP.42E to Cairo in November 1931 — in a leisurely seven-day trip. The jokes about the "built-in headwinds" notwithstanding, the gentlemen's club on wings was beloved by passengers for its elegance and comfort. T. E. Lawrence once observed that: "We export two kinds of Englishmen" those who "went native" (like him) and those who "in reaction to their foreign surroundings take refuge in the England that was theirs". The ponderous HP.42/45 with its plush interiors provided an environment which, remindful of a British suburban drawing room, was reassuring to the Englishman abroad.

Imperial was so pleased with the airliner that they wanted two more HP.42s from Handley Page. But to restart the production line, the manufacturer asked such an exorbitant price that in 1933 the airline ordered a pair of landplane versions of the Kents from Short. An unloved aircraft when compared with the HP.42/45s, the L.17 Scyllas had accommodation for 39 passengers and were fitted with autopilots. One was blown upside down at Brussels Airport in 1935 and the other would survive to be used in BOAC service in 1940.

"See Europe in Comfort By Air" — vintage advertising by Imperial Airways emphasized the meals, the two stewards and toilets on the Heracles and Hannibal. The company worked hard to have its services measured against the standards of a rail compartment on the Simplon Orient Express or a cabin on an ocean liner. Using words like "distinguished" and "exclusive" and "The Greatest Air Service In The World", Imperial's advertisements appealed to the snobbery of their passengers,

---

5 As elephantine as they were, like the Boeing 747s in the 1970s, the HP.42/45s were ideal for movies: *Hadrian*, G-AAUE, appeared in *Song of Freedom* in 1936 starring Paul Robson; and *Helena*, G-AAXF, in 1933 in *Solitaire Man*, in which the hero catches a jewel thief, distracting him by turning off the cabin lights and escaping to the cockpit to radio Scotland Yard to wait for them at Croydon.

encouraging the idea that certain types of sophisticated people travelled by plane. Fares were purposely kept high to eliminate the *hoi polloi* who nowadays could be seen even on the best ships — in steerage of course. The mail bags were Imperial's main source of income, but they didn't feature in the society pages. The airline reveled in snobbery, publishing lists of its distinguished passengers, especially celebrities such as movie stars, famous authors, millionaires, athletes and foreign royalty; always alluding that one might share the cabin with Winston Churchill, Anthony Eden, H.G. Wells, Harry Gordon Selfridge, Mrs. Barbara Hutton or Marie Lloyd.[6]

Unlike airline ads in the United States and Germany, speed and modernity were never mentioned. At 105 miles an hour — the HP.42/45 was barely 20 mph faster than Handley Page's 0/400 — it was an embarrassment for pilots to see trains beating them below. Roland George Ballantine who flew HP.42s remembered that there were no navigational aids and locating Croydon in poor weather depended on finding the twin towers of Crystal Palace, then setting a stopwatch and descending blind. In contrast to the American aircraft with their landing lights enclosed in the wings, the HP.42/45 pilots still used magnesium flares which were under the wingtips and fired electrically by the pilot for night flying — a fire hazard on linen covered wings.

The DC-2/3, Lockheed Electra and Boeing 247 — unsullied by struts and wires — with their retractable landing gear, deicer boots and autopilots to reduce the pilots' load, were now entering airline service, even as the Hannibals and Heracles sallied forth as if escaping from a Ronald Searle cartoon, symbolizing Britain's dated dowdy status in the world. Juan Trippe, who saw his first HP.42 at Karachi, called it "pathetic" — a pterodactyl compared with the sleek KLM DC-2 also at the

---

6   Publicity about its passengers sometimes backfired on the airline. On one occasion, the papers printed that a certain Mr. X and Mrs. X had traveled to Paris together for the weekend. The real Mrs. X read this in the paper with considerable interest and, somehow disentangling itself from the ensuing quarrel, Imperial Airways was no longer as free with this kind of information.

airport.[7] *Time Magazine* joked in 1938 that "there was a fanciful yarn about India's long-delayed independence; the guess was that it might be coming via Imperial." Then there was a tale about a woman who gave birth during a flight to India. Politely taxed by a flight clerk for boarding the plane in her condition, she became highly indignant. "I'll have you know," she replied hotly, "that when I got on this ship I was not pregnant."

But in their eight years of use, the HP.42/45s never killed a passenger (and how many airliners can say that?). Of the aircraft's more memorable endings — *Hengist*, G-AAXE, was destroyed by fire at Karachi in the former airship hangar on May 31, 1937, when someone connected an oxygen bottle to the compressed air starter system. Pressed into RAF service with the war, G-AAXD *Horatius* was damaged beyond repair when returning from France because the pilot lost his way on November 7, 1939 and made a forced landing at Tiverton golf course, Devon.[8] The fate of *Hannibal*, G-AAGX, is unknown. In British Overseas Airways Corporation (BOAC) insignia, it vanished between Jiwani (now Pakistan) and Sharjah on January 1, 1940. Its wreckage has never been found and as it was carrying military officers and an Indian politician (and perhaps a shipment of gold), there is speculation that sabotage, or hijacking was involved.

With their modern-day wealth and architecture, it is difficult to believe that less than 100 years ago Dubai and Abu Dhabi were both medieval sheikdoms dependent on the pearling industry and piracy — the last so the Royal Navy claimed. Forced by the Persian government to relocate from Bushir and Jask, in 1931 Imperial Airways looked to the Trucial States on the opposite side of the Persian Gulf. For refueling and overnight accommodation, the RAF recommended the creek at Ras al Khaimah (today one of the seven United Arab Emirates) — so did the British Resident as it was opposite his house. George Woods Humphery even suggested the Airways depot

---

7   On the same flight he also saw the *Graf Zeppelin* "looking like a clumsy caterpillar."
8   A four-bladed wooden propeller from the aircraft was salvaged and is now on display at Croydon Airport.

ship *Imperia* to be stationed there to ferry passengers from the flying boat ashore.[9] But the Arabs objected to the overnight presence of civilian foreigners, and in particular Western ones. With typical colonial bluster, the Air Ministry then insisted that an onshore "rest house" be found, protected by "machine guns which could, if and when necessary, be manned by Imperial Airways' staff."

A fall in international demand for pearls brought on by the Depression, coupled with the introduction of artificial pearls from Japan, made the local pearling industry go into a decline and the Trucial States had to reconsider accommodating Imperial Airways' demands. Sharjah's Ruler Sultan bin Saqr Al Qasimi agreed — with reservations — to host an airfield. An agreement was made on 22 June 1932 for a monthly rental of 800 Rupees for landing rights and a personal subsidy of 500 Rupees.

The Imperial Airways' Rest House at Sharjah was built as a fort with watchtowers — one of which was the control tower which had a high intensity beacon and a windsock. There were armored parapets, loopholes for rifles, iron-spike palings, and coils of barbed wire. Three dozen retainers of the local sheik stood guard, especially when the aircraft landed. Sharjah was — the "Air Route Book" summed up — a most uncomfortable station. A shower, a change of clothing and dusting with talcum powder to prevent infection and rest in bed was recommended. The aircraft and passengers spent the night behind the barbed wire, the latter warned to stay within the fort at all times. The aircraft's petrol was offloaded from dhows and forwarded by camel to the fort.[10] Food was flown in either from Baghdad or Karachi and, yes, dinner was Brown Windsor soup and mutton. Bathing water was delivered from the creek in water skins on donkey back. The Sharjah Bath with "its thunderous copper plumbing" became an institution for seasoned travelers,

9   The *Imperia* drew 10 feet of water but the depth over the bar at Ras al Khaimah, even at high tide, was only seven feet.
10   The short documentary *Air Outpost* is one of three films commissioned from Strand Films by Imperial Airways in 1936–37 and produced by Paul Rotha. It focused on one overnight stop on the airline's India service: the airfield and town of Sharjah.

Imperial Airways' HP.42 *Hanno* at Sharjah in the 1930s.

Alexander Frater would write, and was almost as celebrated as the Raffles Long Bar, Singapore. When Pan American flew one of its M-130 flying boats around the world in 1936, Juan and Betty Trippe were onboard. They slept at the Imperial Airways guest house at Sharjah and were unimpressed. The Trippes thought it clean, but it had no running water. Compared with it, the Pan American accommodation on Wake Island "with its Simmons beds and private baths, seemed the heart of civilization."[11] Filthy and filled with cobwebs and scorpions, when Frater visited it in 1985, the former Imperial Airways Rest House was in disrepair. But it was reborn in 2000 as the Al Mahatta Museum dedicated to aviation in the UAE.

At first the sector beyond Basra carried mainly airmail but passengers — male only — were accepted, *The Times* reported, upon condition that they understood that catering and accommodation facilities would be "improvised". The cross-Channel route apart, Imperial's average passenger on all other sectors would have been somewhat less glamorous.

---

11   Daley, Robert, *An American Saga: Juan Trippe and His Pan Am Empire.* Riviera Productions, 1980. P 187.

In 2000 the former Imperial Airways Rest House at Sharjah was reborn as the
Al Mahatta Museum, dedicated to aviation in the UAE.

Prospective customers who had believed the hype about
rubbing shoulders with royalty and movie stars on the Empire
routes were surprised to discover how ordinary their travel
companions turned out to be. Flying was still considered too
slow, dangerously uncomfortable and in 1932, only 75 fare-
paying passengers had been carried to India. Typically, they
were senior officers in the British Army going on leave who
didn't want to spend three weeks at sea, engineers from oil
companies and businessmen — usually without their wives.
A somber proof of that was in the casualty lists after an air
crash where the occupation of each passenger was given.
Surprisingly, on the African route, safari tourists and big game
hunters comprised two percent of the list.

The Indian and Australian governments proved as prickly
as the Italian and Persian. Both wanted participation in
Imperial's ambitions through their countries. The Indian
government demanded that the Karachi to Delhi route be

flown by an Indian airline. Using chartered Imperial Airways DH-Hercules aircraft, Indian State Air Service (ISAS) did so, refueling at Jodhpur until December 31, 1931 when it closed down. In what must have been an insult to Imperial and Britain, all mail and passengers were then carried across the subcontinent by KLM, which was cheaper. In the summer of 1933, Indian Trans-Continental Airlines was formed with 51 percent Imperial Airways ownership. Using two AW Atalanta aircraft, it began flying Karachi-Delhi-Calcutta and in October 1933 on to Rangoon and Bangkok with Singapore in December. From here in March 1936 using DH.86s, a spur was opened to Penang, culminating at Kai Tak Airport, Hong Kong.

The Australian government also insisted on an Australian airline flying the remaining section between Singapore and Brisbane and in early 1934, as in India, Imperial was forced to form another airline partnership, this time with Queensland and Northern Territory Aerial Services (Qantas). The deal was negotiated in January 1934 by Imperial's Secretary S. A. Dismore and one of Qantas's founders Hudson Fysh, with Imperial taking 49 percent of the stock to form Qantas Empire Airways (QEA). Meeting the Indian Trans-Continental Airways Atalanta at Singapore, Qantas Empire Airways (QEA), using DH.61 Giant Moths, would continue with the mail to Batavia-Sourabaya-Rambang-Waingapue-Koepang-Darwin-Brisbane. With four types of aircraft, the longest air route in the world from London to Brisbane in 12 days, was opened on December 8, 1934, and, while passengers to Australia still had to go by rail from Paris to Brindisi, it was a triumph for Imperial Airways in its ten years of existence.

That October, the Macpherson Robertson Air Race from Mildenhall to Melbourne had taken place, spotlighting the state of Imperial Airways and the whole British aviation industry. The race began October 20 and, among the entrants, two American airliners: KLM's DC-2 and Roscoe Turner's Boeing 247D were viewed with skepticism when compared with the three purpose-built DH.88 Comets. Yet both the DC-2 and

247D, by then in regular service with airlines, came second and third — the KLM DC-2 even carrying three passengers and thousands of letters to Australia. To its mortification, Imperial did not even have an aircraft to enter with. "Do not run away with the idea that speed is all important," Geddes placated Imperial's shareholders after the race "We have the record of Imperial Airways going its steady, non-spectacular course, and that is the soundest and best in the end."

For Imperial, the writing was clearly on the wall. Dealt a weak hand by the Imperial Air Transport Co. Ltd Act, it had played it with courage under fire. Government's subsidies were the price paid for government interference and "flying the flag" had its price. The restrictive focus on the Empire routes alone, connecting London with Delhi, Cape Town and finally Australia had overstretched it. Whole areas of the world had been ignored — South America, Scandinavia and Eastern Europe. Despite British interests in South America, the continent had been left to German airlines. Because of poor diplomacy by the Foreign Office, British aircraft were forbidden to overfly Spain. The Post Office had been forced to pay £150,000 annually (in gold francs) to the French and German authorities for the use of their services in West Africa and South America.

The 'chosen instrument' was always severely undercapitalized and under-equipped. France had 269 aircraft in civil transport, Germany 177, Pan American alone had 121 — and Imperial only 32 — one for each of its pilots. In March 1933, Imperial's board would propose to the Air Ministry a major capital investment in new aircraft.

Faithful to the requirements of the Hambling Committee, to encourage the national aviation industry for its military potential, Imperial bought aircraft from Armstrong Whitworth, De Havilland, Short and Handley Page — with mixed results. As with the airships, there were no prototypes and all were acquired in such small quantities as to be handcrafted.[12] Even

---

12 The tally was thus — Imperial Airways ordered: three Argosies in 1925/26, four Argosies in 1927/28, five Hercules in 1926/27, five Calcuttas in 1928, three Kents in 1931, eight Hannibal/Heracles in 1929/31 and eight Atalantas in 1930/33. This was hardly enough to maintain the industry's war potential. Except for the second batch of Argosies, all of these aircraft were ordered off the drawing boards, as were the Short Empires of 1934–37.

with Fokker to promote, KLM had no qualms in buying DC-2s in 1934, as did Swiss and LOT Polish Air Lines. Trippe — who would one day see the giant white elephants: the Bristol Brabazon and Saunders-Roe Princess, could have told Woods Humphery that what drove airlines was profit and not prestige.

Seen by some historians as an attempt by Britain to regain its leadership in commercial aviation, the Empire Airmail Scheme (EAMS) was equivalent to the effect that the Penny Post must have had on the public a century before. First proposed in 1932 by S. A. Dismore, the practical details were worked out by Woods Humphery and Sir Eric Geddes onboard a flag-showing flight to South Africa in 1933. On return, Geddes signed a memorandum to the Cabinet with this significant paragraph: "Imperial Airways has conclusively demonstrated its reliability and dependability already, and the Board has every confidence in its ability to carry a vastly increased volume of Empire letter mail. The Board therefore invites H.M. Government to investigate, in conjunction with Imperial Airways, the carriage by air of letter mail in bulk on the London-Cape Town and London-Australasia routes in the next four or five years' time, on revised rates of conveyance to be negotiated." The Cabinet approved the Scheme as did the House of Commons.

In time for Christmas, on December 20, 1934, the Parliamentary Under-Secretary of State for Air, Sir Philip Sassoon (who had been debating rearmament in the House with Churchill), announced that from 1937 onward, Imperial Airways would carry all first class mail throughout the Commonwealth and the Empire without surcharge. The Government had agreed to pay Imperial Airways an economic rate for its carriage.[13] Sassoon suggested a schedule of just over two days to India and East Africa, four days to the Cape and Singapore and seven days to Australia, a journey which took 30 days by ship. He also expressed a preference

---

13 Despite being on opposite sides when it came to rearmament, Sassoon and Churchill remained friends. In August 1934, Sassoon sent his private plane to fly Churchill and Randolph home from France.

for an improved Kent Class flying boat that could carry 24 passengers and half a ton of mail. The RAF and Alan Cobham had proved it was possible to operate flying boats across Africa and to the Far East. Payload not required for mail would be available for freight and passengers. If Dinsmore, Geddes and Woods Humphery are credited with working out the details of the EAMS, it was Sassoon's influence that got it accepted so speedily by the Cabinet. As if to prove its viability, in 1935, he would set off on a grueling 19,000 mile air tour of 14 countries from September 22 to October 29, with the help of the RAF and Imperial Airways.

Even before the announcement, there had been rumors about tenders for a new fleet of aircraft for Imperial Airways that would have transatlantic capability.[14] Pan American was already operating its Sikorsky S-42s on its South American routes and its Martin 130 "Clippers" would be flying across the Pacific in 1935. Impressed with the KLM DC-2 to be entered in the MacRobertson Race that October, Short's designer, Arthur Gouge, tendered to Imperial in late June 1934 the design for the S.23 (C-Class) flying boat. While Gouge used the Short's Scion Senior floatplane as a half-scale model, the S.23 owed much to the clean lines of American aircraft. Imperial and the Air Ministry liked what they saw and in January 1935 gave the instruction to proceed. Company chairman Oswald Short wanted to build a prototype first but was told that there was no time for this. At the end of May, Imperial ordered 14 S.23s off the drawing board, increasing this order on September to 28. Aware of Juan Trippe's Boeing 314s, the airline then ordered three of the larger S.26s (G-class) — both types to be termed "Empire Flying Boats". To replace its landplanes, on May 29, 1935 Imperial would place an order with Armstrong Whitworth for 12 A.W. 27 Ensigns and with De Havilland for 5 DH.91 Albatrosses.

Imperial Airways' choice for a flying boat for long range mail and passenger delivery was born of its 15 year history: without weight restrictions, the flying boats had the payload

---

14 On August 10–11, 1938, the F.W. Condor would fly nonstop from Berlin to Floyd Bennett Airport, New York.

capabilities for the EAMS. There were so few paved runways, even in Europe, let alone in Africa and Asia, but flying boats could put down anywhere there was calm water. Certainly, the flying boat bases would require mail and passenger accommodation, concrete slipways, maintenance hangars and workshops. But with them, Imperial would free itself from the political difficulties of negotiating intermediate landing stages. Best of all for its passengers, it would finally end the train journey from Paris.

4   Juan Trippe and the American dream

Whether Pan American, Qantas or Imperial Airways, every airline that ever used flying boats has evolved from what occurred in St. Petersburg, Florida in the last summer before the Great War. At a time when aircraft were little more than scientific experiments or suicidal vehicles, Percy Fansler saw their commercial potential. An electrical engineer in Jacksonville, Florida, Fansler convinced aviation pioneer Thomas W. Benoist that flying passengers and mail could be commercially viable. Then he somehow persuaded Jacksonville's municipal councilors to subsidize "aerial voyages" to Tampa across the Bay. It must have been a great leap of faith for them as none had ever seen an aircraft. The Wright brothers had performed a few flights in Florida in 1911 and Curtiss opened a flying school next year but both events had been in Miami. Locals were unimpressed with aviation and some even wanted to ban aircraft from flying anywhere in their state. But with the Florida East Coast Railroad bringing more vacationers from up North every year, each up-and-coming city needed a tourist attraction to woo the punters. Besides, it was a 12-hour train journey around the Bay or a two-hour boat ride across it.

The councilors agreed that the city would pay the St. Petersburg-Tampa Airboat Line (SPT) $40 per day to perform two flights daily to Tampa, for a period of three months. The passengers (never weighing more than 200 lbs.) were to be charged $5 for the experience ($10 for the round trip) and mail and packages carried at $5 per 100 lbs. The contract was signed on December 13, 1913 — the tenth anniversary of the

Wright brothers flight, and Benoist brought his hydroplane to St. Petersburg, hiring Tony Jannus, the first federally-licensed pilot in the United States, to fly it.

On January 5, 1914, 3,000 spectators — said to be half the city's population — came down to the beach to watch SPT's inaugural flight. Mayor Abraham C. Pheil had paid $400 to outbid everyone else in a lottery to be the first paying passenger in aviation history. Because many in the crowd didn't believe Jannus and Pheil would make it, Fansler arranged to be telephoned from Tampa when they did. The "airboat" as it was called, never more than 50 foot above the water, at a speed of 75 mph, took 21 minutes to reach Tampa. It must have been a relief for all when the phone call confirmed that they had.

The very next day, Mae Peabody of Dubuque, Iowa (no stranger to adventure, she had travelled across Siberia in 1909) became the first woman to take a commercial flight. At its conclusion, Mae told journalists that she was considering an offer from line's manager to purchase her own airboat at a price of $4,500. The trips sold out for the next 16 weeks with some of the passengers asking to be taken as far as Sarasota and Benoist brought down his second aircraft to cope with the traffic, hiring Jannus' brother, Roger, to fly it.

But once the municipal subsidy ended and the winter vacationers returned home, the first airline in history was grounded, making its last flight on May 5. By then, Benoist and Jannus were busy planning to build a twin-engine flying boat to cross the Atlantic Ocean with and claim the $50,000 prize offered by the *Daily Mail*. When it was ready in 1915, Benoist offered to build more for the Royal Navy, but they preferred the Curtiss aircraft.

In its short life, the St. Petersburg-Tampa Airboat Line had carried 1,205 paying passengers over 11,000 miles in 172 flights, prescient in that given the right conditions (i.e. persuasive founders and a government subsidy), a flying boat airline was feasible. That summer in another St. Petersburg, this one in Czarist Russia, on June 30, 1914, Igor Sikorsky would successfully demonstrate his "Il'ya Muromets". With a

In 1914, the St. Petersburg-Tampa Airboat Line became the world's first airline when they began operating a Benoist Type XIV across Tampa Bay, Florida. Smithsonian National Air and Space Museum.

crew of three and seating for 16 passengers, the four-engine landplane would fly from St. Petersburg to Kiev with a refueling stop at Orsha, an epic journey of 600 miles, accomplished despite a fire onboard. The rivalry between flying boats and landplanes had begun.

If Curtiss's flying boats were the mainstay of naval aviation during the Great War, at its end they were as essential in flouting the Eighteenth Amendment, i.e. Prohibition, in the United States. With so many surplus HS-2Ls available, by 1919 several air companies had emerged, especially wherever the wealthy congregated. Aviation offered a means of escape from the strictures of prohibition and with Havana, Bimini, Nassau or Canada within range of the Curtiss flying boats, shady outfits sprang up to cater to the demand. One was

In 1914, Igor Sikorsky's Ilya Muromets S-27 E (Yeh-2) bomber, made an epic flight of 600 miles from St. Petersburg (Russia) to Kiev.

Aeromarine Airways in Miami which, using HS-2Ls, ferried winter clientele to the "Liquor Islands", the local nickname for the Bahamas.[1] Fly-by-night (sometimes literally) air taxis could be hired wherever the rich were — including Long Island NY., West Palm Beach and Key West, FL., Newport, R.I. and San Pedro CA. If the U.S. Coast Guard and Royal Canadian Mounted Police were somewhat effective in catching rum-runner speedboats and schooners, flying boats were out of their reach, operating as they did from anywhere — secluded coves, and quiet lagoons — a pattern that would be followed in the 1970s with the cocaine flights into the Florida Everglades.

There were legitimate commercial entrepreneurs like Syd Chaplin, the elder brother of the actor Charlie Chaplin, who bought a surplus Curtiss MF (Military Flying Boat) to take sightseers between San Pedro and Santa Catalina, claiming that his was the first domestic airline in the United States. Promising that their "Luxurious Planes Will Carry

---

1 Aeromarine Airways also began the trend of naming its aircraft after explorers like Columbus which would be followed later by Pan American Airways and the Space Shuttle.

A Curtiss HS-2L flying boat preserved at the Canadian Aviation and Space Museum.

Week-Enders To and Fro in 90 Minutes" the New York-Newport Air Service Inc. subsidized by wealthy Newport commuters, flew a Loening Air Yacht between New York and Newport, R.I. Rodman Wannamaker who had sponsored Curtiss in 1914 began American Trans-Oceanic (ATO). His company adapted an HS-2L to carry 11 passengers, squeezing 9 in the main cabin and 2 outside in the gunner's well. Called the *Big Fish*, the flying boat, painted to look like a fish, operated between Miami and Bimini for two summers, making it one of the first international airlines in the United States.

All were out of business within a few years, except for the Seattle-Victoria Airmail Line owned by Edie Hubbard, a friend of Bill Boeing's. His family had made their fortune in Minnesota timber and after graduating from Yale in engineering, Boeing struck out on his own to the Pacific Northwest. In 1916, he purchased the shipyard on the Duwamish River near Seattle where his yacht had been built and began the Pacific Aero

Products Company to build flying boats. He was taught to fly by aviation pioneer (and future rival) Glenn L. Martin. A contract to build HS-2Ls for the Navy kept the company solvent through the war but, at its end, it faced bankruptcy. In desperation, Boeing paid employees out of his wallet and began turning out furniture — dressers, beds and night tables.

The only flying boat that Pacific Aero Products Company (now renamed the Boeing Airplane Company) built was the B-1, a single engine, two seat float-plane. On March 3, 1919, Boeing and Hubbard would fly it the 84 miles between Seattle to Victoria, Canada with a mail bag containing 60 letters. Hubbard would buy the B-1 (Boeing's only sale that year), to begin his own company, the Seattle-Victoria Airmail Line. He became Boeing's test pilot but kept up his contacts with the Post Office. It was Hubbard who suggested to Boeing that his company bid for airmail contracts and build aircraft to service them.

Eddie Hubbard and his Boeing B-1 seaplane at Redondo Beach, CA. 1920.

When ten-year-old Juan Terry Trippe[2] witnessed Wilbur Wright's flight around the Statue of Liberty in 1909, he knew what he wanted to do with his life. He was born in Sea Bright, N.J., on June 27, 1899. Years later, Trippe's biographers and public relations staff were quick to claim that he had been given the name "Juan" because his family had descended from the Spanish conquistadors, but the truth was even more dramatic. His maternal grandmother, Kitty Flynn, was a Liverpool barmaid who fell for a bigamist bank robber, Charles W. Bullard. In time he left her to marry yet again. When Bullard's legal wife had detectives track him down, Kitty left for New York. She moved to Brooklyn and in a social coup worthy of Hollywood, married a wealthy Irish-Venezuelan businessman named Juan Terry. One of her daughters by Bullard, Lucy Adeline, married Charles Trippe, scion of an old money family who could trace his ancestors back to the Norman Conquest and whose grandfather had been awarded the Congressional Medal of Honor in 1805 for fighting Barbary pirates. Their second son was Juan Terry Trippe.

As the son of a New York investment banker and broker, Juan was educated in private schools and, like Boeing, sent to Yale. His professors thought that what Trippe lacked in intellectual abilities he made up with his industriousness and determination. He was exceptionally secretive, and so closemouthed that Yale classmates called him "Mummy." In 1917, with the war in Europe raging, Trippe left Yale to join the U.S. Naval Reserve Flying Corps where he qualified for night flying and received an ensign's[3] commission. The Armistice was signed before he could be sent to France, and Trippe returned to Yale to complete his degree. While there he organized the Yale Aeronautical Society and even represented the university

---

2   It was a name that Trippe hated as it gave him a Spanish-Mexican exoticism, which the patrician in him detested. In later years, when forced to travel on business to Latin America, he called himself "J.T. Trippe".

3   Trippe failed the eye test for a pilot's license and it took a phone call by his father to the Assistant Secretary of the Navy, Franklin D. Roosevelt, to allow him an immediate second chance. This time, he got the eye chart, memorized the lines before the test — and passed.

in an air race, competing with a dozen other "air clubs" from Ivy League colleges. At his father's bequest, on graduation he whiled away his days as a bond salesman — the dullest years of his life he later said — until 1923 when he heard that the Navy was selling off surplus planes.

Trippe bought seven of them and formed Long Island Airways at Rockaway Beach NY with friends. It flew sightseeing tours, operated a charter service and did occasional work for motion picture companies. The Roaring Twenties were the decade of the bull market, holding companies and easy credit, meaning that Trippe had little problem getting former Yale classmates to invest in his next venture, Colonial Air Transport Company (CATC).

The 1925 Contract Airmail Act is the foundation that commercial aviation in the United States is built upon. Signed into law on February 2, 1925, the Act authorized the awarding of government mail contracts to private carriers, established the rates for transporting mail and set airmail rates. It was called the Kelly Act after the bill's congressional voice, Melville Clyde Kelly, a Republican member of the U.S. House of Representatives from Pennsylvania, who was chairman of the House Post Office Committee. Representing McKeesport as he did (where coal, iron and railroads dominated), why Kelly would want to take business away from his railroad constituents (already suffering because of the trucking lobby) is mystifying. Even more so is that he did this at the request of one Alan Magee Scaife from an affluent Pittsburgh family. But then Scaife had been to Yale (Class of 1920) and was pleased to help out his former roommate, one Juan Trippe. Kelly would also sponsor the 1928 Foreign Airmail Act, which helped Pan American in its expansion into South America.[4]

As expected, CATC was awarded a plum route — to fly the mail from Newark N.J. (New York's airport then) to Boston. The carriage of mail was paid by weight making it a lucrative contract, but Trippe was dissatisfied. He had the vision to

---

4   Marilyn Bender and Selig Altshul, *The Chosen Instrument. Pan Am/Juan Trippe. The Rise and Fall of an American Entrepreneur.* New York: Simon & Schuster, 1982.

see past the airmail subsidies to commercial self-sufficiency. Passengers could accompany the mail and be charged to do so, he told Colonial's stockholders, and instead of the single engine Fokker Universals they had chosen, he committed CATC to two large Fokker F.VIIs, each with capacity for 8–12 passengers. The financially cautious stockholders were aghast and resisted this. It was a boardroom coup that failed and in 1926 Trippe withdrew from CATC which eventually became American Airlines.

John T. Hambleton was what Trippe hoped he might have been had the war lasted longer. A former fighter pilot with the 95th Aero Squadron on the Western Front, Hambleton had been awarded the *Croix de Guerre* and Distinguished Service Cross with Oak Leaf Cluster for outstanding bravery. In 1924, Hambleton married Margaret, the daughter of George Blow Elliott, the president of the Atlantic Coast Railway. If that wasn't enough "old money", the usher at their wedding was a boyhood friend, David K.E. Bruce, the son-in-law of the Treasury Secretary Andrew Mellon. A Harvard man with a chest full of medals, Hambleton was urbane and eloquent and Trippe was in awe of him. On June 2, 1927, ten days after Lindbergh's solo flight across the Atlantic, he asked Hambleton to be his Vice President and join him and his Yale classmate "Sonny" Whitney to form the Aviation Corporation of America (ACA), each of the three putting up $25,000 which would be about $350,000 in 2020.

"Let me tell you about the very rich." F. Scott Fitzgerald wrote in 1925 "They are different from you and me." The American dream was power, wealth and, most importantly belonging to the same upper strata of society (which Fitzgerald's protagonist Jay Gatsby, despite the lavish parties, could never reach). For Trippe, it was always about whom he knew — and besides, "Sonny" Whitney (the grandson of Cornelius Vanderbilt II then considered the richest man in the United States) Trippe knew other wealthy Yale alumni like Robert "Bobbie" Lehmann (of Lehmann Brothers) and railroad baron W. Averell Harriman. The word 'networking' wasn't yet invented but Trippe excelled at it. It was said that at one time every one of Pan American's board of directors could sing *The Wiffenpoof Song.*[5] Soon other like-minded men of "comfortable means" wanted shares in ACA — Grover Loening, Sherman M. Fairchild, William A. Rockefeller, and the initial capital was raised to $300,000.

But the real money Trippe understood was in flying overseas. "I could see," he once said, "that there was less competition abroad than at home." This became a cast iron policy for him which he blindly pursued for decades and which would eventually lead to Pan American's demise. Trippe especially wanted FAM (Foreign Airmail) Route 4, which was between Key West, FL on the southern-most tip of the United States and Havana, Cuba. It had just been awarded to a company called Pan American Airways (PAA). Founded on March 14, 1927 by three army officers "Hap" Arnold, Carl Spaatz and John H. Jouett, (later to be joined by John K. Montgomery and Richard B. Bevier), PAA had been created solely to counterbalance a perceived German aviation threat in South America. The German-owned airline SCADTA[6] had been quietly operating Junkers float planes in Colombia since 1920. When SCADTA lobbied for landing rights in the Panama Canal Zone (overflying the Canal by non-American aircraft was forbidden then) for Arnold, Spaatz and Jouett (all of whom would distinguish themselves in the next world war) this was too close to the U.S. military bases on the Canal. Their motive was less profit and more patriotism (or paranoia?), but PAA was only a paper airline, without aircraft, pilots or landing rights in Cuba.

Trippe called Francis White (Yale Class of 1913), the Assistant Secretary of State for Latin America, and asked him to sound out the Cuban president of the day, Gerardo Machado. He then got Anthony Fokker himself to fly down to Havana and give Machado an aerial demonstration of his plane, even taking him up in it. The next day Trippe had a Cuban lawyer draw up a document granting exclusive landing rights to ACA and had Machado sign it, making PAA's FAM 4 contract worthless.

---

5   The signature song of a Yale student, a cappella singing group — Cole Porter was a member in 1913.

6   Sociedad Colombo Alemana de Transportes Aereos.

Arnold, Spaatz and Jouett recognized a preemptive strike when they saw one and their ghost airline was merged with the Trippe-Whitney-Hambleton concern, into a holding company called the Pan American Airways Corporation — a name that Trippe liked. Years later, he would say that he always thought Aviation Corporation of America was "too fussy" for an airline.

A ground crew was rushed to Key West's Meacham Field[7] to level a runway for the two Fokker F.VII trimotors Trippe planned to use — the same ones he had ordered for Colonial. There were already 30,000 pieces of mail waiting, brought in by the Florida East Coast Railway and, to comply with the stipulations set by the Post Office, the first delivery flight had to be completed no later than October 19. But, by October 17, the Fokkers had not arrived and runway construction was hampered by rain. His request for a deadline extension having been refused, Trippe was in danger of forfeiting the coveted route. By chance, sitting out a hurricane threat at Miami, was Cy Caldwell of Nova Scotia who was ferrying a little Fairchild FC-2 float plane to Haiti. He was mobilized (the hurricane threat ignored) and at 8:04 am on October 19, Cy took off with 772 lbs of mail. The aircraft was overloaded far beyond its weight restrictions and the co-pilot was left behind. Caldwell landed at Columbia Airfield in Havana, covering the 103 miles in an hour and two minutes — the co-pilot travelled by steamer to meet him. Pan American was in business. Trippe paid Caldwell $150 for saving the airline and then cabled his success to one Elizabeth "Betty" Stettinius in Paris (where her parents had sent her to escape his intentions). They married the following year, honeymooning in Europe where Trippe managed to fit the Berlin Air Show in. His loving companion and confidante, Betty Trippe, would always be known as the First Lady of Pan American.

Days later, the Fokker F-VIIs arrived and, flown by former Aeromarine Airways pilot Ed Musick, the first official Pan American Airways flight left Meacham Field for Havana on

7 The original Pan American office at Key West is now Kelly's Caribbean Bar, Grill and Brewery, owned by former actress Kelly McGillis who starred as Tom Cruise's girlfriend in the movie *Top Gun*.

The first official flight of Pan American Airways, operated by a Focker F-VII, left Meacham Field in Florida for Havana, Cuba, on October 28, 1927.

October 28, 1927. Passenger service began on January 16, 1928, a date chosen for maximum publicity, typical of Trippe.[8] The Sixth Pan American Conference was then underway in Havana and both President Calvin Coolidge and Cuban President Gerardo Machado greeted Trippe and Joan Whitney as they emerged from the plane. But the star of the show, indeed, then the most famous person on the planet, didn't arrive in Havana until February.

Trippe always claimed that he was present at Roosevelt Field on May 20, 1927 and had seen Charles Lindbergh take-off on his attempt to reach Paris non-stop. A month later, he watched the ticker tape parade accorded Lindbergh from the Union Club. But it was fellow pilot Hambleton who persuaded Lindbergh, then on a goodwill tour of 82 cities, to join Pan American as a technical advisor. For Trippe it was the ultimate publicity coup. Since landing in Paris, Lindbergh had been besieged with promotional offers — his biographer Scott Berg once observed that people thought he had walked on water, not flown over it.

---

8 One of Pan American's first Cuban employees was Fulgencio Batista, the future president and dictator.

The twentieth century's first celebrity superstar, he had been raised with a frontier mentality — shy, forthright and earnest. A survivor of the Suicide Club (which is what the U.S. Airmail pilots called themselves) he was the son of Charles Augustus Lindbergh, the Congressman for Minnesota who in 1917 had campaigned vigorously against the United States entry into a European war. Pan American flew 71 passengers to Havana in January 1928, including Al Capone and his bodyguards. It maybe apocryphal, but Capone is supposed to have growled to the pilots "If anything happens to us, remember, it won't be good for you fellers." Then the gangster dropped a $1,000 tip on the ticket counter.

Now in enclosed cockpits, the Pan American pilots could wear uniforms and, thanks to Trippe's naval service, they were navy blue with white hats. One of the employees at Meacham Field was Basil Rowe who began his career in aviation at a county fair in 1914, when he was 17. He was "watching an old time flier as he 'stubbed his toe' on some treetops and fell into a creek. I went over to help him," Mr. Rowe recounted, "and got myself a job as a fifth-rate mechanic. The next year he taught me to fly as I sat alongside him on the wing of the Wright biplane." In 1927, Rowe helped organize the West Indian Aerial Express, flying between the Virgin Islands and Santiago, Cuba. When his company was absorbed by Pan American in 1928, he was hired by Trippe and assigned to the airmail route between Miami and Puerto Rico. As there were only three pilots then, Rowe would be the most senior pilot in the company, retiring in 1956.

But full loads were seasonal and filling the Fokkers, along with the new Ford Trimotors, was difficult. Virgil (Vic) Chenea who had once owned Florida Airways was now the "Pan American Traffic Man" in Havana and took to hanging around the bar near the ticket office in the Sevilla Biltmore Arcade hotel, plying Americans who had arrived by boat with drinks in the hope of getting them tipsy enough to buy an air ticket home.[9]

---

9   The Sevilla Biltmore Hotel, run by the Mafia, features in Graham Greene's, *Our Man in Havana,* as the place where the mild-mannered vacuum cleaner salesman, James Wormwood, is recruited by MI6.

THE GOLDEN AGE OF FLYING BOATS

When, because of the 1928 Foreign Airmail Act, the government began paying airlines for the carriage of mail by the mile instead of by the pound — (unscrupulous air companies had mailed Sears catalogues and phone books to themselves back and forth across the country) — Pan American moved to Miami, which was as far as they could be in terms of the Fokker's capabilities and still make it back. Miami was also more central for connections and Trippe bought 116 acres of swampland on 36th Street and Le Jeune Road (where the present airport is), and had two runways, two hangars and a modern terminal building constructed. The Pan American Airways terminal was opened on September 15, 1928 by Amelia Earhart and Ruth Elder, two aviatrix celebrities that guaranteed media coverage. Earhart had only been a passenger on a transatlantic flight that June: "a sack of potatoes" she later said, but as the first woman to cross the Atlantic in an aircraft, she had been given a ticker tape parade on Broadway and the public couldn't get enough of her.

If he was to expand across the Caribbean and into South America, Trippe knew he needed flying boats as well as landplanes. When the Spanish exploited the South American continent in the 16th century, they built waterfront cities on the edge of the jungle for their galleons to dock at. Trippe went to the New York Public Library to research their voyages and conceived a network of strategic stopping points along the South American coast for flying boats. Airports were nonexistent in the interior of South America or too expensive to hack out of the jungle, but established harbors allowed passengers to disembark directly downtown. Besides, refueling from a barge and renting a mooring on the waterfront allowed for an expedient escape if the next coup went against the Yankee foreigners. For the hesitant passengers, flying boats were considered safer than landplanes as they could make unscheduled landings anywhere there was a body of water. As Pan American's Chief Engineer André Priester said: "A seaplane carries its own airport on its bottom."

On December 7, 1927 Pan American bought its first flying boat, a S-36 sesquiplane amphibian from Igor Sikorsky. The

The Sikorsky S-36 was the first flying boat to be ordered by Pan American. The aircraft pictured above, owned by Mrs Francis Grayson, was lost during a failed attempt to cross the Atlantic.

Russian émigré who built the massive "Il'ya Muromets" in 1914 had fled the Soviet Union (where his name and achievements were "erased" until 1977) and set up the Sikorsky Aero Engineering Corporation on a farm near Roosevelt Field, Long Island, NY. Five S-36 sesquiplane amphibians were sold to Pan American — and just in time. The latest FAM Routes up for bids by the Post Office were No. 5, which ran from Florida across the Mexican Yucatan to the Panama Canal Zone, and No. 6 to Haiti, Puerto Rico and south to Trinidad. Awarded both, Trippe needed the flying boats to service them.

Sikorsky advertised his S-36 amphibian as "Land Where and When You Want" and with their elegant boat-like hull and retractable undercarriage, they could do just that. But their Whirlwind J5 engines were underpowered and the fuselage was too low in the water to get off the "step" quickly. Room for mail was limited and the six passengers sat on two benches opposite each other. Lindbergh was unimpressed with the S-36, but it allowed Sikorsky to remain in business and develop the superb S-38.

Reminiscent of Curtiss's Nancy boats, the S-38 had a high upper wing and an aesthetically bewildering banana-shaped nose. It's blunt aft end looked as though the hard-pressed Sikorsky firm had run out of materials.[10] But the twin boom was high enough away from the water and the lower wing provided additional lift while supporting the floats. Seating 8-10 passengers, the S-38 had a range of 600 miles and was powered by more reliable Pratt & Whitney R-1340 engines. It made its maiden flight on September 15, 1928 and Sikorsky was immediately swamped with orders. He built one hundred and one and Pan American became his biggest customer. But the first S-38 went to its rival, the New York, Rio and Buenos Aires Line Incorporated (NYRBA) for its survey flight of South America.

Colonel Ralph Ambrose O'Neill had flown Nieuport and Spad fighter aircraft in the 147th Aero Squadron during the Great War and having shot down 6 enemy aircraft had been awarded the Distinguished Service Cross (twice) and the *Croix de Guerre.* Born in Mexico to American parents he was fluent in Spanish and in 1920 was hired by the Mexican government to train its country's air force. By 1927, O'Neill was the exclusive agent for Boeing and Pratt & Whitney in Latin America, and it was while demonstrating Boeing's F2-B fighter aircraft, that he became interested in starting an airline.[11]

A war hero, competent aviator and well known in Latin and South America, O'Neill was ideal to do this. He got the financial backing of influential men on Wall Street like James H. Rand of Remington-Rand, Lewis Pierson of Irving Trust, William B. Mayo of the Ford Motor Company and especially that of aircraft manufacturer Reuben H. Fleet. After years of rubbing shoulders with the South American elite, the airmail contracts for Argentina and Brazil came to O'Neill easily. The flaw in his plans was that he could carry the mail north from South America but, until awarded an FAM route, not vice versa.

---

10   Richard Knott, *The American Flying Boat,* Naval Institute, 1988.; Reprint. edition (January 1, 1988) P. 120.

11   While working for Boeing, O'Neill would fall in love with his executive secretary, Jane Galbraith. They would marry and Jane would join him on many future flying boat trips, becoming the first woman to fly to South America.

A replica Sikorsky S-38, belonging to S C Johnson & Son.

Well-engineered and functional, the S-38 was ideal for millionaire sportsmen, adventurers and industrialists — people who could afford a price tag in excess of $50,000 in 1928 dollars. The playboy Howard Hughes outfitted his S-38 with a leather divan, it was said by scandalized Long Island hostesses, to interview aspiring starlets.[12] So many private owners used their S-38s to commute to work that Manhattan's East River was sometimes congested with tycoons "yachting" in from Long Island. They could alight in water off the foot of Wall Street, then go directly to the office and be home for dinner. Owners included Col. Robert McCormick, publisher of the Chicago Tribune, taxi and rental car mogul John Hertz, C.R. Walgreen of drugstore fame, and H.F. "Hib" Johnson, head of what was once called Johnson Wax (now S C Johnson & Son).

---

12 Nothing demonstrated the S-38's versatility better than the movie, *The Aviator*, in which Howard Hughes (Leonardo Di Caprio) takes Kate Hepburn (Cate Blanchett) skylarking over Beverly Hills at night in an S-38. The cabin's cozy furnishings included curtains, a fridge and the couch. The lovebirds land at dawn on a lawn somewhere and the very same airplane later alights on water, delivering Hughes onto a California beach. The S-38 in the movie was built for Hib's son, Samuel Johnson, who retraced his father's flight in South America.

Because of its ruggedness and amphibious capability, the flying boat was known as "The Explorer's Air Yacht". In 1935, Hib Johnson undertook an epic adventure in his S-38, flying it from his corporate headquarters in Racine, Wis. to the forests of Brazil — 15,500 miles — in search of carnauba palms, which provided the wax used in Johnson's Wax. At a time when few airports existed in the U.S. and there were few in the undeveloped world, an amphibian was the only type of aircraft capable of making such a trip.

Another S-38 would feature in the Matto Grosso Expedition in January, 1931. Financed by E. R. Fenimore Johnson who owned RCA Victor, the expedition using an S-38 with crew from Pan American, studied indigenous culture on the Brazil-Bolivia border. While at Corumbá on the Paraguay River, the Americans offered to take the influential Brazilian explorer General Cândido Mariano da Silva Rondon to his ranch at Cuiabá. As it would be a two-hour flight rather than a week long riverboat journey, Rondon agreed.

He was rowed to the S-38 anchored several hundred yards off-shore but onboarding the crew found that an improvised duralumin patch, plugging a gash in the hull, had failed and water had leaked in, a too common occurrence for flying boats landing on rivers filled with debris. The water was bailed out and the patch resealed, Captain Charles Lorber signaled to start both engines and called for co-pilot/mechanic José Sauceda to lift the anchor. It would not stir, having become entangled on the feed pipe of Corumbá's water plant. Rather than cut the rope and lose the anchor, Johnson told Lorber that he would retrieve it. Forty years later, he remembered "all of us thought that such a swim, brief though it would be, was extremely dangerous, so naturally I did not feel like asking someone else to do the job." He dived in, fearing an attack by jacarés (small crocodiles), but after locating the anchor in 18 feet of fairly clear water and seeing no lurking jacarés, dislodged it and swam up the rope. Halfway to the aircraft he met a sight "which... turned my blood to ice water... layer after layer of piranhas around the anchor line... like the spokes of the Statue of Liberty's crown." Johnson inched up the anchor line anticipating an attack but crawled aboard unbitten. He remembered his fear was so great that it "had frozen me into speechlessness. The plane was well on its way before I could utter a word."[13]

Lindbergh's employment with Pan American began on January 17, 1929. He was to be paid $10,000 annually and allowed to purchase 1/10th of Pan American's shares at half their current value. He had already signed an agreement with Transcontinental Air Transport (TAT) — known for its record of air crashes as "Take A Train"— the airline even advertising itself as "The Lindbergh Line."[14] On February 4, 1929, Lindbergh and Hambleton pioneered future routes for Pan American in an S-38. They circled the Caribbean, from Miami-Havana-Belize-Guatemala City-Managua-Panama City-Barranquilla-Maracaibo-Curacao-Port of Spain-Georgetown-Paramaribo-San Juan-Port au Prince; returning to Miami. No mail was carried but, as Hambleton observed, everywhere they went, people were beginning to realize the possibilities of airmail.

The pair returned home on February 11, in time for Lindbergh to hear Dwight Whitney, the U.S. Ambassador to Mexico, formally announce that his daughter Anne was engaged to him. Although the pair had only been on four dates, they would be married on May 27, 1929 — the kidnapping of their son, the tabloid journalism (in which photographs of the baby's body in the morgue were sold nationwide) and the Nazi controversy were all ahead of them. The tragedies that shaped their lives began soon enough when, on June 8, Hambleton was killed when the Flamingo monoplane he was a passenger in crashed — with his wife watching.[15] Trippe, who would not allow his

---

13 Adapted from H. Hobson, Eric, *Brazil From Above*, 60.3 (2018): Expedition Magazine. Penn Museum, 2018 Web. 18 Mar 2020, P. 32.
14 The onset of the Depression almost bankrupted Transcontinental Air Transport which only carried passengers and, in 1930, at the Postmaster's suggestion, it merged with Western Air Express, which only carried mail, to form what would eventually become Trans World Airlines (TWA), a future rival of Pan American.
15 His son, Lt. Col. John A Hambleton, would retire from the United States Air Force after combat tours in Korea, Vietnam and Cambodia, only to be killed in 2009 when the Mustang replica he had built suffered engine failure.

name to be spoken in his presence, was deeply shaken — as was his board of directors — Hambleton was the only man who could oppose him and get away with it. He was the heart of the airline, a journalist said.

As there were no flying boats yet available that were large enough to carry mail and passengers to make flights to South America financially worthwhile, Lindbergh advised Trippe to use landplanes, build a string of airfields and install beacons and direction-finding equipment from the Canal Zone to Honduras via Managua. On September 20, 1929, a Pan American Fokker F10A, piloted by Lindbergh himself, left Miami for San Juan on an exploratory trip to the Caribbean islands and Latin America. The passengers were his wife Anne, Trippe, Betty and Glenn Curtiss who, in retirement, was living in Florida. The flight would inaugurate Pan American's inflight meal service with Steward Ralph Vega in a "white ducks" uniform serving fried chicken, salad and coffee. In San Juan, they would switch to an S-38A and continue to Paramaribo.

Betty kept a diary of the journey — as she would of other Pan American events. Foreshadowing the Apollo 11 astronaut's goodwill tour thirty years later, the Lindberghs and Trippes were lionized wherever they landed. Betty wrote that there were multiple "pushing, cheering, unwashed crowds", motorcades, the playing of national anthems, bouquets presented to her and Anne, speeches and banquets and Lindbergh standing on flag-bedecked balconies below while crowds shouted "Viva Lindbergh!" She empathized with the newly married Lindberghs who were "practically mauled by the crowds." As the astronauts Neil Armstrong, Buzz Aldrin and Michael Colins would also be, Lindbergh himself was awed by all the acclaim. They covered 9,000 miles in three weeks and the goodwill and publicity generated by his star quality could only help with landing rights for Pan American.

Reuben Fleet left the Army in 1923 to begin the Consolidated Aircraft Corporation in Curtiss's old Buffalo aircraft factory, transferring operations for better flying conditions (as Curtiss had) to San Diego in 1935. Fleet had tried to interest the Navy in his XPY-1 Admiral patrol flying boat but lost out to Glenn Martin. In 1929, Consolidated used the unsold Admiral as the basis for its Commodore, a twin-engine, parasol-winged, monoplane airliner that would be the largest, most luxurious flying boat yet built. Powered by two Pratt & Whitney R-1860 Hornet engines that the pilots loved for their reliability, the Commodore had an all-metal hull and held 32 passengers in short haul configuration, or 14 in long. The cockpit was enclosed and there were two passenger compartments forward, each seating eight, and aft there were either two three-passenger compartments, or one four-passenger compartment. The interior was in pastel colors with carpeted floors and upholstered seats. It was impressive enough for O'Neill's investors to allow him to order ten Commodores from Fleet.

In the short time NYRBA operated them, the flying boat proved its structural soundness. On an early trip along the South American coast, a Commodore's fuel line ruptured in flight and the engine caught fire. Captain Robin McGlohn landed on the nearest river and taxied the burning flying boat up onto a mudflat, the passengers escaping through a rear hatch. The fire burnt off the wing coverings, but the fuselage was intact. On another occasion, Captain Herman E. Sewell had to land one in a field of Cuban sugar cane. The Commodore slid among the stalks and came to a stop — virtually undamaged. It would be disassembled, trucked out, rebuilt and resume flying. Somewhere in the genetic heritage of the PBY Catalina flying boat that five years later Consolidated would build, is the Commodore.

In that summer of 1929, the ominous rumbles of the stock market sliding into an unprecedented crash, made airline investors worry, but it did not deter either Trippe or O'Neill. Both had set their sights on expanding to Brazil and Argentina. In July, O'Neill would pilot his S-28, christened *Washington*, in a historic flight of 8,000 miles from New York to Buenos Aires, the first ever attempted. NYBRA began operations from Miami to Buenos Aires and Montevideo on August 21, and later with multiple stops through the Amazon jungle to Yacuiba, Bolivia.

Exterior and interior of a Pan American Consolidated Commodore. In 1929 it was the world's largest and most luxurious flying boat.

What characterized Trippe, Richard Branson would write, was an uncanny ability to pace his airline's growth with the range of the airliner as it slowly evolved: first crawling from island to island across the Caribbean and into Mexico, then extending to Central and South America. With Sikorsky building a larger version of the S-38, Trippe, preparing to expand to South America, would order it on December 20, 1929.

That month potential rivals on the Atlantic were also dealt with when Trippe discussed a cooperative effort with Aéropostale and Imperial Airways: the three had begun to talk of a shared transatlantic service. This led, in 1930, to a jointly owned subsidiary of the three companies: Pan American–Imperial Airways that would operate from New York to Bermuda, the Azores and finally Lisbon from where Aéropostale would take over. It was a good deal for Trippe as each of the European carriers provided 25 percent of the service and Pan American the remaining 50 percent. The stipulation that would cause future problems was that the transatlantic service had to be initiated simultaneously by all three. In 1930, that was a dream.

The first Commodore named *Rio de Janeiro* was christened by Mrs. Lou Henry Hoover, the president's wife, on October 2, 1929. To O'Neill's horror, she arrived at the launch accompanied by Trippe! As soon as Mrs. Hoover (unaware of the *faux pas*), broke a bottle of seltzer over the aircraft, Trippe seized the microphone to announce that Pan American would soon begin flights to South America on flying boats as luxurious as this. Thinking this was actually a Pan American event, the media lapped it up, making O'Neill furious, as many now thought he worked for Trippe.

The former fighter pilot had influence in several South American capitals, but Trippe had it where it really mattered — Washington. Here he courted President Hoover's new Postmaster General, Walter Folger Brown. With the passage of The McNary-Watres Act (The Airmail Act of 1930) Brown ended competitive bidding for airmail contracts by sharing them out to established, sufficiently financed airlines. Under provisions of the Act, the Post Office paid the airlines for available space on their aircraft rather than actual mail carried. This was the incentive for the airlines to purchase larger, more reliable aircraft which, after loading on the mail, they could then fill with paying passengers. To ensure that O'Neill couldn't compete, Brown shrewdly withheld opening the FM 6 (from San Juan, Puerto Rico to Paramaribo, Surinam) bidding for months, while NYRBA hemorrhaged thousands of dollars. Later cited by the Roosevelt Administration for dictatorial collusion, Brown is seen by many historians as bringing order to the U.S. aviation industry.[16]

NYRBA's attempt to survive exclusively on passenger flights south proved futile — in March 1930, loads were barely 15 percent. The lack of market research in choosing the airline's name NYRBA (always thus abbreviated) didn't help either. It was a public relations nightmare at a time when Pan American's name and blue globe logo was pioneering what we now call corporate branding. Worse was that at many of the outlying South American refueling ports, the central government's authority did not exist and NYRBA's flying boats were pursued by local police and even fired on. The onset of the Depression, combined with Brown's favoritism, caused NYRBA's investors to pull out. The death blow came on August 19, 1930, when James Rand offered to sell his shares to Trippe for 40 cents on the dollar. When NYRBA merged with Pan American as a junior partner on September 15, O'Neill called it "a shotgun wedding after a rape." Trippe would offer him a job but he refused, saying, "They can steal my house, but they can't make me run it for them." O'Neill thought that the battle for South America would be a duel between pilots for South American refueling stops, but he was wrong. Pan American was built in Washington. Mail routes were created in the office of the Postmaster General, the airline was developed in the anterooms of Congress and other corners of the Administration. Ralph O'Neill would

16 In February 1934, after investigating the mail fraud scandal, President Roosevelt ordered the Army Air Corps to fly all airmail across the country. By May eleven pilots had been killed, and the work was returned to the airlines.

disappear from history, forgotten today even in his hometown of Nogales, AZ.

Besides the ten Commodores and their experienced flight crews, Trippe inherited NYRBA's Miami terminal.[17] Dinner Key was a small island in Biscayne Bay where locals camped (hence the name of the "quay"). With dredging, it was made into a peninsula for a naval training base in 1916 and the young Trippe had been stationed there. To combat the rum runners in the 1920s, Dinner Key became a U.S. Coast Guard base until 1926 when a hurricane devastated it. Having bought the land in 1929, O'Neill had a large houseboat built in Cuba towed out to it to be NYBRA's operations facility, the airport was now called Barge Terminal.

Trippe would remake Dinner Key to be Pan American's gateway to the Caribbean and South America. Fred Gelhaus who had built the Miami offices on 36th Street collaborated with New York architects William Delano and Chester Aldrich to create the first terminal building in the world solely for flying boats. In fact, it was the world as Trippe would have wanted it. The centerpiece was a two-story white stucco rectangular building with extensions on either side and at the far end a ramp to bring up the flying boats and 4 hangars. Extending around the terminal building was a frieze of winged globes and rising suns. It opened on March 25, 1934 and the Barge Terminal was happily retired. Passengers were picked up from their Miami hotels by the "Aerocar" — a trailer designed by Curtiss, their first sight of the complex from the palm-lined Pan American Drive. Sightseers flocked to Dinner Key, not only to gape at the Clippers moored outside but also the giant multicolored globe sunk into the terrazzo within. Built by Rand McNally, it depicted the air routes of the world and every two minutes was rotated by an electric motor. The murals near the ceiling traced the history of Flight from Leonardo Da Vinci's designs to Pan American's Clippers.[18]

---

17 Four more Commodores were bought directly from Consolidated.
18 Trippe had a smaller version of the globe in his New York office in the Chrysler building.

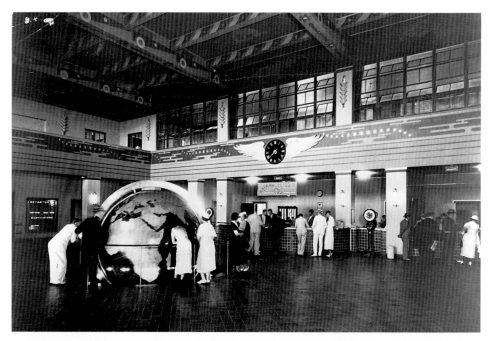

Pan American's Dinner Key terminal in Biscayne Bay, Miami, contained a giant multicoloured globe rotated by an electric motor. Today it is Miami's City Hall.

During the war, with the airline now headquartered in San Francisco and La Guardia, NY, the Miami building served as the Ocean Navigation School to train Royal Air Force navigators who used the four remaining Commodores to practice their skills on. In 1943, President Franklin Roosevelt would board a Boeing Clipper from the terminal to the Casablanca summit — the first time an American president would fly while in office. The last flying boat left Dinner Key on August 9, 1945 and the following year Pan American sold the property to the City of Miami for $1.1 million. The building went through a few uses before being reborn as Miami's City Hall. The murals have since been restored and the mammoth globe donated to the Florida Museum of Science.

With the Commodores, Pan American could now run a service from Miami to Buenos Aires (with a Ford Trimotor flight across to Santiago, Chile) in six days compared with three weeks by ship. It was still a long weary coast-hugging journey requiring six overnight stops. Before touching down in Rio, passengers were put up at hotels in Kingston, Maracaibo, Port of Spain, Belem, Fortazela and Sao Salvador. Some of the hotels remain in business today — worse for wear, like the Excelsior Hotel in Fortaleza, Brazil. This was where Amelia Earhart and Fred Noonan, circumnavigating the globe at the equatorial latitudes in 1937, stayed while Pan American mechanics worked on their Electra for the transoceanic flight to Africa. The pair had just flown over the dense Brazilian jungle, much of it unmapped, and Earhart wrote of her fear coming down in it. She once told the young novelist Gore Vidal that she didn't fear the ocean as much as she did the jungle.

A monoplane with the four 575 horsepower Pratt & Whitney Hornet B engines under a parasol wing, the S-40 was, for a short time, the world's largest amphibian and also the largest transport plane yet built in the United States. Lindbergh didn't like the myriad struts and wires that held the wing and engines together, saying it would be "like flying a forest through the air." The aircraft's weight after the diminutive S-38 had been an engineering challenge, even for Sikorsky and he had difficulty

The Sikorsky S-40 amphibian was, for a time, America's largest transport aircraft. Charles Lindbergh predicted it would be "Like flying a forest through the air."

in finding springs heavy enough for the huge landing gear. He solved this by adapting heavy duty railroad car springs. The S-38's banana nose was replaced with a handsome ship's bow, giving the S-40 the appearance of a square-rigged ship in full sail. Within, an 8 foot ceiling meant that all could walk upright as well as a smoking lounge in mahogany wood paneling. A pantry with a refrigerator and stove meant that pursers (steward) became part of the crew. It could carry up to 40 passengers and had a crew of five — two pilots, an engineer, radio operator and a purser.

On October 10, 1931, Capt. Basil Rowe and crew took delivery of the first S-40 from the Sikorsky plant. They flew it to the Anacosta Naval Station, VA, where Mrs. Hoover christened it *American Clipper*, the first Pan American plane to carry the name *Clipper* — the other two were the *Caribbean Clipper* and the *Southern Clipper*. Pan American never used the S-40 as an amphibian, removing the wheels to save weight. The flying boat's normal range was about 500 miles and it was kept on the Caribbean. Only three were built, all for Pan American and both Lindbergh and Sikorsky were already planning the S-42. The S-40s would provide safe, reliable service for Pan American into World War when they were passed on to the U.S. Navy, the *American Clipper* itself would be scrapped in 1943.

It would enter service on November 19, the three put on the South American routes where Pan American (and the United States) was in danger of losing its monopoly. In January 6, 1931 twelve Savoia-Marchetti S-55 flying boats under the command of General Italo Balbo would fly in formation across the South Atlantic from Bolama, Portuguese Guinea to Natal, Brazil. In France, the Latécoère 300 passenger/mail flying boat was being prepared to operate from Dakar, Senegal to Brazil.[19] With a large German community in South America, in 1932, the *Graf Zeppelin* inaugurated a regular service to Brazil with 20 trips per year. Proof of a revived Germany was Lufthansa's combined flying boat/steamship airmail service in the South

---

19 On December 7, 1936, French aviator Jean Mermoz took off from Dakar, Senegal, in his four-engine Latécoère 300 flying boat for a flight across the South Atlantic to Brazil. It was to be his 24th crossing but, after a brief radio message, *Croix du Sud*, and its veteran five-man crew vanished, never to be seen again.

The only surviving Savoia Marchetti S.55 flying boat was preserved in the (now closed) TAM museum in Brazil.

Atlantic beginning February 3, 1934. The steamship *Westfalen* had a catapult facility for launching and retrieving Dornier Do J Wal flying boats.

But Trippe, not content with just linking both Americas with an air route system had, like Cortez, now set his eyes on the Pacific. Pan American announced its need for an even bigger, faster airplane with a greater range than the S-40 that could fly from San Francisco to Hawaii. Boeing and Douglas were busy with their landplanes and only Sikorsky and Martin responded to the call. Sikorsky offered the S-42, a heavier (17 tons) version of the S-40, and Trippe bought ten.

This flying boat differed from other Sikorsky designs in that the tail surfaces were carried directly by the hull and not on open booms. This made for a longer hull and more spacious cabin accommodations. Inside, a center aisle gave access to all passenger compartments and to the cockpit forward. The

(Above) Pan American's Sikorsky S-42 *Samoan Clipper* alongside Short S.23 Empire *Centaurus* of Imperial Airways in Auckland Harbor in 1937. (Below) Interior of a Pan American Sikorsky S-42.

bulkhead doors were watertight so that it was finally possible to seal off any part of the hull section in case of damage to the plating. Adjustable passenger seats were hung from the bulkheads without legs to the floor. There were two completely equipped toilets and washrooms off the aisle adjacent to the companionway. Between the hatch and tail was all the steward's equipment, life rafts, auxiliary fire-fighting equipment and a combination mail and baggage compartment occupy the space in the hull.

The walls and ceiling in the four passenger compartments were lined with walnut-balsa wood veneer panels, all removable for inspection of underlying structure. Pads of rubberized horsehair between the liner panels and the bulkhead panels dampened out vibration and helped in the sound insulation. Each compartment had the three circular windows on both sides that were fitted with shatterproof glass and non-operable. Ventilation was from two overhead ducts with four adjustable registers in each cabin section. The cross-frames under the floor between the bulkheads were spaced far enough apart so that a man may go down into the bottom without difficulty, and 'stringers' arranged so that no water pockets can form between bulkheads. There were eight elliptical fuel tanks carrying 1,200 gallons of fuel.

In the crew compartment, the chief pilot was on the left and co-pilot on the right in the usual manner. The radio operator occupied the space behind the co-pilot and the flight engineer was stationed behind the pilot. Only the essential navigating and engine control instruments (tachometers and manifold pressure gauges) were on the pilots' boards. The engine indication instruments (such as pressure and temperature gauges, fuel gauges, etc.) were mounted on the rear cockpit bulkhead at the flight engineer's post. The pilots could, for the first time, be concerned only with flying instruments and the flight engineer with all four engines. Another innovation was that the throttle, flap and adjustable pitch controls, ignition switches, master switches, and the fire extinguisher controls were suspended from the cockpit roof, overhead, for easy reach of both pilots. A door in the forward cockpit bulkhead gave access to the anchor winch and to a hatchway in the forward deck.

Beginning with the *Brazilian Clipper* in May 1934, the S-42s served Pan American well, operating between Miami and Rio de Janerio. That few Americans knew where that South American city was — or could afford to fly there made Trippe consider a wildly, imaginative idea. The ultimate publicist, thirty years later he would pull off a major coup in publicity by having the airline's name and logo emblazoned on one of the tallest buildings in Manhattan. Although the company didn't own the building and only occupied 15 floors, everyone from tourists to taxi drivers knew it as the "Pan American Building". The signage was unpopular with city planners (and other airlines) as it dwarfed Grand Central Station and commanded the view on Park Avenue.[20]

In Depression weary America, everyone went to the movies for news on current affairs and to escape real life. The Miami-Rio airfare might be out of reach for the majority of the viewers but if air travel could be portrayed as glamorous, romantic and sexy (with some dance numbers) it would lure the wealthy away from ocean liners and make everyone else forget their troubles for 90 minutes. It is not known whether Trippe asked Merian C. Cooper to make a film that featured his airline's South American route, or the pilot in Cooper was intrigued by the possibility of doing so using real and fake aircraft, but *Flying Down to Rio* was product placement around a musical.

A fighter pilot who had fought in the Polish-Soviet conflict in 1919, Cooper had been invited by Hambleton to join Pan American's board of directors. Attendance couldn't have been onerous as he was able to make movies for RKO Radio Pictures when not at meetings. His most successful was *King Kong* released in 1933, which he co-wrote, co-directed and appeared in. A technological marvel of the day, *King Kong* had stop-motion animation and Cooper pioneered the traveling matte process (comparable to the "blue screen" today).

---

20 It would also be the last time the City of New York would allow corporate names and logos on tall buildings.

The movie, *Flying Down to Rio,* promoted aviation almost as much as Lindbergh's transatlantic flight and hugely benefited Pan American's South American services.

Flying for six continuous days in a deafness-inducing, unpressurised, freezing metal tube was neither glamorous or sexy but that wouldn't be the first (or last) time Hollywood promoted unrealistic expectations or misrepresented real life. Audiences didn't want to see the poverty, disease and corruption typical of a South American city then — in 1933 they could see much of that at home. Using beautiful young people, dances and *double entendres*, the movie made flying from Miami to

Rio (via a Haitian beach), fun and believable. The male lead, Roger Bond, (played by Gene Raymond, an actual pilot who would go on to fly B-17s in the Second World War), has a piano in his aircraft so that he can compose music en route to Rio. The female lead, Belinha del Rezende, is played by gorgeous Dolores del Rio who was Mexican, but her name was an added bonus. She catches Bond's eye, prompting a blonde dancer to ask: "Say, what have these South American girls got below the Equator that we haven't?" In true Hollywood formula, lowly accordion player Fred Ayres (Fred Astaire) is told by the police that the hotel opening that his band is rehearsing for is canceled because there is no entertainment license. Then Roger sees a plane flying overhead and thinks of scantily clad girls (and what pilot hasn't?) dancing on its wings. The "Air Ballet" in traveling matte shows that flying is so safe that an army of showgirls can dance, wave, and even do trapeze stunts on top of an aircraft's wings.[21] The sequence where the girls employ miniature parachutes which then rip their clothes off, dates this as a pre-Code film. It all works out in the end with Fred, now band leader, and Honey Hale (Ginger Rogers) strutting her stuff — the movie would be the first time that Astaire and Rogers would dance together.

And so that Pan American can get its S-40 in, the ancient seafaring power that a ship's captain can perform marriages is now bequeathed to Clipper pilots and the lovebirds tie the knot while cruising in luxury at 5,000 feet. *Flying Down to Rio* promoted aviation almost as much as Lindbergh's transatlantic flight — and with some great dance numbers. It also allowed Cooper to resign from the board and make more movies.

It would happen again. In 1956, when Pan American wanted to announce its round the world flights, the advertising agency J. Walter Thompson was contracted to design ads for *Life, The Saturday Evening Post*, and all other magazines that affluent Americans read. The agency sent the well-known artist Norman Rockwell on a globetrotting tour of cities wherever Pan American flew. Rockwell came back with scenes of pigeons in

---

21 The aircraft used in the movie were a Fairchild 71, a Buhl Bull Pup LA1, a Lockheed Vega, a Monocoupe 90 and the S-40.

Trafalgar Square, beggar-thronged Karachi streets, priests, monkey tamers and snake charmers. Trippe was not pleased — those real-life drawings wouldn't sell tickets. "Americans can see pigeons in St. Louis if they want." an airline spokesperson huffed. Rockwell who always drew what he saw, would later write of the whole experience: "...the agency and Pan American did not want pictures of the strange lands and people. 'Those would only frighten tourists,' they said; 'we want pictures of smart-looking tourists sunning on smart beaches in front of smart hotels.'" The advertising agency hired someone else and Americans saw another version of *Flying Down to Rio.*

5   Romancing the Clippers

With his secretive and imperious nature, Trippe announcing, "We are now ready to fly the Pacific," at a board meeting, must have shocked his listeners. He proposed that Pan American fly — not just to Hawaii — but to the Philippines and China. In 1934, the enormity of crossing the Pacific by aircraft was equivalent to space travel — both equally unforgiving. Had Trippe forgotten the Dole Derby?

Four days after Lindbergh landed in Paris, James Dole, the Hawaiian pineapple king, offered a First Prize of $25,000 and Second of $10,000 for the first persons to fly from Oakland, San Francisco to Honolulu. Everyone wanted a piece of Lindbergh then and the city of Oakland constructed an airport, hoping like Dole that Lindbergh himself would enter the race. He didn't but a number of would be "Pacific Lindberghs" did. On August 16, 1927, they took off from Oakland Airport (all in landplanes), aiming for Hawaii, almost a half-hemisphere away. Before it was called off, the Dole Derby had killed 10 aviators — three preparing for the race, five during it, and two in the search for survivors. Parts of bodies and aircraft thought to be from the Derby washed up on Californian and Hawaiian shores for months after. Dole had hoped that, like Raymond Orteig, his prize would stimulate transoceanic aviation, but all it did was reinforce the public's opinion that the vast and unforgiving oceans could not be crossed by aircraft — certainly not by landplanes.

The Hawaiian Islands are the most isolated pieces of land from any continent in the world — even the Galapagos are closer to Chile — and the 2,410 miles between Oakland and Honolulu remains the longest landless air route today. Ignorant about, and ill prepared for, what lay ahead, the participants of the Dole Derby died because their planes fell apart, or they ran out of fuel and put down in the ocean, or got lost in the San Francisco fog and slammed into a cliff. The entire Pacific Ocean would be conquered on October 3–5, 1931 when Clyde E. Pangborn and Hugh Herndon, Jr flew nonstop from Japan to the United States in a Bellanca Pacemaker, covering 4,448 miles in 41 hours 13 minutes. They were competing with the Japanese who had bought two copies of Lindbergh's Ryan monoplane and wanted their own pilots to be the first to cross the Pacific. Arrested as spies, Pangborn and Herndon were detained for seven weeks — which allowed them to meticulously plan their flight.

Locked out of the northerly Pacific, Trippe must have consulted his globe, searching for specks of land in mid-ocean. He chose a more central route that went from San Francisco to Honolulu and then island-hopping to Midway, Wake and Guam (the islands belonging to the United States), then to Manila, the Philippines before terminating in China.

At a time when airliners barely had a 500 mile range and most pilots still navigated by landmarks, this was equivalent to voyaging out of our planetary system and into Deep Space. A relay station for the transpacific underwater cable, Midway, was 1,380 miles from Honolulu. The uninhabited coral atoll that British captain Samuel Wake discovered in 1796 (and named after himself) was 1,250 miles from Midway. Guam, a former Spanish colony ceded to the United States in 1898, was 1,560 miles from Wake and Manila was 1,600 miles from it.

Rather than be party to Trippe's insane proposal, two of the board members resigned. Not only were commercial flights across the Pacific impractical, but the logistics of constructing refueling stations in the mid-ocean were beyond the company's abilities. The country's leading expert on aeronautical research Dr. George Lewis, Director of the National Advisory Committee on Aeronautics, attempted to dissuade Trippe and personally offered to provide "a public relations cover" if he wanted to back out of the plan. Airships, not aircraft, were the future of global air travel and Lewis would prove this soon after by taking

TRANSPACIFIC FLIGHT

IT'S A SMALL WORLD BY

PAN AMERICAN AIRWAYS

the *Hindenburg* to Germany. Aware of the harm that Lewis's pronouncement could do, Trippe worked hard to placate him. A director of the Pacific Zeppelin Transport Corporation since 1929, Trippe and his wife would later also embark on the *Hindenburg* (probably to check out the competition), taking it from Frankfurt to Rio de Janeiro.[1]

The diplomatic hurdles that a Pacific commercial air service would face were almost as insurmountable as the technical. The Japanese were aggressively asserting themselves in Asia and, to the disgust of Major General Douglas MacArthur the U.S. Military Advisor to the Philippines, President Franklin Roosevelt had promised to remove all U.S. military bases from that country. Taking advantage of this, in September, 1934 Japan gave notice that it would withdraw from the Five Power Treaty of 1920. This had limited the Japanese Navy to a lesser number of capital ships vis a vis the United States.

But Trippe was always able to align his plans with that of his government's. On October 3, 1934, he wrote to the Secretary of the Navy, requesting a five-year lease on Wake Island, Midway and Guam to construct refueling stations, with an option for four-year renewals. Roosevelt was hesitant to provoke the Japanese by militarizing these strategic islands but a civilian airline refueling on them was another matter. In an attempt to disguise the Navy's military intentions, Rear Admiral Harry E. Yarnell even designated Wake Island as a bird sanctuary. On December 29, President Roosevelt issued Executive Order 6935, which placed Wake Island, Sand Island at Midway and the almost submerged Kingman Reef under the control of the Department of the Navy's (i.e. Pan American's) jurisdiction. Although he always said that he was apolitical, Trippe's close ties with Hoover and Walter Folger Brown made Roosevelt circumspect of his lobbying. The President may have thought Trippe a "gangster" for padding his invoices to the government but his administration gave Pan American *carte blanche* on the Pacific with the understanding that it could help serve the

---

1 Founded in 1929, the Pacific Zeppelin Transport Corporation, subsidized by Goodyear president, Paul Litchfield, had plans that would never be realized to operate a 36-hour Zeppelin service between California and Hawaii.

national interest, in the event of war with Japan. Renting the islands for $100 annually, the airline was to act as a surrogate for the Navy which disavowed any official knowledge of what Pan American was doing but allowed its personnel to take contract jobs with the airline in civilian clothes. Not militarizing the islands would cost the Americans dearly when war came.

In a show of force, on the 10–11th January 1934, U.S. Navy pilot, Lt. Cdr. Knefler "Sock" McGinnis, had led six of the new P2Y-3 flying boats on a 24-hour flight from San Francisco to Honolulu. To Pan American, the 2,410 miles between the two cities now looked achievable by its latest aircraft, the S-42. The first one had been ready for trials by Christmas, 1933 but because of the ice on the Housatonic River at Stratford, these were delayed until March. On August 1, 1934 test pilot Boris Sergievsky, the controls shared by Lindbergh and Musick, put the S-42 through its paces.[2]

The 311 mile prearranged course was from the Stratford light house to the George Washington Bridge NJ, over Staten Island to Long Island, Rhode Island and back to Stratford. The flying boat lifted off the river at 9.24 am, flew four round trips over the course and was in the air for seven hours, 53 minutes and 58 seconds, covering 1,242 miles. By the end of the tests, it had captured nine world records in aviation previously held by France and Germany for the United States. In November, Musick took delivery of the second S-42 christened the *Pan American Clipper* equipped with long range tanks and special instrumentation to use on Pacific survey flights.

Ten S-42 flying boats were built; five were involved in air crashes, the first on April 11, 1936 when it struck a fishing boat while taxiing across the harbor of Port of Spain, Trinidad. With 18 passengers that included Jose Iturbi, the noted Spanish pianist and a crew of seven, the S-42 caught a pontoon

---

2   *Airplanes, Women and Song*, the title of Sergievsky's, memoirs is apt. He flew with the Tsarist air force, Sikorsky and the Office of Strategic Services during the war. His fondness for beautiful women was a passion of equal intensity to flying and he had three wives and numerous mistresses. A Park Avenue matron seated next to Sergievsky at a dinner party asked him to describe a high point in his life. He replied, "...bathing a princess in champagne." They don't make them like that anymore.

Of the ten Sikorsky S-42s built, five would be lost in accidents and one destroyed by enemy action.

on the bow of the fishing craft, tearing a hole in the forward compartment. Trapped in the submerged cabin of the plane, three drowned including Amadeo Lopez, the cabin steward. One S-42 would be destroyed by enemy action at Kai Tak, Hong Kong on December 8, 1941. Four survived the Second World War and were broken up for salvage in 1946.

The airline's focus officially moved away from Miami to the Pacific in January, 1935 and the Pan American Airways station was opened at Alameda, on San Francisco Bay. The airline signed an agreement with the Matson Navigation Company and the Inter-Island Steam Navigation Company on June 20, 1935 to provide meteorological forecasts from their ships for the Clippers.

It is safe to say that none of the Pan American crews groping their way across the unknown knew they owed their lives to a professor of Ancient History at Cambridge University. During the First World War, because of his fluency in German (and his skill at completing the *Times* crossword in record time), Frank Adcock had been recruited by the Admiralty to work at their "Room 40" — the predecessor of Bletchley Park. Here he decrypted German radio messages for naval intelligence which were vital in the Battle of Jutland. Tracking Zeppelins and U-boats by their radio transmissions, Adcock improved on the loop direction finding equipment then being used with symmetrically connected pairs of pole antennas. Although he would be made an Officer of the Order of the British Empire and later knighted for his wartime services, Frank Adcock was prouder of his translation of Thucydides and published writings on Greek and Roman literature. The Cambridge don's development of direction finding did for commercial aviation what satellite communications systems would decades later. Installing the Adcock Direction Finding (DF) sites across the Pacific was a priority for Pan American to ensure its crews got accurate bearings from shore transmissions. It allowed a ground operator to get a bearing on an aircraft at a range of 1,500 miles and with a bearing of two stations, a Clipper could fix its own position with great accuracy.

Having just graduated from the Massachusetts Institute of Technology, twenty-year old John Borger was hired to help build the transpacific air route. Sixty years later, he would recount the adventure. "What's amazing is that eight of us in the Chrysler Building in New York City planned this expedition in two months. Captain L.L. Odell, Pan American's Chief Airport Engineer, was in charge of planning, and Charles Russell was in charge of the expedition. I was just out of college, and was chief clerk. I remember our Request for Capital Appropriation was over a million dollars, one of the biggest RCA's at the time; the Board okayed it immediately."

The S.S. *North Haven,* a 6,700-ton freighter that had been taking cannery workers to Alaska, was ideal to transport the necessary men and materials to the island bases. It left San Francisco on March 27, 1935, its huge refrigerators packed with food for six months and its lower deck a dormitory with double bunks for the 80 construction workers — carpenters, plumbers and electricians hired by the airline, some of whom had worked on the Boulder Dam. There were also 24 Pan American employees, 12 each for Midway and Wake.

Loaded on the ship were prefabricated buildings, 12 each for Midway and Wake. For each base there were two diesel engines to generate electricity; two windmills to pump water up and get water pressure; a Caterpillar tractor with an interchangeable bulldozer blade and crane and tanks that held 4,000 gallons for both aviation gas and water. Two 38-foot power launches, one each for Midway and Wake, and a 26-foot launch for Guam for air-sea rescue were loaded on deck as were seven barges to tow the cargo ashore.

"At Midway," Borger wrote, "we had to unload in the open sea. We loaded the cargo onto the barges, and the power launches towed them four or five miles through the reef to the beach on Sand Island. When we got to the shore, we loaded the cargo onto 4 x 20-foot sleds we'd designed, and the tractors towed them into place. First we set up a temporary power plant; we had electricity the first night. Then we set up the food storage building, with a walk-in refrigerator and freezer, so the ship could leave. Then the construction workers started setting up the mess hall and kitchen; two crew buildings, one for base personnel and one for transiting aircrews (the hotel wasn't built until 1936); the Station Office for operations, the radio operator, and dispatch; buildings for the radio transmitter and the Adcock direction finder; a repair shop for the chief mechanic; the windmills to pump water, and the station manager's quarters. We also buried the tanks for gas and water, though not deeply.

Wake is made up of three islands. It's true it was uninhabited except for birds. We had to wear hats. We'd planned to put the station on Wilkes Island, which is open to the sea, but the survey team found it was too low in the water. So was Wake Island. But Peale Island, on the far side of the lagoon, was okay. We unloaded the cargo into a storage yard on Wilkes Island, then built a 50-yard railroad to the lagoon (somebody by inspiration had brought light-gauge railroad track). We put the small launch on a barge and, with the help of the tractor, we shoved it across the knee-deep channel between Wake and Wilkes. The launch towed the barges of cargo across the lagoon to Peale Island, where we did the same song and dance as at Midway. Wake depended on rainfall for water, so we rigged canvases on the roofs, drained them into underground tanks, then pumped the water up with the windmills."[3]

The coral heads had to be blasted out of the lagoon so they wouldn't rip the bottom of the flying boats. This took months of blasting and five tons of dynamite. Distillation plants had to be shipped in and as the sand on Wake would not support vegetation, several tons of topsoil were imported from Guam. This was used to grow vegetables and reduce the cost of transporting them from California to feed the islanders. Worst were the colonies of rats, descendants of the castaways from Captain Wake's landing. They welcomed the unexpected new source of food and armed with air rifles; employees based on the island fought them for years in a series of battles. With Guam, Wake was occupied by the Japanese from 1941 to 1945. Cut off from supplies, the Japanese hunted down all the rats for food. The story might be apocryphal but when the Americans returned, the rat population had vanished.

On March 31st, 1935 Musick brought the S-42 *Pan American Clipper* to San Francisco for the survey flight from Alameda and Honolulu. Although the Sikorsky was "factory fresh" he had it taken apart, testing every engine, fuel line, screw, nut and bolt. "Meticulous Musick" never took chances. Trippe arrived from New York by train on April 15th and conferred with Hugo C. Leuteritz, his radio genius. Would the Adcock signals work from that far away? Leuteritz had made improvements to them and assured Trippe they would — the DF system at Mokapu Point near Diamond Head, Hawaii was operating.

They left the next day. Musick's crew were First Officer R.O.D. (Rod) Sullivan, Flight Engineer Victor A. Wright, Navigator Fred Noonan, Radio Operator Wilson T. Jarboe, Jr. and Flight Officer Harry Canaday. The flight took 18 hours, 37 minutes

---

3 *When We Built the Transpacific Air Route,* by John Borger (Originally printed in the PAHF Clipper Newsletter, Spring 1995).

Ed Musick (left) and Rod Sullivan in the cockpit of a Pan American Sikorsky S-42.
Pan Am Historical Foundation.

and, as the flying boat approached Hawaii, squadrons of U.S. Army and Navy airplanes joined it, providing a ceremonial escort to Pearl Harbor. When asked by the media to describe the flight, Musick shrugged it off as routine.

But the Pacific gods had saved their wrath for the return flight. Throughout, Musick fought headwinds that made the Clipper barely crawl across the ocean. They had enough fuel for 24 hours and while Vic Wright "worked" the engines trying to get every drop of fuel out of them, Noonan tried in vain to get a sighting through the clouds for a "fix". With fuel dangerously low, they were lost, aware that Trippe had the media waiting to interview them at Alameda. Then a break in the clouds showed them the California coast and Musick was able to nurse the plane, now on fumes, down. It had been a close call, the S-42 had been flying for 23 hours and forty-one minutes.

Fred Noonan's navigation of the two Honolulu flights earned him a congratulatory letter from the world's foremost expert on air navigation, P.V.H. Weems, who had taught pilots at the Naval Academy. Noonan later wrote to Weems, that navigation during the Honolulu flight "was comparable with such as would be practiced afloat — fixes were determined entirely by stellar observations at night."

There were more survey flights and when Musick returned to the mainland in October to test the new Martin M-130, Rod Sullivan captained the S-42 to Honolulu, then Midway and Wake. This last base was not quite ready for a flying boat as despite months of blasting, the coral heads in the lagoon were still protruding out of the water like so many mines. A channel marked by buoys had been cleared but it was barely deep or long enough for a landing. With the nearest "alternate" hundreds of miles away, Sullivan (who was known to be heavy handed with aircraft controls and people), brought the S-42 in — his approach too fast and too long to land in the marked channel. The second time he again brought the flying boat in too fast but this time managed to stop — a few feet from running aground. Sullivan's explosion of temper began in the cockpit and continued to the dock and the mess hall.

Guam was a military base, closed to all ships except the U.S. Navy and the governor was a naval officer. After the tensions at Wake, the welcome for Sullivan's crew at Apra Harbor by the friendly Polynesian natives was much appreciated. Second Officer Marius Lodeesen (Lodi), who would himself become a Clipper captain, kept a diary of the flight and the reception. "As soon as we had docked we met the Governor, then the usual pictures and then we had to pass through a platoon or so of girl scouts who saluted and then pounced upon us and pinned little bouquets on our lapels. Vic says that was the hardest part of the entire trip. People came up and shook our hands and smiled like we were the Pope himself. Finally we got away and to bed for some rest. In the afternoon a formal reception at the Governor's mansion where we met all the notables, and were presented with a beautiful inlaid wood cribbage board. That evening we divided our attention between a dance given by the Elks and a party at the officer's club given by the officers. Everyone danced together; officers, enlisted men, natives and what not. Extremely interesting. The natives are very nice and well-built and most of them handsome, especially the women. They made me think very much of the Dutch East Indies... very polite and very much unspoiled. No tourist ever comes here."[4]

Glenn Luther Martin got into aviation as a boy by building kites on his mother's kitchen table and selling them to his friends for 25 cents. As a young man he would barnstorm, then go to Hollywood and fly with Mary Pickford (he refused to kiss her onscreen in case his mother saw the movie). In 1911, he started a company to make flying boats for the Navy. His first flight was 33 miles to Catalina Island after which Martin is supposed to have said: "Some day you'll see men flying across the Pacific, just as they now travel by ship." When his company built the *China Clipper*, to honor him Trippe would fly Martin to Catalina Island once more. Today the Baltimore company he built is part of the Lockheed-Martin Corporation which still owns the original buildings where many of Martin's famous airplanes were made. One of them is the old "A" Building from which the three M-130's were rolled down to Dark Head Cove and launched into Middle River.

Trippe wanted a flying boat that had the range to reach Europe or Hawaii while carrying a payload equal to its own weight. Lindbergh, who had been involved with all of Sikorsky's designs, was at the time suffering the trauma of his son's kidnapping and murder and didn't take part in this. Those who did were Martin's Chief Engineer Lessiter C. Milburn, Project Engineer L.D. McCarthy, Test Pilot William K. "Ken" Ebel and, especially, Pan American's Chief Engineer, André Priester, who had written the demanding specifications for such an aircraft. The required range was 2,500 miles against 30-mile

4 An author and raconteur, Marius Lodiseen would begin his career with Pan American, flying S-38s, even landing once at Devil's Island, French Guyana: www.panam.org/pan-am-stories/622-all-the-way-to-guam

headwinds. Trippe split the order evenly, taking three M-130s from Martin and three S-42Bs from Sikorsky. Not subtle about its intentions, Pan American would name its M-130s the *China Clipper, Hawaii Clipper* and *Philippine Clipper.*"

Accepting the contract to build flying boats for Pan American hadn't been unanimous at the Martin company. C.A. Van Dusen, "whose job it was to keep the company solvent" told Martin that the project would bankrupt them. The airline had only ordered three — the company would never recoup the investment and Martin had made four M-130s, selling the last to the Soviet Union. But, famously obdurate, Martin had made up his mind (or his mother "Minta" had) and he followed through with it. He had just been awarded the Collier Trophy for his B-10 bomber, the U.S. military's first all-metal monoplane and wanted to break into the commercial aircraft

One of Pan American's three Martin M-130s is chistened *Hawaii Clipper*, May 1936. Pan Am Historical Foundation.

business that his former chief engineer Donald Douglas (who had left after one too many fights with him), now had a lock on. Even Boeing, primarily known for its military aircraft, was now turning out airliners, albeit its 247 had lost it money.

Martin counted on Trippe remembering the loss he had taken with building three when Pan American ordered the next generation of flying boats. In hope of a sale, he built the even larger M-156 which had higher fuel capacity and more powerful Wright Cyclone engines. When Trippe wasn't interested, Martin sold it to the Soviet Union in 1937, the sale included all engineering plans and licenses. He continued to build giant flying boats during the war in the Mars series as troop and medivac transports. Obsolete on completion in 1947, five of them found new lives as water bombers in British Columbia. One was still being used for that purpose in 2020 and the other was retired to the Naval Air Museum, Pensacola, FL.

Coming full circle, in 1952 Martin's company would build the Marlin, the last flying boat to be used by the U.S. Navy. On November 6, 1967 in a final tribute to flying boat operations in the U.S. Navy, a Marlin would make one last pass over San Diego Bay's Naval Air Station North Island — once the sandy little island where in 1910 Glen Curtiss had opened a flying school.

When Pan American rejected the Martin M-156 it was sold to the Soviet Union.

The M-130 was 90 feet, 10.5 inches long, 24 feet, 7 inches high with a wingspan of 130 feet. The M-130's maximum take-off weight was 52,252 pounds. As shown in the newsreels of the *China Clipper* launch, the top and bottom of the hull were covered with corrugated aluminum alloy sheeting. The total wing area was 2,315 square feet, including the sponsons used for stability on the water (they also carried 1,900 gallons of fuel). The Dornier Do X had popularized the use of the "sea wings" as they stabilized the metal behemoth turning on the water. Arthur Gouge, who designed the Short's Empire flying boats, disagreed with their use, preferring the more economical wing floats instead.

Four air-cooled, supercharged R-1830 Pratt & Whitney Twin Wasp S2A5-G two-row 14-cylinder radial engines powered the M-130. They had a normal power rating of 830 horsepower at 2,400 r.p.m., and 950 horsepower at 2,550 r.p.m. for take-off. The engines drove one of the great aviation innovations of the 20th century — the three-bladed Hamilton Standard Hydromatic constant-speed propellers. Called the "gearshift of propellers", it would earn its inventor, Frank Caldwell, the Collier Trophy of 1933. The M-130 had a cruise speed of 130 miles per hour and a maximum speed of 180 miles per hour. Its service ceiling was 10,000 feet and hypothetical range was 3,200 miles. Because the aircraft were not pressurized, they generally flew at about 8,000 feet.

Thirty-two passengers could be carried with sleeping accommodation that fluctuated, depending on the number of passengers. The M-130's fuel consumption on Alameda-Honolulu leg for the first year averaged 126.6 gallons per hour until the 87-octane fuel was introduced. Without passengers and a minimum mail and cargo load, its range could be extended to 4,000 miles, but if 12–14 passengers were carried with a mail and cargo load of 2,000 pounds, this decreased to 3,000 miles. This meant that no more than eight or nine passengers could be carried to Hawaii which was the lynchpin of the whole route. Sandwiched between the Sikorsky and Boeing aircraft, the M-130 was good but not outstanding and events would prove that Trippe had been intuitive in only ordering three. Sadly, in the best tradition of beautiful opera heroines, each of the Martin Clippers met a violent end.

The aircraft's interior was the vision of the industrial and theater designer, Norman Bel Geddes, who had been inspired by the Do X.[5] He was known for his theater designs, cocktail shakers, radios, a teardrop double-decker bus and the model of the city of the future in the General Motors exhibit of the New York World's Fair. In January 1934, Bel Geddes proposed that Pan American consider the total flying experience from the point of view of the passenger — not the flight crew or engineer. He proposed a complete redesign with a single unifying standard not only of the aircraft's interior but of everything that a passenger might encounter, from terminal facilities to dinnerware, uniforms and menus. He didn't need to convince Trippe who had thought this as far back as Dinner Key. Both Sikorsky and Martin were less sure and it took some persuasion to convince engineers to pay heed to the instructions of a designer asking them to adjust the position of windows or relocate a gangway for aesthetic reasons.[6]

Flights were long and dreary and passengers who could afford to fly were wealthy and fastidious. To enhance what was a claustrophobic metal box below thundering engines, Bel Geddes used all the theatrical illusions he could. Bulkheads were paneled in simple light-colors that were easy on the eyes. Their entrances, traditionally at the spine of an aircraft, were moved to the side, creating large compartments on the left side of the cabin, and smaller ones on the right. At night, this allowed for beds to be arranged at a right angle to the aisle in the larger compartments, and parallel to the aisle in the smaller ones. The off-center aisle had a single seat on one side and, across the aisle, three abreast seating on a thickly upholstered

---

5   In 1929, Bel Geddes designed "Airliner Number 4," a 9-deck amphibian airliner that incorporated areas for deck games, an orchestra, a gymnasium, a solarium, and two airplane hangars.

6   Dieter Scholz, *Pan Am's Historic Contributions to Aircraft Cabin,* Hamburg University of Applied Sciences, German Aerospace Society, Hamburg Branch. Hamburg Aerospace Lecture Series 2017.

The interior of the Martin M-130 was designed by Norman Bel Gedes, using all the theatrical illusions that he could.

high, straight-backed sofa in a light tubular frame. Sofa arms could be removed and the sofas converted into sleeping berths curtained off from the aisle for privacy.[7]

The forty-by-eleven-foot passenger quarters of the Martin M-130 were divided into three compartments and a large central lounge, providing accommodation for up to 36 passengers on shorter daylight flights and for 18 on long flights requiring night-time settings. Bel Geddes gave the passenger cabin the appearance of a club with soft grey fabric walls and generously proportioned sofas and adjustable lean-back chairs. Each Martin M-130 had its own color scheme. The Green Scheme called for seats in green with gold piping, and corresponding colors for the striped night curtains. The Brown Scheme called for brown seats with eggshell white piping, the Yellow Scheme

7 Gregory Votolato, *Transport Design: A Travel History,* Trowbridge: Cromwell Press, 2007. P. 180.

combined yellow and green with an emphasis on yellow. All colors were sufficiently subdued to provide a pleasant ambience for long distance flights.[8]

In the larger compartments, the backs of the sofas doubled as mattresses for the upper berth beds, the seats formed the mattresses for the lower berths. Similarly, the upper and lower berth beds were formed in the smaller compartments. At bedtime, the lounge was divided by curtains into dressing rooms for men and women, and two wash basins were placed on the magazine table with hot and cold water. In addition, there were wash basins in the separate men's and women's toilets.

In previous Clippers, as in all unpressurised airliners then, passengers could count on being partially deaf for days after a flight. Thus, sound-proofing the M-130 was very much on Bel Geddes' mind. He covered the walls and ceiling of the cabin with doped fabric held in place with zippers so that it could be removed for cleaning and routine inspections of the cabin walls. The fabric itself was in a ribbed pattern, a damper of the engine noise. Cork flooring and wainscoting up to the window sills provided additional sound absorption.

All fabrics used were tested for sound-proofing qualities, and, like the upholstery, were fire-proofed to permit smoking in any part of the aircraft. The flooring could be rolled up like a rug for cleaning or removal. Adjustable curtains at the windows prevented the glare from the water and tropical sun and regulated the amount of light in the compartments and the lounge.

The M-130 ushered in the era of custom-made aircraft galleys that Pan American would continue with its Boeing 707s and 747s. Previously, passengers ate off paper plates at their seats, using wooden utensils. This was to be the first Clipper with a compact galley that utilized every square inch of space, with storage for linens, silver, cigars, food, etc. A suspended glass and china closet, insulated against vibration by spring steel construction, was added so that the glassware,

---

8   Ibid Dieter Scholz, *Pan Am's Historic Contributions to Aircraft Cabin*, 3.2.1

cups and dishes would not rattle or break. Beetleware, a thin high-quality plastic invented in Britain in the mid-1920s, was chosen for the table service instead of china because it took up little space, was light in weight and had the appearance of high quality china. Borrowing from the maritime world, Bel Geddes had all crockery fitted with vacuum bottoms that allowed them to cling to the table in rough weather.

There was an electric stove, a refrigerator, a sink with hot and cold water, a garbage receptacle and a soiled-laundry container. The wooden top of the refrigerator was surfaced to double as a draining board. Food came in four one-gallon containers. It had been precooked ashore, to be stored in the thermos containers, and given the final touch onboard. When Pan American allowed the consumption of alcohol onboard, a wine closet was added with a variety of liquors and the correct glasses for each type.

Reminiscent of the Boeing 747 to come, the Pan American airline ads were right — the three Clippers really were tomorrow's aircraft today. On December 20, 1934, Ken Ebel took the first M-130 the *China Clipper* down to Middle River for its test flight. It was delivered to Pan American on October 9, 1935 — over a year behind schedule, and at a time when a Douglas DC-2 sold for $78,000, its $417,200 cost was almost twice that of the S-42.

In the midst of the 1930s, silver-hulled and majestic, the Clippers — Martin and Boeing — were more than flying boats. They gave hope to millions of Americans beaten down by the Depression. It wasn't just that ordinary people could soon afford a vacation in Europe or Hawaii. It was the Romance of Flight, well represented in the aviation posters of the day — which was about as close as most got to exotic travel. Taking a Clipper, rhapsodized the airline, is to: "Sail beyond the sunset and the paths of Western stars in a modern way that would have thrilled Ulysses."

For Americans, the flying boats also symbolized their country's coming of age, a patriotic consciousness in their technological and cultural might that the world would soon know. The first flight by a commercial aircraft to Hawaii was comparable to the Apollo launches in the 1960s — the dawn of an era that promised Americans much. Unlike previous flying boats, it even evoked a romanticism from Pan American personnel who called the *China Clipper* — *Sweet Sixteen*, referring to its Civil Aeronautics Board registration number, NC14716.

The day November 22, 1935 had been auspiciously chosen because it was the 100th anniversary of the first Clipper sailing ship to enter San Francisco harbor. It was a weekday but 20,000 people somehow made it to Alameda to witness the first transpacific mail flight. Millions across the country listened to the launch on radio and soon would thrill to it at the movies. Nor was the audience confined to Alameda; an estimated 150,000 people watched from San Francisco, the Marin Headlands and other points around the Bay.[9]

Pan American milked the event for as much as it was able to. All three radio networks were there as were movie news cameras, some in aircraft circling overhead. The original plan had called for two NBC journalists to be on the flight but the flood of mail prevented that. The U.S. Post Office was about to issue a 25 cent airmail stamp featuring a Pan American Clipper and prominently photographed with the stacked mail sacks were Postmaster General James Farley, Assistant Postmaster General Harllee Branch.

Trippe ceremoniously handed Musick his written orders. Musick had already flown the Clipper on a shakedown cruise from Baltimore to Miami, Puerto Rico and then across Mexico to California. The night before, he had conducted a blind flight test, scrupulously checking everything. In his barnstorming days, Ed Musick had earned the name "The Jeweler" for good reason.

Farley made a great show of "loading" the sacks of mail into the plane himself and to emphasize the progress made since the 19th century, a horse-drawn Concord coach drew up to deposit the final sack of letters. The loading completed, there

---

9   A plaque in front of 950 West Mall Square, Naval Air Station Mall, Building No. 1, Alameda Naval Air Station, commemorates the inauguration of ocean airmail service and commercial flights across the Pacific.

20,000 people witnessed Pan American's *China Clipper* make the first transpacific mail flight from Alameda on November 22, 1935. San Francisco Museum.

were 58 sacks in the cargo hold, totaling some 110,865 pieces of mail that weighed 1,837 pounds — even without passengers, the government's FAM-14 contract rate of $2 a mile would be very profitable for the airline. No wonder the cynics called it *The Taxpayer Clipper.*

The author, Robert Gandt, describes the scene that day at Alameda thus. "The departure ceremony was scheduled for two-forty-five. The band played a Sousa march while the guest speakers mounted the platform. Behind the reviewing stand waited the great ship, her massive wings forming the backdrop for the scene. A gigantic flag was stretched across the grass, guarded by 170 boy scouts. Bombs and rockets were bursting overhead. Sirens wailed from boats across the bay."[10]

10 Gandt, Robert. *China Clipper* (P. 1–2). Naval Institute Press. Kindle Edition.

There was the ceremonial reading of a letter from President Roosevelt in Washington who proclaimed himself "an air-minded sailor" and said "Even at this distance, I thrill to the wonder of it all." Then in keeping with the nautical theme, Farley commanded: "Captain Musick, you have your sailing orders. Cast off and depart for Manila forthwith." The Twin Wasp engines sputtered to life one after the other and soon the *China Clipper* had made its way beyond the protective breakwater and onto the broad bay. At 3:36 pm, the 26 ton flying boat lifted off, the band playing *The Star Spangled Banner* as it did so. It must have been, for the audience, like watching on television, 34 years later, the Apollo 11 astronaut Buzz Aldrin saluting the American flag on the lunar surface. Every Wednesday after that, spectators would gather at Alameda to watch the weekly Clipper leave for Honolulu at 3 pm. The World had become a little smaller.

But that inaugural flight almost ended as it began. Heavy with fuel, the *China Clipper* nearly hit the unfinished Golden Gate bridge. The bridge's roadbed hadn't been built yet, but the suspension cables that linked the towers had wires dangling below them like a metal fringe. "It had been our intention to fly over the bridge," Second Engineering Officer Victor Wright recalled years later, "but Musick quickly saw that with the engine cowl flaps open he wouldn't be able to get up enough speed to clear the wires, so he nosed the Clipper down at the last moment and went under the bridge cables, threading his way through dangling construction wires. We all ducked and held our breath until we were in the clear." The pilots of accompanying aircraft thought this dramatic flying was intentional and some of them did the same.

The *China Clipper* landed at Pearl Harbor at 10.15 am the next day to an audience of cheering naval personnel from the U.S. Pacific Fleet. The flight had taken 21 hours and 4 minutes. On November 24th, at 6:35 am, it would leave Honolulu with mail, fresh food and 14 passengers to replace staff on Midway and Wake. When the Clipper touched down at Cavite on Manila Bay on the 29th at 3:33 pm, 300,000 Filipinos and a flotilla of

Pan American's Martin M-130 flying boat, NC14716, *China Clipper,* made history by operating the first scheduled airmail service across the Pacific Ocean.

boats greeted it. It was met by President Manuel Quezon of the Philippines who declared a nationwide holiday.

On the survey flights the crew had lived off sandwiches in waxed paper and coffee from thermos jugs. It would not be until June 20, 1936, that the Clippers carried a steward/purser on the Pacific route who catered to all onboard. But by that date the airline's Eastern Division Pursers had already flown over a million miles and begun a "Million Mile Club". Joseph Fernandez, Nilo Borges, Mario Borges, Joie Carrero and Rafael Kerr were original Pan American pursers. Fluent in English and Spanish, conversational French and Portuese, they had worked the routes to Cuba, Mexico, Columbia, Venezuela, Panama, Trinidad, Rio and Buenos Aires and back to Miami.

Bill Taylor, a young engineer hired by Pan American to set up the bases was in Guam when the *China Clipper* was on its return flight from Manila. In an interview in September, 1993 he would relate the experience. "We got word that the *China Clipper* had left Manila, and as the progress reports came in by radio, we knew that it was going to be later than planned. It was going to be a night landing. So we towed the landing light floats out into the harbor and lined them up into the wind.

I went out with one of them to be there when the airplane came in. We waited and after about half an hour we were out there when it finally came in, it came in low over the Orote Peninsula, and landed perfectly right in alongside these floats. Everything was fine until he started taxiing over to the float. He had to turn and taxi across wind. The wind was so strong that the airplane had difficulty in taxiing without dipping one of his wings. But he worked with it, and I was alongside with the launch to help him get the bow line to get up to the float and he finally made it and everything was okay. It was the first time I had ever done anything like this, and being a new boy on the street, I was a little concerned that I could do everything just as it should be done. But it worked out alright. They had not had a night landing on this run before — they'd all been daylight landings, because flying westbound they were flying with the sun, but coming back it's a different story, so they had night landings to contend with. And this was the first night landing they'd had on the trip. But it worked out alright. The airplane was there, of course, overnight, and I was all excited, because I knew I was going back on it. So I had everything all prepared.

"We had an early take-off next morning, before dawn, and just getting in the airplane and being on the *China Clipper*, was just the most fantastic event from my standpoint, because it was only the second time I'd ever been on an airplane, and to be on the *China Clipper* in the Pacific Ocean was just a really exciting event! And then, to meet Captain Musick, really have a chance to talk with him on the flight, was great. And to talk to Fred Noonan... that time he was doing a great job, and I watched him doing his navigation, and he was an expert at that, and we hit Wake right on the nose. It made me very happy to know that the Adcock direction finder was working properly which I had laid out before leaving there."[11]

The mid-1930s were the birth of American super-heroes: Superman, Batman, The Shadow, The Phantom — on the radio, in the movies, comic books and newspapers. Visual artists

11 www.panam.org/pan-am-stories/599-china-clipper-the-return

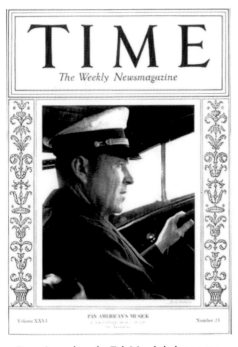

TIME
The Weekly Newsmagazine

Volume XXVI   PAN AMERICAN'S MUSICK   Number 23

Pan American's Ed Musick became so famous he was featured on a *Time* cover.

Jerry Siegel and Joe Shuster would create "Superman" in 1935 to fight the anti-Semitism they daily encountered. The American Dream had morphed into a nightmare where banks foreclosed, gangsters proliferated and racist organisations marched openly. Only in pulp fiction, it seemed, did larger than life brave men arise and, with courage and charisma, do the impossible. The transpacific flights, equivalent in the 20th century to Magellan navigating the Pacific, begged for such a hero and for Pan American's publicity department it was cometh the hour, cometh the man... Even before the *Ligue Internationale des Aviateurs* named Captain Edwin C. Musick the recipient of the Harmon Trophy in 1936, as the world's outstanding aviator and ablest flying boat pilot, Van Dusen, the head of the airline's publicity department, saw his opportunity. Only two Americans: Charles Lindbergh and Wiley Post, had been accorded this honor and when Musick accepted the award, all he had said was, "There must be some mistake."

"He lives quietly", reported *Time Magazine* which put him on their December 2, 1935 cover, "with his blonde wife, Cleo, has no children, likes baseball, Buicks, apples, ham & cheese sandwiches and vacations in Manhattan." His home daily flooded with fan mail and his phone rang off the hook with offers (until Musick got the bemused phone company to give them an unlisted number) he hated the attention that was thrust upon him. The magazine commented, "He refuses to show off or make wisecracks for newsmen. Completely lacking in vanity, he refuses to discuss his career even with such close friends as Navigator Noonan, with whom he bunks when on flights."

Lindbergh and Earhart were photogenic and, by now, media savvy but, out of the cockpit, Musick was uncomfortable with reporters who were looking for a wisecrack. Van Dusen was torn between trying to get the monosyllabic hero to cooperate with him, or simply presenting him as the strong, silent Gary Cooper type that he was. He even pressured Musick to shave with various different types of razors to eliminate the almost permanent 5 o'clock shadow that showed through in press photographs. When Musick was preparing to depart on *China Clipper's* historic flight across the Pacific, Van Dusen is supposed to have asked him to send some comments over the radio that would make good copy for the newspapers. Musick protested that he wouldn't know what to say, so Van Dusen suggested that he say something about the sunset over the Pacific, and Musick agreed. Several hours later, over the Pacific ocean, Musick phlegmatically radioed back: "Sunset, 0639 hours."

As he had in 1922, raising capital and publicity by networking with his old Yale classmates, Trippe used the lure of the Clippers to do so yet again. On October 14, 1936, the *Philippine Clipper* carried Trippe and other VIP passengers across the Pacific as a final preview flight before regular passenger service began. The other passengers were Sonny Whitney, the Chairman of Pan American Airways, Senator William McAdoo, Chairman of the Senate Commerce Committee, Wallace Alexander, Chairman of the Matson Steamship Line, William Roth, President of the Matson Steamship Line, Roy Howard, Chairman of the Scripps-Howard newspaper chain, Paul Patterson, President of the *Baltimore Sun* and Amon Carter, the publisher of the *Fort Worth Star Telegram.*

In Hawaii the passengers and crew would stay at the pink Royal Hawaiian Hotel which had opened on Waikiki Beach in 1927 and in Guam at the brand new Pan American Skyways

Hotel. At Wake and Midway, the airline put up its own prefabricated hotels which Trippe ensured sat in landscaped gardens with soil imported from Guam. On completion, Pan American invited the pictorial magazine, *Life*, to photograph the accommodation and they did so, complete with the requisite pretty young passenger unpacking for the night. *The New York Times* covered their construction thus on January 15, 1936:

PACIFIC AIRLINE SHIPS TWO HOTELS

Prefabricated Buildings Sent to Midway and Wake Islands to Care for Plane Travelers.

Two complete, prefabricated hotels of forty-five rooms each were among the 6,000-ton cargo of the Pan American chartered supply ship *North Haven*, it was disclosed yesterday, when she sailed from San Francisco on Monday night for the island bases of the airline across the Pacific Ocean. The two hotels will be erected at Midway Island and Wake Island. The prefabricated hotels of frame construction, are complete in all details, including furnishings. Designed for the special conditions on tropical islands, they consist of two wings built with a central, circular lobby. They have wide verandas. Each room has a shower bath with hot water.

Full furniture for the social rooms and bedrooms, down to coat hangers and ash trays, is in the vessel's cargo, as well as cashier's cages, desks, draperies, inter-room telephones and scores of other items.

After that first flight, the *China Clipper* and its crew became instant heroes and "Clipper mania" swept the land. The airline licensed the production of *China Clipper* toys, gifts and souvenirs and there were Clipper labels on everything from farm produce to household insurance. There was a Clipper beer and a *China Clipper* song which inspired a dance step. Chevrolet connected the steel construction in its cars to the same technique used in building the *China Clipper*. Restaurants and inns had *China Clipper*-themed dining rooms with "decor just like on the *China Clipper*".[12] And as

---

12   The original Hong Kong Airport, Kai Tak, had a "Clipper Bar" and Clipper models decorated its paneled walls. For more information on the airport see the author's *Kai Tak: The History of Aviation in Hong Kong*.

Indiana Jones would, in the movie *The Raiders of the Lost Ark*, fictional heroes Jack Armstrong and the Phantom flew by *China Clipper* to battle villains — who were always foreign.

As happened with *Flying Down to Rio*, both Hollywood and Pan American capitalized on the Clipper craze. Warner Brothers approached the airline and arranged for its subsidiary, First National Pictures, to make a romanticized movie about the *China Clipper*. A "B" production that was rushed out in August 1936, the movie touted in the trailer as "the most heroic adventure of the 20th century" had a grizzled Humphrey Bogart in a secondary role as the taciturn Clipper pilot Hap Stuart (he did somewhat resemble Ed Musick). Pat O'Brien (looking vaguely like Juan Trippe) who had played a heroic pilot in *Airmail* was the lead as the "driven and cold hearted Dave Logan, the president of Trans-Ocean Airways, who sacrifices everything for his dream of a transpacific airline." Bogart later said that, given the wooden script, he was embarrassed to be in the movie.

The real star is the *China Clipper* — even the studio model of the M-130 used in some of the shots cannot detract from its silver beauty. The flying boat makes its maiden flight in the film, cutting a white wake into the waters off San Francisco before soaring in the air and passing over the almost completed Golden Gate Bridge. As it crosses the Pacific, bursting through clouds and battling a typhoon, audiences thrill to the team of "ground control" radiomen and meteorologists that follow its course, relaying updated weather information to the pilots. It ends with the Clipper arriving in China to a harbor packed with cheering spectators and beaming government officials.[13]

The movie *China Clipper* (followed by the even worse B movie *Bombay Clipper)* was shot with Trippe's cooperation and received his approval. A film reviewer for *The New York Times*

---

13   Made in 1968, the year Trippe retired from Pan American, Stanley Kubrick's science-fiction epic, *2001: A Space Odyssey*, had product placement for Pan Am's moon ambitions. In one scene, the fictional Pan Am *Space Clipper* — emblazoned with the carrier's unmistakable logo — docks inside a gigantic space station. For millions of Americans, as the airline had done with its South American and later Asian fights, it made the future easy to imagine.\

Pan American's *China Clipper* inspired one of Hollywood's less memorable movies. Humphrey Bogart later admitted to being embarrassed by his role.

described the O'Brien character thus: "He goads himself and his aides mercilessly toward the realization of his vision. Marriage, friendship, consideration of himself — these are sacrificed upon the altar of his ambition." Everyone at Pan American was surprised that Trippe did not object to his portrayal in the movie — especially when Musick (Bogart) delivers a Hollywood punch to his jaw. Thanks to the Warner Brothers distribution, the movie played to packed houses. Today it is a cinematic curiosity — its redemption is the film footage of the M-130 and the bases at Midway, Wake and Guam which in five years would be brutally occupied by the Japanese. As for Bogart.... his great films were definitely ahead of him.

With the overnight accommodation in place, as planned, the mail route also became a passenger route. Delivered to Pan American on December 24, 1935 and declared airworthy on

July 23, 1936, the *Hawaii Clipper* was the last of the three Martin flying boats and Trippe was already considering its replacement. On July 21, 1936 he signed a contract for six Boeing 314 flying boats. The *Hawaii Clipper* flew to Honolulu in May, where a 14-year-old girl christened it with coconut water. It would be used for the inaugural passenger flight scheduled for October 21, 1936. The airline offered seven tickets by lottery and more than 1,000 people applied for them with Richard F. Bradley, the San Francisco aviation manager for Standard Oil winning Ticket No. 1. Among the passengers was the famous "first-flighter" Clara Adams. A wealthy widow, Adams held the record for being on first flights — the first woman to fly the Atlantic on the *Graf Zeppelin* and then on the Dornier X and in 1939 would be on the *Dixie Clipper* across the Atlantic.

On arrival at the Alameda office, the passengers were weighed, as was their baggage, which the airline warned was limited to 55 lbs without exception. Every extra pound swallowed up more fuel and on the San Francisco-Honolulu leg, every gallon was precious.

Pan Am's flying boats were boarded with something of ceremonial pageantry. At the sound of first bell, the captain and his seven-man crew would ceremoniously board the M-130 beside the floating pier; their double-breasted dark blue tunics and white caps giving the scene a nautical air. When the bell rang twice, the passengers would follow. When they boarded, a white-uniformed steward ushered them into the two cabins where they would sit, offering each a package containing gum and cotton wool. All kept their overcoats and hats on as the interior would become chilly when the aircraft gained altitude. To their disappointment, photography from the air was not permitted, especially of Pearl Harbor, Midway, Wake and Guam. With a "Panair" launch scouting ahead for floating obstructions, the big flying boat would be wending its way out of the "Port of the Trade Winds", as the little harbor was known, to the bay where it would make its take-off run.

That first night, as the *Hawaii Clipper* winged across the Pacific, it entered an almost purple twilight. The passengers moved about the cabin freely, exploring the Clipper, their every wish catered to by the steward.[14]

As the plane was unpressurized, when it got stuffy, he would allow each passenger to put their head out of the back cockpit for a breath of fresh air, one at a time. Publicity photos show men and women playing cards, backgammon and checkers while seated in comfy wicker chairs. Strangely, nothing seems to be bolted down and seat belts are nowhere to be seen.

The only overnight onboard was the first one and before retiring to their sleeping berths, the voyagers assembled at the dining lounge for a meal complete with fine china, silverware and white tablecloths. "It was a conventional supper — grapefruit, celery and olives, soup, steak, vegetables, salad, ice cream, cake and coffee," wrote passenger Charles McKew Parr. "The captain acted as though we were his guests."

Trippe's fascination with maritime tradition was everywhere. "The Clipper was a ship, not a plane. Time was marked by bells, the crew's watches were set at Greenwich Mean Time, and everything onboard moves according to the best merchant marine practice." wrote *New York Times* reporter Lauren "Deac" Lyman, who was a passenger in 1936.[15]

As on ships, a steward oversaw the passenger cabin, helping with customs and immigration forms, and organizing luggage. He kept smokers stocked with a steady supply of gum to help them cope with the "no smoking" rule. He made the beds, served the meals, which were prepared in advance and stored in insulated containers to keep them hot. With lunch and dinner, there were regular snacks and tea throughout the flight. On the ground, the stewards ran errands for the passengers (who probably also had servants at home) and at some stops even

---

14   One of Pan American's first stewards was Charles (Bebe) Rebozo. In 1943, after training as a navigator, Rebozo helped ferry about 100 warplanes to North Africa for the Army's Air Transport Command. He became a good friend to President Richard Nixon — the media would say his "bagman" — and was investigated by the Senate in the Watergate scandal for converting campaign contributions for Nixon's personal use.

15   The year before, Lyman (whose first story for the newspaper was witnessing Lindbergh's take-off from Roosevelt Field in 1927) had been awarded the Pulitzer Prize for coverage of the Lindbergh family's exile to England.

assisted with the docking of the flying boat — which was why it was a male occupation.

The imbibing of alcohol on all Pan American aircraft was forbidden which, given their Caribbean flights, must have been difficult to police. This was due to Chief Engineer André Priester who fought to keep pilots and passengers from alcohol. The reason was posted on his office wall: "Aviation is not in itself inherently dangerous. But to an even greater extent than the sea, it is terribly unforgiving of any carelessness, incapacity, or neglect." Alcohol was not allowed inflight on any domestic airline in North America then as, although Prohibition had ended, some states (and Canadian provinces) flown over were still "dry". But Trippe was acutely aware that his airline's wealthy clientele was used to enjoying cocktails before and wine with dinner. He also knew that on Imperial Airways aircraft stewards trained as bartenders assuaged passenger fears with liberal amounts of liquor. As a result, those Pan American passengers who brought their own supplies for the long flights were winked at by stewards. Trippe deferred to Priester's anti-alcohol rule until his return to power in 1940 (after the "Sonny" Whitney interlude) when inflight bar service was begun, once out of U.S. airspace.

The reciprocating engine noise apart, a Clipper flight was unforgettable. The view from eight thousand feet offered its own entertainment: lonely ships traversing the vast stretch of ocean below, a cavalcade of cloud formations, sometimes a thunderstorm, and spectacular sunrises and sunsets. At night, the moon played on the ocean while constellations danced across the sky.[16]

Trippe had wanted sleeping space for twenty passengers, but with the M-130s' range had to settle for a limited number of sleeping berths. The steward erected a Pullman curtain that divided the main lounge into separate dressing rooms for men and women. After putting on their pajamas, the passengers could retreat to one of the sleeping berths, which were the size of a camp cot. "The bunks were like Turkish baths" complained Helen Gierding of Orange County CA., who was traveling to

16 Meredith Hindley, Longreads, February 2015

Manilla to marry her fiancé and would keep a diary about her flight, "as the heat of the plane came through the ceiling." But she slept well because of "the sound of the motors." Eighteen hours after leaving Alameda, the Clipper would taxi up to Ford Island, past rows of naval vessels. The early morning departures and constantly changing time zones led many passengers to retreat to their berths after takeoff and reemerge for lunch. The 60-hour flight from San Francisco to Manila took six days, the $950 fare covering all accommodation and meals.[17]

HONOLULU - Hawaiian hips are shaking and shoulders quivering to a brand new island dance — the "Clipper Hula" — dedicated to Pan American Airways

The novel hula telling the story of Pan American's conquest of the Pacific was danced for the first time recently at the 10th anniversary ball of the Royal Hawaiian Hotel on the beach at Waikiki. Among those applauding the new story-in-dance were Governor Joseph B. Poindexter; Maj. Gen. Hugh A. Drum, commanding the Hawaiian department, U.S.A.; Admiral Orin G. Murfin, commanding the Pearl Harbor naval base; Mr. and Mrs. Biddle Duke of New York, in Hawaii on their honeymoon, and 1,000 other guests at the birthday ball.

The setting for the *Clipper Hula* was in keeping with the theme. As the guests were dined along the beach, a large model of the Hawaii Clipper swung onto the dance floor. From the illuminated cabin stepped ten hula dancers. These danced to the music of Louise Akea and her Royal Hawaiian Girls Glee Club. Miss Akea is employed by the Inter-Island Steam Navigation Co., Ltd., general traffic agents in Hawaii for Pan American Airways.

A description of the *Clipper Hula* and accompanying festivities centering around the plane model was broadcasted throughout the territory."

Virgin Islands Daily News, June 11, 1937. *Clipper Hula* New Dance In Hawaii

If the Clipper was on schedule, the passengers would spend an afternoon and a night at Midway — ample time, the literature claimed, to sample the island's great golf course. What wasn't in the literature were the safety precautions onboard every Pacific Clipper in case of a ditching. Helen Gierding might have noticed onboarding that there were the four "international orange" stripes on the wings and guessed they were to help search and rescue personnel find the flying boat if forced down at sea. The M-130 had six watertight compartments — any two of which could keep it afloat. Besides the balloons that could be released as search markers, safety equipment included inflatable life rafts, signal flares, a shotgun, a saltwater still, fishing tackle and enough food to keep 15 people alive for a month.

By 1936, Japanese atrocities in China were increasing and Pan American wanted to terminate its transpacific flights in Hong Kong instead of Shanghai. Although the Japanese Army was only 60 miles away, the British colony of Hong Kong called the "Gibraltar of the East" was thought more secure. But it was already being served by the pretty little DH.86s of Imperial Airways and the British government refused Pan American access to it. Not so the sleepy Portuguese colony of Macao next door. In the ultimate one-upmanship over rival Hong Kong, although it didn't have an airport, Macao was quite pleased to have Pan American bring the Shanghai mail and passengers to them. On August 14, 1935, Pan American's director in China, Harold Bixby, left Shanghai in a CNAC Sikorsky S-38 flown by Pan American pilot William S. Grooch and co-pilot/radio operator William Ehmer. It refueled at Foochow (now Fuzhou) and arrived in Hong Kong where Bixby conferred with the American consul. The British wanted Philippine landing rights for Imperial Airways and also the right to fly British airliners in China on CNAC routes, neither of which Pan American had the power to grant. Bixby said that it was like trading a button for a full coat. But by New Year's Day 1936, landing rights with the Portuguese had been successfully negotiated and CNAC could now fly passengers to Macao and put them on a ferry to Hong Kong. Bixby and Trippe knew that the real power in Hong Kong was not the British governor but its *taipans* and it would only be a matter of time before they would demand transpacific airmail access and force the governor to change course. This occurred on January 19, 1937 with Bixby securing a five-year contract for Pan American in Hong Kong.

During the 1930s Imperial Airways served Hong Kong with the relatively small DH 86 de Havilland Express.

The first Clipper arrived at Hong Kong via Macao on April 28, 1937 from Manila. *The South China Morning Post* reported that the S-42B *Hong Kong Clipper II* "...brought 2,500 pounds of American cargo, including 100,000 letters and newspapers from the United States only six days old. The papers left Alameda, Calif., last Thursday aboard the *China Clipper*, being transferred to the *Hong Kong Clipper* at Manilla. A large crowd welcomed the clipper at Kai Tak Airport. Included were Acting Governor N. L. Smith and representatives of all of the colony's government and commercial activities. The Clippers' pilot, A. E. Laporte, and crew were escorted to a dais at the hangar, where the acting governor gave a speech of welcome."

Within sight of Kai Tak Airport was then the Peninsula Hotel and as it did not require taking the Star Ferry to Hong Kong island, it was where the crew stayed. Built by the Kadoorie family in 1928, the "Penn's" guest books are filled with the rich and famous — from Emperor Haile Selassie to HRH. Princess Margaret and the Aga Khan, from Frank Sinatra, Tennessee Williams, Elton John to Yul Brynner and Sylvester Stallone. The locals believe that the hotel has a lot of ghosts. Prewar

Hong Kong was an isolated outpost of the Empire which the British were willing to sacrifice — Prime Minister Winston Churchill would famously acknowledge that there was "not the slightest chance" of being able to defend it. Although the third floor of the Peninsula Hotel has been remodeled several times, Japanese tour groups still ask to see it. It is where on Christmas Day, 1941, the Japanese would hold the Colony's surrender ceremonies. Major General Michael Maltby, the General Officer Commanding (GOC) and Sir Mark Aitchison Young the British governor would sign the surrender documents by candlelight. Both were incarcerated as prisoners of war until August 1945 with Maltby calling his hut at the Argyll Street POW Camp "Flagstaff House", the name of the official residence of the GOC. The hut remains today in Hong Kong, although it is now a tea museum — which would have appealed to the Japanese.

Bixby knew that with Hong Kong done, Trippe would be pushing for routes to Hanoi, Bangkok and other Asian cities. He also knew that it was time for PAA-CNAC to quit Shanghai — immediately. Writing in *Topside Ricksha*, (his self-published, limited-print memoir, circa 1938) Bixby recorded what happened in the city on August 14, 1937: "Outside, small-arms fire and automatic rat-a-tat punctuated the nerve-fraying rhythm of artillery-shell and aerial-bomb concussions." Less than a mile away on Shanghai's Central Post Office roof, he watched Chinese Air Force bombers dive at the Japanese warship, *Idzumo* anchored in the Whangpoo River, which had been firing into the city point-blank. "Inexperienced pilots released bombs early — most fell into the river, but several exploded in refugee-packed Nanking Road between the upscale Cathay Hotel and the equally plush Palace Hotel."

After shuttering the PAA-CNAC office, Bixby entered the blood-soaked downtown streets and walked home. He wrote, "Did you know that it's impossible to walk through blood? It is extremely slippery. I had to make a detour. Pieces of people were hanging on the telephone wires." Using the CNAC DC-2s, Bixby managed to evacuate all employees to Hong Kong. But by 1938,

even the British colony was no longer safe. On January 24, a Pan American-CNAC DC-2 would be shot down by Japanese fighters soon after take-off from Kai Tak Airport, killing 12 of the 17 onboard. Capt. Hugh Woods who had flown the Clippers in South America put the plane in a tight spiral and landed in the Pearl River, swimming to shore. In a testament to

Pan American's Juan Trippe with his famous globe.

both man and machine, the DC-2 was later salvaged to be re-flown and during the war Woods would fly "The Hump" between Burma and China.

With the San Francisco-Hong Kong route in operation and Pan American awarded the Collier Trophy (the only airline ever to be so honored), Juan Trippe was riding high. The media hung on his every word, his alma mater gave him an honorary degree and Clarke Gable's wife, Carole Lombard (who was soon to die in a plane crash), told *Look* magazine that she found Mr. Trippe one of the world's ten most interesting men — along with George Bernard Shaw and Chiang Kai-Shek.[18] A lesser man would have "reposed on his laurels." Instead, Trippe went once more to his office globe with a piece of string to see where else Pan American could fly to.[19]

---

18   In the School of Management at Yale University there is a professorship entitled "The Juan Trippe Professor in the Practice of International Trade, Finance, and Business."

19   Made in the late 1800s, Trippe's globe is now in the National Air and Space Museum Collection.

Since the days of Alcock and Brown, the crown jewel of commercial aviation had always been flying the ocean between London and New York. The most dangerous segment of the crossing was between Newfoundland and Ireland and it wasn't only because of the prevailing westerly winds and poor winter weather. The distance was beyond the capabilities of the aircraft then in use. The idea of constructing floating islands in the mid-Atlantic to refuel aircraft had been studied, especially by the French who were confined to flying to Brazil from their colony in Senegal. Without colonies, the Germans were limited to the use of their Blohm and Voss Ha 139 planes catapult-launched from the *Schwabenland* and *Friesenland*. Carrying passengers would have been difficult with this method because of the 4.5 G acceleration.

More fortunate than everyone else, were the British who had the islands of Bermuda and Newfoundland. But their focus was the Middle East, Asia and Africa, not the Atlantic. Besides, the generation of statesmen then in Whitehall were pro-airship and threw enormous sums of money at the Burney Airship Development Scheme. As late as April, 1937, their faith in airships was such that the Imperial Airways' London to Budapest flights were rerouted to call at Frankfurt, the only terminus in Europe for Zeppelin services to Rio de Janeiro and New York. Even before the *Hindenburg* disaster on May 6, 1937, Germany's Nazi government had abandoned airship development and was testing the Focke Wulf Condor, a four-engine, 26-seat airliner that had transatlantic capability.

The United States which had kept German airship ambitions of flying from New York to San Francisco at bay by refusing to provide helium, now did the same with landing rights for a Lufthansa commercial service. While this did not help Roosevelt's isolationist policy, especially in the Mid West, it gave Pan American some breathing space. Both Trippe and Woods Humphery were aware that their mutually exclusive "Gentleman's Agreement" of 1935 was running out of time and their respective companies had to begin scheduled transatlantic flights soon. An airline's reach is dictated by

By 1937 Germany was testing the Focke Wulf Condor, a four-engine, 26-seat airliner with transatlantic capability.

its aircraft's range and in 1937, Pan American's S-42Bs were barely capable (even with refueling stops) of crossing the Atlantic. The new Imperial Airways' Empire flying boats could not at all. Although the Short's Mayo composite and Cobham's refueling gave some hope both were, so far, for mail only. Gouge (now Sir Arthur) was building the S.30 and designing the S.26 flying boats, each with more range, but in 1937 all Imperial had were the S.23s.

At 800 miles from the mainland, Bermuda was within range of both the Sikorsky and Empire flying boats and by making scheduled flights there from New York, British honor would be upheld. For the Atlantic survey flights, Imperial modified two of the first S.23s, the *Caledonia* and *Cambria*, putting six additional fuel tanks between the engine nacelles and across the top of the cabin to give them a range of 3,300 miles. At the same time *Cavalier* was dismantled and shipped to Bermuda on SS *Loch Katrine*, arriving on 20 December 1936. Negotiations were successfully conducted in 1937 for a reciprocal scheduled service from Port Washington, NY (and Baltimore when icing prevented it) to Bermuda. With Lufthansa's Dornier flying boats, sporting Nazi swastikas, using Bermuda from September, 1936 onward, both Pan American and Imperial Airways were pressured to look for a base on the island. During the Boer War, the British government had transported Boer prisoners to Bermuda, incarcerating them on tiny rocky Darrell's Island — thus bestowing on local sharks unexpected largesse as at night the prisoners attempted to swim away. Unfortunately, as the local cemeteries attest, the POWs brought with them enteric fever which decimated the local civilian population, the British Army garrison and crews of visiting ships. With such a haunted past, Darrell's Island had been abandoned until converted into a flying boat base in 1937.

Both airlines conducted survey flights from Port Washington to Bermuda, in May 1937, progressing to weekly passenger flights on June 16 and twice weekly on August 25. As this route wasn't part of the EAMS, the *Cavalier* was the only Empire flying boat fitted for 24 passengers and staffed by two stewards.

Testing radio bearings from shore stations and meteorological forecasts, Imperial decided on a series of transatlantic survey flights through 1937 on both the northern and southern crossings. "Taffy" Powell took *Cambria* on a tour of eastern Canada, touching down on 3 September on the river in Ottawa where, six years before, Charles and Anne Lindbergh had moored *Sirius*. They continued to Toronto where the *Cambria* lost a float. Spare parts and two Imperial Airways' engineers were sent over to New York on the RMS *Queen Mary* while the crew were dinner guests at several local homes and taken to see Niagara Falls. When the flying boat left on 23 September, crowds gathered at the waterfront to watch as she would soar over the city skyline, land in a cloud of spray to roar off in another take-off while the crew tested the new float. The *Cambria*'s most eventful flight was two years ahead of her.

The first Empire flying boat ditching occurred on this route on January 21, 1939. *Cavalier* was on the Port Washington–Bermuda run when it suffered carburetor icing in three of its

Imperial Airways Short S.23 *Cambria* was taken on a tour of eastern Canada in 1937. In 1938 she took part in air-to-air refuelling trials conducted by Alan Cobham with an AW.23.

engines and ditched in the ocean, 285 miles off Long Island. One of the reasons for the choice of flying boats for the EAMS was the assumption that they could put down on the open sea in times of emergency, with some degree of safety. But "holed" on landing, *Cavalier* began to sink immediately. The eight passengers and four crew clambered on top of the hull until it disappeared beneath the water. Fearful of sharks, they intertwined arms and legs. The Empire flying boats did not carry life rafts until later and, other than their Moseley Life-Saving Seat Cushions, the survivors had nothing. Their good fortune was that they had landed in the warm Gulf Stream and with the exception of two — one of whom was the purser — survived in the water for ten hours until rescued by a passing tanker. One of the passengers claimed wilful negligence on the part of the airline which had been aware of carburetor icing and sued for $200,000. *Cavalier,* the fifth Empire flying boat to be lost was replaced by *Champion*, the first S.30 boat to be built.

As the Portuguese hadn't given the Americans landing rights in the Azores yet, Pan American initially used the northern route. The three refueling stops chosen were Botwood, Newfoundland, Boucherville outside Montreal and Foynes in Ireland. In 1935, the governments of the United States, Great Britain, Canada and the Irish Free State signed the Montreal Agreement ruling that one day when transatlantic travel was a certainty, flying boats would refuel at Foynes, a port on the south side of the River Shannon estuary.

Capt. Harold Gray flew the S-42B *Clipper III* on July 5, 1937 from Port Washington, NY to Shediac, New Brunswick, then to the Bay of Exploits, Botwood, Newfoundland, arriving at Southampton on the 8th where Woods Humphery took the crew to dinner in London. On the same day, in the opposite direction, the first crossing of the Atlantic by an Empire flying boat took place when *Caledonia,* stripped of everything except the fuel tanks and piloted by Captain W. N. Cummings, flew from Southampton to Foynes and then on to Botwood. Shortly after 03:00 GMT, the two aircraft had passed each other by 60 miles. Prime Minister Mackenzie King was returning to Canada from the Coronation of King George VI on the *Empress of Australia*. On July 8th, on deck for his morning "constitutional", he saw the *Caledonia* following the ship up the St. Lawrence and then overtaking her. Thrilled about aviation matters (when meeting Lindbergh in 1927, he had called him "this young god descended from the skies") King wrote in his diary, "it was like a great seagull, heaving in flight." When the prime minister sent the crew a message of congratulations, the flying boat circled the ship twice in salute. The *Caledonia* continued over Quebec City and touched down at Boucherville to a welcome of ship' sirens. The next day, the Imperial crew arrived in Port Washington NY and were feted by Trippe at the Pan American Chrysler building office.

In allowing the use of Shediac and Boucherville, the Canadian government had hoped that the transatlantic flights would terminate in Montreal where, with Trans Canada Airlines, it would link Vancouver to London. But both the Americans and British saw New York as the prize and Mackenzie King accepted this. Shediac would be chosen by Pan American because it

LIFE Magazine's photograph of Imperial Airways S.23, *Caledonia*, over New York in 1937 — the first east to west crossing of the Atlantic by a flying boat. A Pan American S-42B, *Clipper III*, crossed from west to east on the same day.

was on the direct route between New York and Botwood and in June, 1937 a wireless station, a Customs House and administration offices were built at Pointe du Chêne. As it had rail links to central Canada and New England, mail could be added to the Clipper's cargo during the brief stop.

The Bay of Exploits had been charted by Captain James Cook in 1774 for its sheltered, deep and fog-free harbor. On its western shore, the tiny port of Botwood was plucked out of obscurity to become the "Gander" of the flying boat era (first receiving international attention in 1933 when Charles and Anne Lindbergh refueled the Sirius there). A slipway was built and *Oscar,* a refueling barge "of generous proportions", was stationed there. The "alternate" to Botwood, in case of fog, was Gleneagles on Gander Lake, 30 miles away. The Lake's name would be transferred to Hatties Camp, the nearby airfield.

Botwood would play host to the flying boats of Pan American, Imperial Airways, American Export Airlines (AEA) and later BOAC. Sanford B. Kauffman (Yale Class of 1921) had been hired by Trippe in 1928 to be the airline's general manager. Kauffman was sent by Pan American to reconnoiter the suitability of the Newfoundland port as a stopover for the airline. He got to St. John's, Newfoundland and after a train journey "that stopped in the middle of nowhere", Kauffman sat in the station for a long time until the mailman drove him to Botwood in an old ramshackle car. He thought it "a godforsaken place". There was no hotel but the general store which also sold furniture had a bed in its window. Kauffman made a deal with store owner and was allowed to sleep in the window with the shades drawn during the night. In the daytime, the railway engineer who was on the night shift, used it.[20]

Botwood's other claim to fame is that its villagers had performed the first act of belligerence in North America when the Second World War was declared. On September 3, 1939 the town's lone constable and a group of citizens arrested the surprised crew of the German freighter *Christoph V. Doornum* in the harbor.

---

20   Sanford Kaufmann: *Pan Am Pioneer: A Manager's Memoirs.* Texas Tech University Press, 1996.

Aware that Botwood's easterly position allowed the convoy protection flights to fly 450 miles further into the Atlantic than the nearest Canadian base, in 1940 the Canadian government sent troops to protect the British colony and the RCAF's Cansos fought the Battle of the Atlantic from its harbor. The port's passenger accommodations, named "Caledonia Camp" after the first Imperial Airways flying boat to alight there, counted Prime Minister Winston Churchill (who was trapped here overnight by bad weather), President Roosevelt and Bob Hope as guests.

Apart from its heritage museum with flying boat photos and models (and a chapter in the 1991 Ken Follett novel *Night Over Water*) Botwood will always have a tragic remnant of its flying boat days. On October 1, 1942, *Excalibur*, an AEA Sikorsky VS-44 flying boat carrying 37 passengers to Foynes, "porpoised" on take-off from the harbor. It got to an altitude of 10 feet before settling back into the water and on the second run reached 35 feet before crashing. The force of the fuselage hitting the water created a wave that caught the propellers. The V-44's tail broke off and the aircraft quickly sank. Only twenty-six of those onboard could be rescued from the aircraft and taken to a local hospital, where three later died. As the wreckage is in 90 feet of water, there have been several attempts to recover the remains.

Consulting his globe, Trippe's next logical choices for expansion on the Pacific would have been Singapore and Australia but both were about to be served by Imperial Airways. To end their country's isolation, the New Zealand government had lobbied unsuccessfully for years to have Imperial Airways extend their Empire route across the Tasman Straits. In frustration, on March 11, 1937 New Zealand's minister of public works broke rank with Australia and Britain and invited Pan American to fly to Auckland.

For airlines, route planning evaluation is dominated by economic considerations and forecasts of potential passenger and freight revenues are essential. New Zealand was historically, socially and economically tied to Australia and Britain, not to the distant United States. Joseph Conrad, another admirer of the great clippers, wrote that any fool can carry on, but a wise man knows how to shorten sail in time. Was this route planning being led by Trippe's ego rather than economics? An airmail service connecting New Zealand with the United States over vast lengths of the Pacific would hardly be profitable — nor did the airline have the technical capability for it. But Trippe, who had challenged his board members as far back as Colonial Air Transport in 1927, now searched for specks of land that the Clippers could refuel at to reach New Zealand. As they were British colonies, Fiji and Canton Island were out (until 1941) and the French wanted the hefty fee of $200,000 for the use of Nomea, New Caledonia but Pago Pago was part of American Samoa. And then there was Kingman Reef...

Previously called "Danger Reef" for good reason, it was named by Captain W. E. Kingman, who discovered it in 1853. Before it could be claimed by the Japanese, Hawaiian politician Lorrin A. Thurston hoisted the American flag over it on May 10, 1922. Usually submerged and barely 5 foot above sea level when it wasn't, Kingman Reef is 925 miles south by west of Honolulu. Unlike Wake or Midway, there was no terra firma for permanent buildings and to use it as a refueling base meant stationing a ship permanently there.

American Samoa, 1,400 miles south west of the Reef, was not that much better — but for Trippe, at least it was American. Its capital, Pago Pago, is surrounded by high steep hills on three sides with the open ocean breaking over reefs on the remaining side. Landing or taking off from Pago Pago's harbor needed skill, experience and luck. The approach required a short, steep, precise turning dive, and a quick stop once on the water, to avoid the deadly reefs. Auckland was a long 1,800 miles away and the flying boat would require a maximum fuel load. Having to return to Pago Pago "heavy" (as would be the case if a flight had to be canceled shortly after takeoff) would mean disaster.

The company's chartered freighter the S.S. *North Wind* (sister ship to the *North Haven*) left Honolulu on March 11, 1937 with all that would be needed to support the survey flight when it came through Kingman Reef. Until the flying boat base at Auckland's Mechanics Bay was built, Pan American sent its own meteorologist Al Francis to set up a radio station at St. Heliers, an Auckland seaside suburb to maintain contact with Pago Pago.

Captain Musick left Alameda for Honolulu on March 17 in the new S-42B, christened *Pan American Clipper II*. Shortly after take-off they sighted Amelia Earhart's Electra which had left Oakland Airport to fly west on an around-the-world attempt. Onboard her aircraft were Albert Paul Mantz who worked the radio, the former Pan American Chief Navigator Fred Noonan and co-pilot Harry Manning.[21]

After refueling in Honolulu, Earhart ground-looped the plane on the runway because of a blown tire. The Lockheed was damaged and shipped back to California for repairs for the second (and fateful) attempt. Musick too was delayed at Honolulu with an engine leak and would not leave until the 23rd. They located the *North Wind* off Kingman Reef and stayed overnight on it, its crew trying hard to cheer up a tired and apprehensive Musick. The next morning in the driving rain, always his careful self, Musick took an hour to warm up the four Hornet engines before he was ready to depart for Pago Pago. There they were delayed for six days by the weather.

On March 29, crowds gathered around Auckland's Waitemata Harbor to welcome the S-42B. At 4.43 pm. word came from the Auckland Harbor Board's signal station on Tiritiri Matangi Island that the aircraft had just passed overhead. After a circuit up the harbor, Musick took the Sikorsky east and banked again just off Orakei. "Lower and lower she came, her four propellers just turning over," wrote a *Weekly News* eyewitness. "Off the end of the tide deflector her shadow appeared on the water below her and then the lowest point of her keel neatly broke the surface. In a moment she was afloat, gradually losing way as a white wave foamed up on either side of her hull."

21 Earhart had already enlisted the marine officer Harry Manning as her navigator, but her husband George P. Putnam wanted Noonan because of his experience with Pan American. Noonan accepted her offer, he had gone as far as he could with the airline and, newly married, was reportedly considering settling down and starting a school for navigation.

"Onlookers, too caught up in the moment to cheer, silently followed the action: the rapid dash forward of two shepherding air force launches, the gentle rock of the Sikorsky's brick-red wings, the dip and rise of its floats. A man in white appeared at one of the hatches and took a rope which had been rowed out from the mooring pontoon. As he did so, a workplace siren somewhere ashore sounded the five o'clock knock-off. It was a fitting salute. Thirty thousand New Zealanders turned out to greet Musick and his crew. A man of few words, he addressed the wildly cheering crowd by saying only, "We are glad to be here." Over the course of 12-and-a-half days and just under 50 hours of flying time, Pan American had signaled the end of New Zealand's isolation, opening up speculation on what the emerging technology of flight held for life in these remote islands."[22]

Earhart and Noonan's disappearance on July 2, 1937, somewhere near Howland Island, shocked and grieved the world but especially so the airline's employees. Across the Pacific, Pan American DF operators had heard her last transmissions and, aware that the temporary U.S. Navy DF site on Howland Island was unreliable, had tried to help. They couldn't reach her, possibly because, to save weight, Earhart had her aircraft's trailing antenna and associated radio gear removed. Noonan's skill at celestial navigation was unequaled but before she left Oakland, Earhart had asked George Angus, the Pan American superintendent responsible for radio communication and direction finding for help. Despite Noonan's navigation, she also wanted to rely on radio bearings. Angus had shown her what transmissions the airline used. Was Earhart having doubts about Noonan? That both the celestial and DF systems failed them will always be a mystery.

When Musick returned to Auckland on another survey flight on December 26, the *Pan American Clipper II* (now christened *Samoan Clipper*) was not to be the only flying boat in the harbor. The Imperial Airways flying boat *Centaurus*, piloted by expatriate New Zealander Capt. John Burgess would touch down on the Waitemata the next day, to a gala welcome. On

---

22   Vaughan Yarwood, *Wings Of Desire*, New Zealand Geographic, October–December 1998.

arrival, Burgess taxied in and moored alongside the *Samoan Clipper*. Musick and Burgess congratulated each other and shook hands over a Union Jack-covered table. The *Centaurus* went on to the South Island, landing off Erskine Point, Lyttelton Harbor, Christchurch on 3 January 1938. "Freedom of the Port — Lyttelton Extends Warm Welcome — Congratulations to Captain Burgess." was the headline in the local newspaper. It was actually "freedom of the port" as The Harbor Board had not yet taken legal steps to enable it to charge harbor dues for flying boats. At the official reception on the Akaroa jetty, the Mayor of Lyttelton, Mr F. E. Sutton reminded all that it was almost the anniversary of the First Four Ships to arrive in Canterbury 87 years ago. The crew were the guests of the Mayor of Christchurch at dinner at Warner's Hotel. Unlike Pan American, Imperial Airways encouraged local publicity — Geddes and Woods Humphrey wanted an all-Imperial Airways route to New Zealand — and locals were invited onboard to inspect the flying boat. The visitors, one of whom was the reporter from "The Press", tried the seats, admired the tiny kitchen — not much tinier than those of some small flats, they commented — and stood on the promenade deck "gazing through the windows in an attempt to envisage the view that the lucky passengers had, and listened eagerly to the description of the outstanding points of the vessel given by their guide."

Musick left Auckland on January 3, 1938 for Honolulu, and once there, was immediately sent back on a return flight on the 9th. He was tired and was due for a well deserved return flight home to Cleo. A month before, he managed to fly the *Hawaii Clipper* through a typhoon – a flight that taxed him and the plane severely. This time when they arrived at Kingman Reef, they were met by the *Trade Wind*, one of the last four-masted schooners built in Victoria, B.C. for the Australian trade. They made it to Pago Pago and left the next day at 5:37 am on January 11th for Auckland, heavy with fuel — 1,150 gallons in the hull and the same amount in the wing tanks. As before, one of the Clipper's engines sprang an oil leak and Musick had no choice but to return to Pago Pago.

Pan American's Martin M-130 *Hawaii Clipper* photographed in 1938.

Renowned for his caution, he could have circled the island while the Clipper burned off enough gasoline to attempt a landing in the small harbor. It was early morning, the weather was clear, the winds calm and water surface smooth. Musick knew, from previous experience, the risks of dumping fuel with the S-42B — once it had left the drains at the rear of the wing, it tended to flow back over the wing, toward the engines. He knew too that gasoline fumes could build up inside the wing itself. The last radio message was: "We are going to dump gas — cannot use the radio while dumping — stand by." Shortly after, there was an explosion that was seen for many miles and what was left of the *Samoan Clipper* fell into the Pacific as a ball of fire. The US. Navy seaplane tender *Avocet* (one of the naval ships that had searched for Earhart and Noonan) was sent out from Pago Pago to the scene but found only an oil slick and a few bits of wreckage.[23]

The board of enquiry concluded that either the heated engine exhaust or the fuel vapors may have entered the

---

23 The *Avocet* has one more claim to fame. At Pearl Harbor, on December 7, 1941, her single gun was able to shoot down one of the attacking Japanese planes.

wing and begun a fire that spread to the fuel tanks in the hull, causing the explosion. Musick's death, coming after Noonan's, was a great loss and not only to Pan American — his record-breaking flights had made him a hero to millions. Besieged with offers to write his biography, his widow Cleo asked Musick's colleague and good friend William S. Grooch to do so and *From Crate to Clipper with Capt. Musick, Pioneer Pilot* was published in 1939. The New Zealanders honored him with the Musick Memorial Radio Station at Bucklands Point, Auckland where a bronze plaque and photos of Musick and the S-42B are on permanent display. After the crash, the dump chutes on all other S-45s were modified to extend aft to jettison fuel clear of the aircraft. In February 1939, the B-314 replaced the M-130 flying boats on the Pacific and it would not be until July 1940, that Trippe would reopen the South Pacific route from California to New Zealand.

Perhaps to punish commercial aviation for its hubris about "conquering the oceans", Tyche the goddess of ill fortune struck (after all, her father was Oceanus) and she claimed the most experienced of all. A war hero and pioneering airmail pilot, Jean Mermoz, was France's answer to Lindbergh. When Aéropostale began flying the mail across the Atlantic in 1930, using a Latécoère 28 float-equipped monoplane, Mermoz took off from St. Louis, Senegal on May 12 for Natal with a navigator, a radio operator and sacks of mail. That night, they battled through a series of waterspouts that rose into stormy clouds. Fellow Aéropostale pilot Antoine de Saint-Exupéry writing of the ordeal in his *Wind, Sand and Stars* recalled: "...this spectacle was so overwhelming that only after he had got through the Black Hole did Mermoz awaken to the fact that he had not been afraid." Mermoz's luck ran out on his 28th Atlantic crossing. On December 7, 1936 he and a crew of four left Natal for West Africa in *Croix du Sud* the Latécoère flying boat. During the night, a message was transmitted from it: "Coupons moteur arrière droit",[24] and nothing further. Despite an intensive search, no trace of Mermoz and his crew has ever been found and he is honored today both in France and Brazil.

---

24   Shutting down the right-rear engine.

In 1936 the Latécoère flying boat *Croix du Sud* piloted by Jean Mermoz was lost without trace on a flight from Natal to West Africa. Painting by Guillaume Favre.

On the early morning of July 29, 1938 Capt. Leonard Terletzky taxied the *Hawaii Clipper* out of Apra Harbor, Guam. Ahead was Manila, Macao and Hong Kong. It would take 12 ½ hours to do the 1,600 miles between Guam and Manila and Terletzky knew that with 2,550 gallons of gasoline onboard, the Clipper would have a cruising time of 17 hours. With sunset at Manilla at 6:39 pm, they had a safe 14 hours of daylight to make the flight. Ahead, there were scattered thunderstorms, typical of summer weather in the Pacific, and Terletzky plotted a course south of them.

A senior Pan American pilot, he had more than 9,000 flying hours, 1,600 of which had been spent over the Pacific in an M-130. First Officer Mark "Tex" Walker had more than 1,900 hours flying time, the majority in transpacific operations. Second Officer George M. Davis had 1,000 hours of transpacific flight logged. Radio officer William McCarty had 1,352 hours in transpacific operations. Even the cabin steward, Ivan Parker

Jr, soon to be preparing a lunch of consommé, creamed tuna on toast and fruit cocktail, was making his 26th Pacific crossing.

The passenger list gives an insight into the select few who could then afford to travel by air: Fred C. Meier, the principal plant pathologist at the U.S. Department of Agriculture in Washington, D.C. was going to the Philippines, where he planned to study disease transmission in the upper atmosphere. Dr. Earl B. McKinley, a noted bacteriologist and the dean of George Washington University's Medical School, was carrying two new serums to test at the Culion Leprosy Colony in the Philippines. Kenneth A. Kennedy, Pan American's Pacific Division traffic manager, was checking out the company's overseas operations, which had been disrupted by the Japanese invasion of China. Major Howard C. French, commander of the 321st Observation Squadron, was on his way to monitor the Japanese bombing of Canton. Edward E. Wyman, was vice president of export sales for the Curtiss-Wright Corporation, who wanted to sell P-36 Hawk fighter aircraft to the Chinese Nationalist government; and finally, there was Wah-Sun "Watson" Choy, an American of Chinese descent who owned a New Jersey–based restaurant company. As many restaurant owners did then, Choy had named two of his cafes after the *China Clipper*. Going to Hong Kong to visit his mother and sister, Choy wanted also to meet his brother Frank, an air force pilot with the Nationalists. Choy was carrying $3 million in gold certificates on behalf of the Chinese War Relief Committee which they were donating to Chiang Kai-Shek.

The *Hawaii Clipper* had already completed 35 round trips between Alameda and Manila and, as per the airline's and Glenn L. Martin maintenance programs, the engines and propellers had been each overhauled after every three round trips or 300 hours. The day before leaving Alameda, the company's routine procedure called for a three-hour familiarization flight by the same crew scheduled to make the trip. During the exercise, a routine emergency landing was made and an "abandon ship" drill carried out in which the life raft was inflated, and got over the side with the crew and emergency rations aboard. An emergency radio was set up and communication with shore stations established.

At the Midway and Wake overnight stops, in the inspection of engines and vital parts of the aircraft, no irregularities were discovered. At Guam, the flying boat had been hauled out of the water for a detailed inspection, and everything appeared to be in working order. At Wake, the *Hawaii Clipper* had met with the *Philippine Clipper* going in the opposite direction and the crew of the latter remembered that Terletzky's crew were "in the best of spirits."[25]

McCarty sent routine position reports every half hour and at 12:11 p.m. local time, he sent the following message: "Flying in rough air at 9,100 feet. Temperature 13 degrees centigrade. Wind 19 knots per hour... Position Latitude 12 degree 27' North, Longitude 130 degree 40' East dead reckoning... Rain... sky above covered by stratocumulus clouds, base 9,200 feet... flying last half-hour on instruments."

Eduardo Fernandez, the radio operator on Panay Island, near the Philippine coast, acknowledged receipt of the message. But when Fernandez indicated that he wanted to transmit the latest weather report, McCarty responded: "Stand by for one minute before sending as I am having trouble with rain static." Fernandez did as he was told but when he tried raising the *Hawaii Clipper* 60 seconds later, there was no response. This wasn't unusual but as time passed and he still couldn't contact Terletzky's plane, he became concerned.

At 12:49 p.m. Fernandez alerted all stations to stand by on emergency frequencies. As McCarty's last reported position was 300 miles off the Philippine coast, airline personnel originally hoped that they had landed safely in the water. Even when the 5 pm arrival time at Manilla was missed, there was still hope that their radio was out. Then at 6:30 pm the Navy ordered all naval vessels at Manilla to refuel and put out to sea. In all, 14 ships from the 16th Naval District, Manilla, including six submarines and three destroyers, left port. The troop transport *Meigs* the nearest ship to the Clipper's last reported position,

25   Information on the *Hawaiian Clipper's* last flight has been taken from Air Commerce Bulletin Vol. 10, July 15, 1938. U.S. Dept. Of Commerce.

altered course to the coordinates. The U.S. Army Air Corps sent six long-range Martin B-10 bombers to survey the flying boat's last known position. On August 2nd, Pan American had the *China Clipper* retraced the route of its missing sister ship without success. The U.S. State Department even asked the Japanese government for help and Tokyo redirected the liner *Canberra Maru* to the scene, but its crew found nothing. Only an oil slick was discovered and a sample later sent to laboratories in New York showed that it wasn't from the Clipper's engines. The intensive search on land and sea was abandoned on August 5th.[26]

Since then, the disappearance has spawned conjectures and conspiracy theories — Japanese agents hidden in the hold, a bomb in the luggage, tropical storm etc. as to how and why the Hawaiian Clipper vanished without a trace — almost as many as those concerning Amelia Earhart.

The other two Martin Clippers also met tragic ends. The *Philippine Clipper* was caught and damaged in the Japanese attack on Wake Island on 8 December, 1941, and, as soon as the air raid ended, filled with Pan American employees, took off for Midway. The U.S. forces on Wake Island surrendered to the Japanese on December 23 and of those who survived the attack most later died when the ship that was transporting them to POW camps in Japan was mistakenly torpedoed by a U.S. submarine. The flag that flew over the Pan American building at Wake Island was given to William Van Dusen, the head of Public Relations.

Having escaped the Japanese, the *Philippine Clipper* met its end on 21 January, 1943 on a flight from Hawaii to San

---

26   Nineteen years later, another Pan American Airways Clipper, this time a Boeing 377, would vanish between San Francisco and Hawaii. On November 9, 1957 the Clipper *Romance of the Skies,* crashed in the Pacific, killing 44 people. Nineteen bodies and floating wreckage were discovered about 1,000 miles northeast of Honolulu. What amazed the Civil Aeronautics Board (CAB) crash investigators was that there had been no distress call, the location of the debris showed that the Clipper was far off course and headed away from a Coast Guard ship that could have helped; and, finally, elevated levels of carbon monoxide were found in several of the recovered bodies. In January 1959, after a long investigation, the CAB officials found no probable cause for the crash, and formally closed the case.

Francisco. To escape storms in the San Francisco area, Capt Robert Elzey elected to fly a holding pattern until conditions improved. Rather than San Diego, he chose to land at Clear Lake near Ukiah and Boonville which had been used as an alternate for flying boats before. The Clipper slammed into the mountainous terrain, killing all 19 onboard. The report of the Civil Aeronautics Board blamed Captain Elzey for failing to determine his position accurately before descent.

Finally, the *China Clipper* that, ten years before, with Capt. Ed Musick at the controls began commercial transpacific flights, was lost while attempting a night landing at Port of Spain, Trinidad. Flown by veteran pilot Captain Leonard Cramer, it had left Miami on 8 January, 1945 at 6:30 am, its final destination Leopoldville in the Belgian Congo, via San Juan, Puerto Rico and Port of Spain. There were 30 occupants onboard —18 passengers and 12 crew, mainly employees. The Clipper refueled at San Juan, at 2:39 pm and made for Port of Spain. Landing there in the evening darkness, it missed an approach and went around for a second one. This time the M-130 came down too low, hitting the water at a high speed and nose down which caused the hull to break in two. Rapidly flooding, the aircraft sank and nine of the 12 crew and 14 of the 18 passengers drowned — a sad end to an aircraft that had heralded a new era in commercial aviation.

6   The trimph over distance

rthur Gouge grew up in Gravesend, Kent across from the port of Tilbury. Perhaps it was seeing the maritime traffic on the Thames that made him want to design boats that had wings. Like Claude Dornier and Pierre-Georges Latécoère, he envisioned giant flying boats, telling a journalist in 1938 that someday they would be carrying 250 passengers. Fittingly, his career would culminate with the Saunders-Roe Princess in 1952.

Gouge joined Short Brothers at Rochester in 1915 just as the Seaplane Works were opened on the River Medway. A carpenter apprentice, by 1926 he had risen to Chief Designer. While other flying boat manufacturers were building the all-wood Felixstowe F.3s and F.5s, Oswald Short began experimenting with aluminum alloys in the construction of aircraft. For brothers that had begun as balloon builders under a London railway arch in 1906, they would consistently invest in research, building one of the first hull-testing tanks in Britain.

Metal was thought to be unsuitable for marine aircraft because of corrosion, particularly by salt water. Fixing them to the jetty pilings in the River Medway at Rochester, Oswald Short tested light alloy samples for the effects of corrosion, with the ebb and flow of the tide alternatively exposing them to the water and the air. After thirty-six weeks the steel samples had rusted away, but the alloy showed no significant signs of corrosion. Experimentation of suitable alloys for flying boat hulls would occupy Short and Gouge for the next twenty years, culminating in the Empire flying boat series. They rightly claimed, "We don't build aircraft that float, we build ships that fly."

Both men designed and built the Silver Streak in 1920, the first all-metal aircraft in Britain. Oswald Short kept the workforce of about fourteen thousand men employed through the lean years making bus bodies, children's pedal cars, prams and domestic flat irons. That allowed the company to stay in business and produce a series of flying boats for the RAF and Imperial Airways. Sponsored by Short's and Rolls-Royce, in 1929 Alan Cobham tested the metal-hulled Short Singapore S.5 (the company's design index number of the aircraft) on an odyssey around Africa.[1] This gave them enough confidence to build the Sarafand S.14.

A year before the Dornier Do X with its duralumin hull made its first flight, Oswald Short planned the Sarafand (named for an Phoenician seaport) as the first British flying boat for the Atlantic. Its hull was made of Alclad, a corrosion-resistant fixed sheet alloy that would be used on the Empire flying boats. Nothing as large as the 72,000 lb six-engine biplane had ever been attempted in Britain. At a length of 89.5 foot, a wingspan of 120 foot and a height of 30.3 foot, it was larger than its contemporary, the S-42, and almost exactly the dimensions of the future Empire flying boat.

The Sarafand had a max. speed of 153 mph, a theoretical 1,450 mile range and a 13,000 foot ceiling. Its interior was spacious enough for a crew of ten with ample accommodations that included a wardroom, six folding bunks in various crew rooms, a full galley, a maintenance area and a lavatory — all legacies that the Short Sunderland flying boats would inherit. A large all-metal flying boat was a financial risk for Short's but a personal triumph for both men, as it vindicated their theories on stressed-metal construction for aircraft, especially flying boats.

Looking like a stately galleon in flight, it was launched on June 30, 1932. By then, Oswald Short's dream of a transatlantic flight had ended as on August 18, 1930, Wolfgang von Gronau made the first east-west crossing in a Dornier Wal flying boat. The Sarafand's future was sealed when the Marine Aircraft Experimental Establishment (MAEE) at Felixstowe found vibration issues caused by the push-pull

1   His book, *Twenty Thousand Miles in a Flying Boat : My Flight Round Africa*, was reissued in 2007.

Launched in 1932, the Short S.4 Sarafand was designed for the Atlantic and built from corrosion-resistant alloy. Although unsuccessful, the later Empire flying boats owe much to lessons learned from the Sarafand.

Rolls-Royce Buzzard engines and that on landing, the flying boat had a tendency to "porpoise".

A loss to aviation archeology, the Sarafand was broken up in 1936. Its value to Short's would be in the exploratory use of metallurgy in so large a hull, in finding suitable engines and the culmination of the biplane configuration. When Imperial Airways asked Shorts to consider an enlarged metal flying boat that could serve its Empire routes transporting large amounts of mail, Gouge, having experimented with the Sarafand, was prepared. The airline was impressed enough with the S.23 design offered that in May 1935, it ordered 28 of them "off the drawing board", (each costing £41,000) followed by three of the larger S.26s. The progression from a metal-hulled flying boat to an almost completely metal aircraft had taken years of experimentation by the Short's team.

The S.23 was to be a high-wing, four-engine monoplane, its basic aerodynamic design derived from the Short Scion Senior floatplane and the unwieldy looking Knuckleduster flying boat — neither were commercially successful but both had given Gouge familiarity with shoulder-mounted high wing

177

monoplanes. To get the engines high enough away from the water spray, the wing was initially to be housed in a hump above the fuselage but a hull redesign made that unnecessary. With its 18-tonne weight, it precluded the wide planing bottoms that Shorts had used with the Singapore series and Gouge's team designed a 17 foot deep, narrow hull that would allow the huge aircraft to free itself from the water. It had vertical sides from chine to wing root for minimum drag-inducing with maximum internal volume. It wasn't quite all-metal — the fin, tail planes and the flight control surfaces were fabric covered and the trim and servo tabs were solid mahogany.

The S.23's wing root allowed for upper and lower decks — the upper, or flight deck, would be forward of the wing spar. A single main spar with 'T'-shaped alloy lengths running through the wings would provide the necessary support for the engines. The proposed wing loading was higher than contemporary biplanes and for that Gouge designed the fully retractable trailing edge flap, known as the 'Gouge flap'. This allowed the lift coefficient to be increased by 30 percent and the landing speed reduced by 12 mph with little increase in drag. So large a flying boat turning on the water was one of the considerations that led Gouge to select wing floats rather than the sponsons which the Dornier Do X, the M-130 and later the Boeing 314 used. Floats could be "lost" turning in rough water but the flying boat would not capsize. He designed wingtip floats mounted on wire-braced struts that allowed them to rock fore and aft, reducing the shock loading that would have otherwise been transferred to the wing.

Completing one S.23 a month was onerous for Short's which lacked suitable machine tools and skilled labor to do so. What it did have was Arthur E. Bibby, the formidable Works Manager and, to quote Oswald Short, there were: "Very skilled foremen, leading hands and first-class workmen" who were able to mentor new recruits. Deliveries of the Empire flying boats to Imperial Airways were five in 1936, twenty-two in 1937, five in 1938, seven in 1939 and three and three quarters in 1940 — at which point the plant was bombed.

ONE OF THE 28 *EMPIRE* FLYING - BOATS ➤ **IMPERIAL AIRWAYS**
TWO DECKS . 200 MILES-AN-HOUR . 18 TONS
EUROPE · AFRICA · INDIA · THE FAR EAST · AUSTRALIA

SHORT EMPIRE S.23 FLYING BOAT

88 foot in length
31 foot in height
Wingspan of 114 foot with area 1,500 foot
Empty it weighed 23,500 lbs and gross 40,500 lbs
The basic performance figures were:
Max level speed: 174 kt. (200 mph).
Max cruise: 142 kt (164 mph)
Rate of Climb: 95-0 foot. per min.
Ceiling: 20,000 foot.
Range: 600-703 miles
Endurance 4.5 hrs.

Having learned from the Sarafand's in-line Buzzards, the S.23's powerplants were four 9-cylinder, air-cooled, Bristol Pegasus XC radial engines of 920 horsepower. These drove three-bladed variable pitch de Havilland propellers. But without feathering or fire extinguishers, engine failures would be all the more perilous. Fuel was carried in two 326-gallon tanks between the engines that rested on plywood floors to prevent chafing. Seven flying boats were fitted with 1B and M1 fuel systems, which had fuel tanks in the hull. The S.23 flying boats were originally not fitted with deicing equipment for the airscrews or life rafts until later. But they were the first British commercial aircraft to use 87-octane aviation spirit which had been developed by British Petroleum for the RAF and was used by the contestants in the MacRobertson race.

The "greenhouse" flight deck was not soundproofed and leaked continuously. On either side of it, cupolas had been fitted but the windshield had no shading or wipers and the pilots endured the glare off the water. The captain and first officer sat side by side, each with their own control wheel. The wooden floor beneath them was soon oil-soaked after oil leaking from the Exactor hydraulic controls and the autopilots. The wireless operator sat behind the captain and faced aft, looking at his two wireless sets. Behind him was the mail storage area and against the wall, the retractable DF loop aerial and the hatch to the flying boat's roof which was used for wing inspection and refueling. It was only opened when the aircraft was on the surface. Below was the hatchway and the stairwell that led to the galley with the two chemical toilets, one each for men and women. On the lower deck was the mooring equipment storage, four passenger cabins and the baggage area. In the flying boat's nose were the drogues to help with maneuvering, the anchor and the retracting landing light. On the roof was the telescopic aerial mast, navigation and steaming lights. In place of the pyrotechnic wing tip flares that Imperial Airways aircraft had used previously, the Empire flying boats were fitted with searchlights for use during night operations.

The passenger cabins began with the seven-seat "smoking saloon" directly beneath the flight deck, soon to be converted to mail storage and the steward's office. The amidships cabin was a three seat saloon with two sleeping berths opposite. It was originally intended that the EAMS should be flown by day and night, so accommodation for sixteen bunks was provided in the passenger cabins, the seats folding down to allow the

The day cabin of an Imperial Airways Short S.23 Empire flying boat.

bunks to be rigged over them. While it was possible to fit the bunks when the aircraft was on the water, trying the same while flying was impossible. The airframe flexed so much in the air, especially in rough weather and it was impossible to assemble the bunks in flight. Thus, the idea of passengers sleeping onboard the flying boats while on normal services, was abandoned and the bunks never used.

The promenade saloon which featured in the airline's publicity, was behind the main bulkhead and had double seat reclining chairs on the starboard side with room to stretch one's legs opposite, with four large windows and an elbow rail beneath them. The leather-upholstered chairs (made by Rumbolds of Camberley who would also make the seating for the de Havilland Comet and Aérospatiale Concorde) seated eight in the day and could be adjusted at night to sleep four. In the ceiling above was the bedding storage. Behind the promenade

deck were two steps (literally on the flying boat "step") to the rear cabin which seated six and had the passenger hatch to the aircraft. Finally there was the luggage storage in the tail.

Imperial Airways had traditionally named its aircraft after cities, Greek mythological figures or legendary monsters. What to name 42 Empire flying boats had to be imaginative and memorable. Following the custom begun in 1931, (with "A" for Armstrong Whitworth, "B" for Boulton Paul, "D" for De Havilland etc.) "C" was still unused. Thus, rather than "S" for Shorts, in the British registry all the Empire flying boats were given names beginning with the letter "C". They were either classical (*Calypso),* literary (Byron's *Corsair*), Shakespearean (*Corialanus*) regional (*Caledonia*), historical (*Cordelia,* a Burgundian duchess) or stellar (*Cassiopeia*). When the flying boats were re-registered in Australia for Qantas Empire Airways and in New Zealand for Tasman Empire Airways Ltd. (TEAL), they were christened with names of local significance like the onomatopoetic *Cooee,* an aboriginal call representing the state of Tasmania, and *Aotearoa*, the Maori name for New Zealand.

Simultaneous with this huge order, Shorts also began building the S.20/21 composite, an ingenious project of the Imperial Airways Technical General Manager Major R.H. Mayo who had originated the scheme in Britain. First considered in 1915 by Cdr. John Cyril Porte with his Porte Baby carrying a Bristol Scout fighter aircraft high enough to reach the out-of-range Zeppelins, the pick-a-back concept was then in its heyday. A Sparrowhawk fighter aircraft would hook onto the airship *Los Angeles* on October 27, 1931 and the Soviet Zveno-1, a heavy bomber that carried two parasite fighter aircraft was successfully flown on December 3 the same year. The originality of Mayo's idea was to use it commercially — the "porter" aircraft lifting a small "parasite" which carried a payload to a height from which it could be released to cross the Atlantic. When he broached the concept in 1932, the Air Ministry supported it, judging this more practical than the catapult-launched mail planes that the Germans were using. Designed by Gouge, *Mercury,* a small, four-engined float plane would separate from the porter aircraft *Maia*, to make it across the Atlantic. *Maia* was similar to an S.23 except its Pegasus engines were installed further outboard away from the *Mercury's* float structure. Crucial to the success of this scheme was that there had to be a second launch aircraft on the North American side to get *Mercury* home, but no provision was ever made for this.[2]

Mayo's rival was Sir Alan Cobham and his company Flight Refuelling Ltd (FRL). Beginning with the looped-hose system that required a hose lowered from the tanker to the receiver aircraft (where the co-pilot would catch it with a shepherd's crook), Cobham planned to operate a fleet of tankers stationed wherever in the world aircraft didn't have the range to cross oceans. The Air Ministry, Imperial Airways and the Shell Oil company supported him in this imaginative scheme. For their part Imperial ordered nine S.30 C Class flying boats from Shorts, each with a strengthened structure and tankerage for 2,500 gallons. The extra fuel would give them a range of 2,500 miles and 15 hours endurance. Two went to Tasman Empire Airways Ltd (*Aotearoa* and *Awarua*) and of the remaining seven, four: *Cabot*, *Caribou*, *Clyde* and *Connemara* were fitted with refueling equipment.

Handley Page modified their Harrow bombers into tankers (as they would one day do the same with their Victors) and they would take-off from Gander and Rineanna (now Shannon Airport) to meet the flying boat.[3] At the rendezvous, the receiving aircraft would let down 200 foot of wire at the end of which was a lead weight — originally a lead-filled condom. The co-pilot in the tanker below and behind, would then shoot a cable to the flying boat with a rocket-propelled harpoon to intercept the wire. When contact was made, the hose on the end of the cable was reeled in by the receiving aircraft. The tanker then flew above the flying boat so the fuel could flow by

---

2   The Germans had the *Schwabenland* steam across the Atlantic after each double-launch in order to start the flying boats on their next trips.
3   A Harrow was dismantled and sent over to Canada by ship. It was kept in Ottawa through the war before being scrapped.

The Short Mayo Composite was a long-range seaplane/flying boat combination designed to provide a reliable long-range air transport service to North America, as well as the British Empire and Commonwealth.

gravity. Once the hose was secure, (as radio could not be used) the fueling was choreographed by flag signals.

In 1937, despite a vigorous campaign by the Portsmouth Corporation (who were willing to develop Langstone harbor as a seadrome as Singapore had), the Air Ministry announced that the port of Southampton was to be the center for the EAMS flying boat services and that the aircraft would be serviced at Hythe, across from Southampton Water.[4] When asked in Parliament if other sites had been considered, Capt. H. H. Balfour, the Undersecretary of State for Air, replied that nine had and, "Once account of cost, construction and

4   The suspicion is that it was the Admiralty that used its considerable influence to prevent Portsmouth from getting the Imperial Airways location. As the main naval base of the British Empire, it could not have commercial flying boats so close to the Fleet.

operational convenience had been taken into consideration",
Southampton had been chosen. The requirement for a mile-
long strip of water and a lit flare path at night for the flying
boats must have raised a few eyebrows in Southampton which,
in the 1930s, was more concerned with its lucrative ocean liner
traffic. The location wasn't ideal — the wash of passing liners
made beaching a flying boat hazardous and the Southampton
fog taxiing risky. It prevented Capt. Jimmy Alger from landing
on September 13, 1937 and he had to put the aircraft down in
the Channel, off Foreland, the Isle of Wight, and taxi two miles
to his mooring.

Hythe had been part of maritime aviation since the Great War
when the shipbuilders "May, Harden & May Ltd" erected large
sheds (hangars) to build flying boat hulls for the Admiralty.
When Supermarine took over the hangars for R. J. Mitchell's
Schneider trophy floatplanes *Walrus* and *Stranraer*, flying boats
were familiar sights on the Water. One of the companies that
Imperial Airways inherited in 1924 had been the British Marine
Air Navigation Company. It had operated a pair of Supermarine
Sea Eagle flying boats from Southampton to the Channel
Islands until they, and the company, fell apart. That the South
Western Railway had property at Hythe was coincidental and
Imperial contacted Supermarine to share space at its hangar
at Hythe. In June 1936, when Supermarine moved to Itchen
Bridge and Southampton Airport, Eastleigh, it leased the
sheds to Imperial Airways as a maintenance base for its flying
boats. Other Imperial maintenance bases — more modest in
scale — were at Alexandria, Kisumu (Kenya), Durban, Karachi,
Calcutta and Singapore. All shared the hazards of working on
flying boats afloat where a dropped spanner disappeared into
the water below. To remedy this, lines with cork floats were
attached to all tools. In clearer water, mechanics could "fish"
for dropped tools with an electromagnet or one of the locals
could be induced to dive for them.

On return from its Empire route, the flying boat was moored
off the slipway at Hythe for an overhaul. All interior equipment
like tables, chairs, carpets, life belts and galley pots and pans

(Above) Imperial Airways' flying boat facilities at Hythe, Hampshire.
(Below) Flying boats of Imperial Airways and Qantas at Southampton.

were removed to lose weight. With the depth of the water checked to a maximum displacement of 4 foot, 6 inches, the flying boat was then towed to a mooring. Here a wheeled beaching leg was fitted under each wing root and a steerable wheeled cradle secured under the tail. A tractor then pulled the aircraft rearwards up the slipway. As soon as it was clear of the water, a high-pressure hose washed the salt and slime off the exposed hull. Once the beaching gear was checked again, the aircraft was winched into the hangar. Working in two shifts, the maintenance crew inspected and overhauled wing floats, pipes, batteries, radios, propellers and engines — which were removed and tested on the apron. If all was well for its Certificate of Airworthiness, a test flight followed with bags of ballast loaded onboard to simulate a full load of passengers and mail. A normal "turnaround" was accomplished in two days.

On the day of departure, the flying boat fueled and oiled, was towed up the Water, and warped into the pontoon tail first, the electric cables connected, provisions and mail bags brought in, ready to receive passengers.

The last Imperial Airways landplane with mail from Africa landed at Croydon on March 4, 1937, the airport, from then on, used only for European services. The Hythe base was opened the next day with passengers entrained from London to Southampton to be taken by launch to the flying boat. This ended in 1938 when a terminal was built on the Southampton side at 108 Berth. Another new terminal would be built in 1948.[5]

To catch the daylight hours, flying boats had to leave at dawn and getting the passengers from London down to Southampton by early morning for the departure was solved by picking them up by train the night before and having them overnight in Southampton. Thus the air journeys to anywhere in the Empire began Tuesday, Wednesday and Friday evenings

---

5   All that remains of the Marine Air Terminal (this one built in 1948) can be seen from a public car park at the end of Town Quay (at the seaward end of the High Street), close to the Isle of Wight car ferry terminus. The pontoons can be seen as you leave Southampton.

from either Waterloo or Victoria railway stations. Passengers left on the 8:30 pm train from Waterloo (Platform 9 or 11) for the 90-minute ride to Southampton.

The first EAMS flight on February 6,1937 was exceptional in that the eight passengers left Waterloo Station in the morning. At Hythe, the flying boat *Castor* awaited them, bound for Alexandria. In what had the ingredients for a good mystery story, loaded with the mail were five large cases of gold bullion. *Castor* took off at 11:40 am but returned to Hythe soon after because of oiled up plugs in an engine. The bullion was then offloaded and guarded by the police while the passengers were put up at the Lawn Hotel in Hythe. All waited out the weather to begin again on the 8th. Now two days behind schedule, it was imperative that Capt. Jimmy Alger make up the lost time or Imperial would be fined. The press made a play of this with headlines "Castor Oiled" but through quick turnarounds at Marseilles and Brindisi, Alger got to Alexandria on time, landing illegally at night amongst the Fleet. All in all, it was an unpromising beginning to the EAMS.

Alger was an experienced landplane pilot, having flown with Mollard as far as Kupang in 1931 and captained the inaugural Imperial Airways flight to Cape Town in 1933. But like all flight crews for the new Empire flying boats, he was sent to 'school' at Hamble. There, a three-month course converted landplane pilots into flying boat captains. This was followed by 12 hours, solo and dual, in one of two Saunders-Roe Cutty Sark amphibians, finishing with 20 hours, solo and dual in a Short Calcutta flying boat.

When the graduates got to the controls of an Empire flying boat for the first time, how they flew, it was noticed, depended on previous aircraft to which they had been accustomed. Their misuse of flaps and engines on landing sometimes had fatal results. Former HP.42 pilots, tended to glide in to alight slowly, with full flap. Their turning on the final approach was at low level, until realizing that the wing float on the inside of the turn was in danger, they pulled up sharply to level off, splashing in with the risk of porpoising.

Those pilots who had no knowledge of seamanship were then given an intensive two-week sailing course on a ten ton ketch, skippered by a retired sea captain. Having learnt the tides and phases of the moon and to put out drogues instead of the brakes, the former landplane pilots were now seafarers, joining the ancient guild which counted Odysseus and Jason, Magellan and Cook amongst its members.

Imperial was fortunate that some of its captains were already old hands, having earned their stripes in flying boats while with the RAF. One was New Zealander Captain J. W. Burgess who had flown Rangoon flying boats with 203 Squadron. Having made a triumphant tour of Australia and New Zealand with *Centaurus* in late 1937, he was returning to Southampton. On 18 February 1938, Burgess was attempting to take-off from Lake Tiberias, Palestine with a dead port outer engine. The first attempts to take-off with three engines failed and the calm lake surface did not help. Burgess then tried an operational procedure learnt during his days on the Rangoon flying boats. He got the crew to stand forward on the lower deck with instructions to run aft on his command as fast as possible. Alone on the upper deck, he opened the throttles and ran out the flaps to a quarter. As the flying boat came up onto the step, at their captain's shout, the crew rushed aft. The rapid rearward movement of the center of gravity made *Centaurus* leap off the surface water and she was airborne in 2 minutes, 47 seconds.

The dream of a Cape to Cairo air route by flying boat was fulfilled on 2 June, 1937 when *Canopus* landed in Durban, South Africa. The Statute of Westminster had made South Africa a sovereign state and the flying boat's arrival was as much a "show-the-flag" exercise as it was commercial. State-owned South African Airways had consistently shied away from British-built aircraft, first with Dutch Fokkers and later German Junkers Ju.52s and, in 1936, buying 18 Junkers Ju.86s. This, the first through flying boat service to South Africa was via Marseilles-Rome-Brindisi-Athens-Alexandria-Cairo-Wadi Halfa-Khartoum-Malakal-Butiaba-Port

In 1937, Imperial Airways Empire flying boats reached Durban, and the dream of a Cape to Cairo air route was finally fulfilled.

Bell-Kisumu-Mombasa-Dar es Salaam-Lindi-Mozambique-Beira-Lourenço Marques-Durban.

This itinerary had been made possible because of the first two stops — Marignane north west of Marseilles and Lake Bracciano (Rome). The alighting area at Marignane was on the eastern arm of l'Etang de Berre and while passengers were allowed ashore to stretch their legs, only Air France could drop off or pick up traffic here.

With the Italian government permitting the use of Lake Bracciano at Vigna di Valle (where the Italian Air Force Museum is today) as an overnight stop, the train interlude to Brindisi would finally end. The fascist government's conditions were that Imperial Airways was not allowed to discharge or pick up passengers and permission to use Lake Bracciano could be terminated with three-days notice. The pilots thought the approach to the extinct volcanic crater hazardous because of the low cloud over the Lake and understood why Italian flying boats used the mouth of the Tiber instead. Imperial was poorly treated by the Italian government — passengers were ferried ashore from the flying boat in a bouncing dinghy with an aged boatman wrestling with one oar while his grandson tugged manfully at the other. The Vigna di Valle customs inspectors were known to be overly thorough to the point of rudeness, even rummaging through the crew's baggage.

The passengers and crew were taken by bus to the Grande Hotel de Russie in Rome. Situated between the Spanish Steps and Piazza del Popolo with its obelisk expropriated from Egypt by Caesar Augustus, the hotel had been built by the Russian Imperial family to hold extravagant parties. The Spanish artist Pablo Picasso lived at the hotel for three months in 1917, paying for his suite with a series of lithographs that were displayed. Having to be back on the bus by 5 am, the passengers would have had little time to enjoy them or the hotel's huge marble bathrooms.

Edith Sherry took the flying boat *Castor* from Southampton to Durban that summer and kept a short diary of the trip:

20/8/37: Left Waterloo at 7.30 pm traveled by Imperial Airways Pullman Car to Southampton. Spent night at South Western Hotel.

Saturday 21/8/37: Was called at 6.45 am. Got an awful shock had £13.2.6d. excess luggage to pay. Left by Hotel Bus for Docks. Left Docks by Motor Boat, the Flying Boat *CASTOR* looked lovely out in Southampton Water. Took off at 8.30 am. Glorious morning bright and sunny. Perfect take-off. Passengers — 5 men and myself. Coffee or Bovril served at 10.30 am. Arrived Marseilles 12.30 pm, and went ashore. Left one passenger. Left Marseilles 2 pm. Had lunch onboard. Wonderful view of cloud effects. Also had wonderful view of Swiss Alps en route.

Arrived Rome 4.30 pm. An hour's drive by Imperial Airways Bus to Grand Hotel De Russie. Tea ready on arrival.

I had tea with two gentlemen, one traveling to Durban and the other to Alexandria. Very nice suite of rooms. Dinner at 8 pm. In garden of Hotel, fairy lights and lanterns hanging from the trees and a lamp on each table, very pretty effect. After dinner had walk through the gardens with one of the Officers. I asked him if was possible for us to come down on land and his reply was "only once" — we landed on the sea, river, or lake each time, and in case of a forced landing on land, the flying boat would be damaged badly.

Navigating through Africa by flying boat brought with it a unique set of problems. Electrical storms made the Adcock radio direction finding sites between Cairo and Durban unreliable and the pilots continued to rely on what they knew best — the highway of the Nile or handheld maps and compass courses.

On the rivers and lakes the flying boats had to contend with unique local hazards. On the Nile, a felucca hit *Champion* when it was cast adrift by young boys. There were also the Nile's 'suds' (islands of papyrus and elephant grass weighing tons), floating ice, semi-submerged hippopotami in Lake Victoria, and flotsam of varying size up to whole trees.

As the river at Juba had silted up, the Empire flying boat stopped to refuel at Laropi, Port Bell, Uganda where passengers were taken by bus to the Silver Springs hotel at Bugalobi, Entebbe. When crocodiles ate the rubber mooring buoys that Eustace Short had invented, the airline replaced them with metal ones. The airways staff here could be counted on to entertain the passengers with "experiences" that they could take back to Tunbridge Wells with them. The best story was about the crocodile "Lutembe" reputed to be about 200 years old and so tame that he put on a show for the guests. When his name was called, he swam up to be rewarded with a lump of rotten meat — a habit that supposedly began when local tribes summoned him to dispose of living prisoners of war.[6]

Nairobi was 5,000 foot above sea level and Kisumu, at 1,000 foot higher, strained the aircraft engines. In 1933, Herbert and Ann Sparks opened a five-room hotel at Kisumu known as the Lake Hotel, and when Imperial Airways arrived in 1937, it developed into the Lake Naivasha Country Club. Here guests watched the sun in all its technicolor glory set into the lake. They slept in the hotel's thatched cottages, listening to the lions roar. Nearby was Joy and George Adamson's home where Elsa the lion cub grew up. Now a conservation center, its story was later told in the movie *Born Free*.

After Kisumu, the Imperial Airways route turned toward the Indian Ocean for Mombasa and Mozambique. The passengers

---

6   *Airlines at War — British Civil Aviation, 1939–1944* by Air World Books.

lunched at the quirky Manor Hotel at Mombasa. Begun by two British sisters in 1914, the hotel was more of a club for expatriates than a hotel. It was celebrated for its giant pet tortoise that was 2 feet tall and 4 feet long and which children rode, sometimes down to the ferry to watch the flying boats. Inevitably, the tortoise was run over by a taxi.

As one of the crucial refueling stops before Durban, use of Mozambique Island in Portuguese East Africa had been negotiated by the British. During the Second World War, because of Portuguese neutrality, military passengers passing through were not allowed to wear their uniforms. Imperial first based its traffic officers and engineers in Lumbo, the historic port of the slave trade. Crew and passengers spent the night at the Hotel do Lumbo, reputedly haunted as it had been built for the slave traders waiting for ships while their slaves were shackled in the basement. In 1939, Imperial bought a Durban tugboat hulk, had it towed to Mozambique and with electricity provided by an array of batteries (which were charged during the day) converted it into a houseboat with hotel facilities for 30 passengers. Called the *Richard King* it was nicknamed by staff the *Wretched Thing.*

The last stops before Durban were in what had recently been German East Africa — at Lindi on the southern tip of Tanganyika and Dar es Salaam, a dangerous place to taxi flying boats as its port was littered with wreckage from ships sunk by the Germans in 1915 to block it. When Imperial Airways arrived, there were still many locals who hoped that Hitler's resurgent Germany would reclaim Dar es Salaam and the squat, grey German Lutheran Mission building was known to be a center for espionage.

The Indian Ocean at Mozambique proved vicious to flying boats. On 9 March 1939, *Cambria* with Capt. Alcock, First Officer Geoffrey Shakespeare, Radio Officer "Paddy" Cussans, Flight Clerk Parsons and Steward John Riddock and six passengers was making for Mozambique when the weather changed rapidly and a storm enveloped them. Wireless contact with Lumbo was lost and Alcock knew he had to land the flying boat somewhere before nightfall. They continued up the coast looking for a bay to shelter in, parallel to the storm front, counting as they did seven water spouts about 100 yards apart. Then there was a deadly silence as all four engines stopped, despite there being fuel in the tank. Kroosi Bay was one and half miles due east, too far to glide to. With minimal visibility, eight to ten foot waves below and gale force winds, Alcock was faced with an impossible task i.e. bringing the flying boat down without cartwheeling it. Using all his skill, he put *Cambria* into a steep glide, pushing its nose into a wave between the crest and the trough. The idea was to ride through the trough and then up the next crest without porpoising. As green water hammered at the cockpit windows, the flying boat bucked up the next crest and teetered at the top of a wave. Alcock then gave a violent kick on the rudder and heaved the control column as far back as it would go. *Cambria* stopped, dead in the water. Using aileron, rudder and elevator as a sail, Alcock then tacked the flying boat towards the safety of Kroosi Bay.

The passengers were brought ashore in the darkness by a local boat that the crew was afraid would ram them. The next day, aid came in the form of the passing German liner, *Columbus,* and a Junkers Ju. 52 from DETA, the Portuguese airline in Mozambique. The first relayed a message from Cussan's dying radio to Limbo and the second guided a launch with fuel and company engineers to Kroosi Bay. A vapour lock in the fuel system (and the heavy rain) had doused the engines but all onboard knew they owed their lives to Alcock's skill and that his late brother, who had conquered the Atlantic, would have been proud of him. On March 12, the crew continued on to Durban in *Cambria*, and then returned to Kisumu to pick up the next flying boat for the same run. This was *Corsair* and with what was to come, in hindsight, Alcock wished he had given the crew some time off. As to *Cambria*, it would soldier on through the war until ignominiously scrapped at Hythe in January, 1946.

Less fortunate were the crew on *Challenger* two months later. On May 1, 1939 as it was coming in to land at Lumbo Bay, it porpoised just short of the jetty, killing Tom Webb, the radio Officer and George Knight the flight clerk. Both are buried in the cemetery on the island.

Alcock's crew would pick up *Corsair* at Kisumu on March 14, leaving Port Bell for Juba. As the flight was going well, still exhausted from the Kroosi Bay ordeal, Alcock left Shakespeare in command and went down to the cabin to rest. When he returned to the cockpit, he found Shakespeare and Cussans relaxing — after what they had been through, it was forgivable. The autopilot was on and the flying boat cruising smoothly at 4,000 foot. But Cussans couldn't get a DF fix and was uncertain as to where they were.[7] Fuel was now low and the captain looked to put the flying boat down wherever he could. Even now, it is unclear how they were one hour's flying time west of the track. Alcock descended into a straight stretch of the River Dangu, near Faradje in the Belgian Congo. Coming in, he saw a large rock on the port side and skidded the plane to avoid it. The touchdown was successful but they had hit a submerged rock and the planning bottom was holed. Realising what had happened, Alcock applied power and ran the boat towards the shallows. *Corsair* settled tail-down quickly. With the rear and forward entrances already awash, the crew used the fire axe to cut through the roof of the command deck and all escaped. The local Belgian authorities helped with shelter but Cussans had suffered a concussion and was taken to the local hospital. They were found by *Clio* passing through and Geoffrey Pett, the station superintendent at Rejaf, set off in the company Ford V-8 with other transport from the Sudan Railways Hotel to pick up the passengers, one of whom was Prime Minister Neville Chamberlain's sister. Once in Juba, the passengers continued on their way with Capt. Foy on *Centurion*. A salvage team from Short's was assembled under Hugh Gordon and sent down to the Congo. Gordon had recently returned from Habbaniyah where *Calpurnia* had been wrecked in November,

---

7 It was later discovered that the DF sensors onboard *Corsair* had been fitted in the reverse and the direction-finding loop had reversed its polarity.

Imperial Airways Empire flying boat *Capella* under maintenance at Hythe.

1938. When they arrived, the *Corsair* crew left for England with Alcock under pressure to get the flying boat back in operation soon. Labor from the local prison was employed to pull *Corsair* out of the mud, which by now had settled like cement. Shackled and harshly treated by their guards, to the watching Englishmen, the prisoners were a pitiful sight. When Gordon died in 2009, his obituary in *The Daily Telegraph* informed that while at Faradje, he and his team ate snake sandwiches. He particularly remembered the visit of a local Belgian health official who arrived on a sedan chair, followed by his African mistress, who was carrying a tin kettle and naked but for a trilby hat.

Alcock returned to Faradje to try a take-off on 14 July but, with an engine problem, aborted it. By now exhausted, worried about their health and news of the impending war, the Short's team returned home. Gouge told Gordon that *Corsair* was to be

This grainy photograph shows S.23 Empire flying boat, G-ADVB, *Corsair*, half-submerged in the River Dangu, following a forced landing in 1939.

abandoned with the engines, propellers and radios removed. An Imperial Airways team from Alexandria led by Jock Halliday the engineer-in-charge was sent down to do so and arrived in Faradje on 11 September.[8]

They resolved to repair *Corsair* — the war was a week old and Britain would need every aircraft now. The flying boat was refloated, the swollen river bringing with it poisonous snakes that entered the fuselage by the hole in the keel. The engines were laboriously overhauled and *Corsair* was secured onto a slipway where the keel was repaired. On 19 November it was floated back on the water — only to find there was now insufficient length for a take-off. The team decided to dam the river and the locals who built the palisades to do so made themselves a little village called "Corsairville."[9] On 6 January, 1940 Capt. John Kelly Rogers (who would soon fly Prime Minister Winston Churchill — sorry — allow Churchill

---

8   Jock Halliday would be made a Member of the Most Excellent Order of the British Empire (MBE) for this.

9   The village, now in the Democratic Republic of Congo, still stands. One of the most enjoyable books on flying boats I have read is Graham Coster's *Corsairville: The Lost Domain of the Flying Boat*. Penguin Books, 2000.

to fly his Boeing 314), First Officer Garner and Radio Officer "Ginger" Dangerfield flew *Corsair* out. "When we started," Kelly Rogers recalled, "the river was only 50 yards wide and *Corsair* spanned 38 yards. We took careful soundings, adjusted the load and let her go. When she started lifting, I knew, somehow, we were going to make it. But I don't think anyone else did."[10]

At Alexandria, the flying boat that had almost been left to rot was put through a two-day refit — the engineers there commenting how clean and oil-free the engines were. *Corsair* was flown back to Hythe, which it had left 14 months before. Short's, Imperial Airways, the Belgians and the Congolese — all who worked setting the flying boat free, might take credit from Byron's original poem *Corsair*.

> *O'er the glad waters of the dark blue sea,*
> *Our thoughts as boundless, and our souls as free,*
> *Far as the breeze can bear, the billows foam,*
> *Survey our Empire and behold our home!*

The first Imperial flying boat to arrive in Durban was *Cambria*. On a survey flight, it landed on the bay near the Point Docks on 22 May 1937. On 29 May *Courtier*, flown by Capt. Alcock followed. The flying boats were moored to buoys off Salisbury Island in Durban and passengers were ferried to them from the Gardiner Street jetty. After the African stations, Durban provided the crews with amenities such as medical examinations and there was a thorough inspection of the flying boat by a resident company engineer. But, even here, there was increasing landplane competition as South African Airways was operating a service to Lusaka with Junkers Ju.52s.

The Union government had the Maydon Channel within the Congella basin dredged and in 1939, Imperial Airways would build a hangar and slipway next to the Prince Edward Graving Dock. Early in the war when the Middle East and Mediterranean were being denied to the British by enemy action, Durban was considered as a possible BOAC headquarters. Taxiing in the

---

10   Stephan Wilkinson, *Flight of The River Phoenix*, Aviation History, March 2013.

Early in the war, Durban (seen here with RAF Sunderlands moored and beached) was considered as a possible headquarters for BOAC.

busy harbor, *Champion* would collide with a hospital ship. On 1 December, 1942, *Ceres,* which had run aground at Lake Dingari and was being refueled in the BOAC hangar, would catch fire. The ground crew towed her out and extinguished the flames and sabotage was suspected. During the war, with U-boats sinking Allied shipping off the east coat of South Africa, the Empire flying boats shared the Congella basin with an RAF Catalina squadron. As the U-boats prowled further up the Indian Ocean, the RAF moved to Lake St. Lucia above Durban and in November 1944, equipped with Sunderlands, to Lake Umsingazi.[11]

---

11   As they flew along the Lake, the bored RAF crewmen in the Catalinas used to shoot at the basking crocodiles with their heavy-caliber machine guns — until the local game warden stopped it.

Flying as we do today at 30,000 feet, with the window shade down and engrossed in our personal entertainment devices, it is difficult to comprehend that in the 1930s, the entertainment was outside your window. As the flying boats wallowed along at a slow 164 mph, the passengers gazed for hours out of the large windows in the Promenade Deck. Flying boats did not have an oxygen system and rarely went over 9,000 feet and pilots flew low to steer by ground features like railways and rivers. No one watched movies or played video games behind closed window blinds. Onboard entertainment in those days consisted of sightseeing, chatting, playing cards, diary writing and reading. As all Imperial Airways flying was done in daylight hours and, if fortunate, in fair weather, the passengers could count on a panorama of scenery beneath them — herds of animals that changed direction when the shadow of the flying boat flew over, the Murchison Falls at the northern end of Lake Albert and the snow-covered, majestic Mount Kilimanjaro.

The name Imperial Airways had been chosen with good reason. Those passengers who were British could witness, at first hand, some of the more visible results of imperialism. As they flew over the African continent, they saw beneath them towns laid out with straight streets (as Kitchener had redesigned Khartoum with) coffee plantations that "remittance men" from England had begun, railways that Cecil Rhodes had financed and laborers brought over from India had built; along with schools that had maps of the Empire on their walls and were surrounded by lawns for cricket and garden parties. A further extract from Edith Sherry's diary gives some of the flavor of those journeys:

Monday 23/8/37: Called at 5.15 am. Left Hotel 6.15am. Officers in summer Khaki Uniforms this morning. Have taken on another passenger, now 3 men and myself. Arrived Cairo 7.45 am. Had Breakfast on deck of Imperial Airways Houseboat. Lovely cool breeze blowing. Took off again 8.30 am. Two more men passengers came onboard. Nice view of Pyramids and the Valley of the Kings from the air. Arrived Luxor 10.45am. Nice trip on River Nile by Motor Launch, sipping iced coffee. Left Luxor 11.15 am. Lovely view of ruins. Arrived Wadi Halfa 1.15 pm. but did not go ashore. Left again 1.50 pm.

Arrived Khartoum 5.pm. Long drive to Grand Hotel. Lovely rooms. Iced coffee and cakes served on Balcony on arrival. Dinner at 8 pm, with young fellow from Durban, then chatted on the Verandah until 10.30 pm. Weather very hot.

Tuesday 24/8/37: Up at 4.30 am. Lovely drive to boat, glorious morning, beautiful sunrise. Took off at 6 am. Back to three passengers. Arrived Malakal at 8.45 am. had breakfast at Imperial Airways Station, very nice house on river bank, lovely garden. Left again 10.30 am. Reached Beauty Harbor 2.15 pm. Went for motor boat ride on Lake Albert. Glorious lake. Had wonderful view of Murchison Falls en route. Saw enormous swarm of locusts stretching for miles. Very bumpy flight to Port Bell. Arrived Port Bell 4.30 pm. (time on 30 minutes here, now 5 pm.) Nice drive to Hotel at Kampala. Lovely rooms. Quite a pretty town. Weather lovely, no sticky heat here altitude about 4,000 feet.

The airline supplied booklets on the flora and fauna you were flying over but better than them was the captain. With complete autonomy over the flight that their counterparts would envy today, the captains were tour guides. Air traffic control ended outside the airport perimeter and space-based tracking systems for aircraft were decades away. Because there were so few aircraft in the air at any given moment, the captain could decide where he would fly and at what height. As a result, they often deviated from their flight plan to show passengers points of interest along the way, such as the Pyramids, waterfalls, pearl divers, temples, elephant herds, basking sharks and pagodas — sometimes at very low heights. One pilot described the African route thus: "We often used to fly low over herds of wild elephants, or give the passengers a view of a charging rhino, or the lope of cantering giraffes. One of the most popular sites was the river just below the Murchison Falls; the area teemed with countless hippos."

Flying from Southampton to Durban in 1938 meant that you were a tourist as soon as you got on the plane — in contrast with today where tourism begins when you get off. From your seat you were treated to the whole panoply of civilizations — Egyptian, Roman, Greek, Cretan — and British colonial. The temples at Thebes and Horus, the riverside villages in Kenya, the Colossi of Memnon, the former slave market at Mozambique

— these were not theme parks with tour guides. On a ship you saw little more than the ports and the coast but flying down the Nile to Lake Victoria and onto the Indian Ocean, you were off the beaten track.

Golf, on the Promenade Deck of an Empire flying boat.

Mass tourism and environmental pollution were yet to despoil Africa and, in the 1930s, the "dark continent" was little changed from the days of Livingstone, Rider Haggard and Speke. Flying here in the 1930s has been called the last romance of the white man and what those Imperial Airways passengers experienced lives on today only in the writings of Ernest Hemingway, Beryl Markham and Karen Blix-

en. The prolific author, Elspeth Huxley, came to Kenya as a child in 1913 and witnessed the beginning of aviation in East Africa. She was a passenger on the Imperial Airways HP.42 *Horsa* and wrote of the experience in *Nine Faces of Kenya*. One cannot choose one's family and even less whom one shares the cabin with on a plane. It was Huxley's misfortune to share a flight from Cairo to Khartoum with "... two of the most lousy, affected, giggly, selfish English girls you've ever seen going to Entebbe." When the aircraft broke down in the desert, a not infrequent occurrence then, "the lousy girls got worse, wilting and grousing" in front of the locals and Elspeth "had to speak quite sharply" to them.

Huxley's love for the continent and its wildlife comes through in her celebrated memoir, *The Flame Trees of Thika,* but her outdated crime novels (with the bumbling Canadian detective Supt. Vachell) portray well the British expatriates in Kenya in the 1930s that Imperial Airways would have known. The women are always in corduroy slacks and silk shirts, the men are bounders and everyone drinks sundowners and Pimms, smokes Balkan Sobranies, has affairs out of boredom and, occasionally, murders. In the three books, she tells of the wicked young wife known to flyers on the Imperial Airways route as "Pilots' Pleasure" and the aviatrix with a contract from the Slimforall Corset Company to fly around the world promoting the sale of Aviator Brassieres.

When the television series *The Flame Trees of Thika* was being shot in Kenya in 1980, Elspeth Huxley came on location to watch and (to everyone's relief), approved. After seeing her old home, she would write: "The avenue of flame trees had long since been cut down... There were ghosts around. The small white community that had cleared bush and planted the first coffee here had been young and hopeful, laughing off their troubles, charged with optimism, believing in themselves and in the worth of their task. All are dead." It was an appropriate epitaph for that golden era of flying boats in Africa before the war began.

In what was to be the last year of peace, Imperial Airways met equally with triumph and disaster. The antipodes, Australia and New Zealand, had been reached with Qantas Empire Airways ordering six Empire flying boats.[12] Given the large tracts of land in their country, Australians had been skeptical about using flying boats, pointing to KLM's success with DC-2s. But Cobham had demonstrated how a sea/landplane combination could work when he and Sergeant Ward arrived in Darwin on 5 August 1926. The floats were removed from the DH.50 and, as a landplane, it continued on to Melbourne, returning to Darwin where the floats were refitted for the return trip to Britain. As the Italians used flying boats for propaganda value so too did the British. To commemorate the sesquicentenary in January, 1938 of the First Fleet's arrival in Sydney, the RAF

---

12   *Coogee, Corio, Coorong, Carpentaria, Coolangatta* and *Cooee*.

sent five Saro-London flying boats fitted with external long-range fuel tanks to the celebrations. Leaving Plymouth on 1 December 1937, they arrived in Brisbane, on schedule, on 21 January 1938, and were in Sydney by 25 January, where they were joined by the Empire flying boat *Centaurus*. Having flown 29,800 miles, the five were a good advertisement for the suitability of flying boats over long distances. The Australian Parliament passed the Empire Airmail Services Act on 1 July, 1938, in which all mail would enter the country through Darwin with letters for Brisbane and Sydney continuing on by flying boat and those for Perth by landplane.

As in India and South Africa, here too, Imperial Airways faced competition from landplanes that were faster and more convenient. The Australian government allowed KLM and its East Indies subsidiary (KNILM) to continue their service with DC-3s and Lockheed 14s from Amsterdam to Batavia and on to Sydney. Not only were they a full day faster but passengers knew they wouldn't be off-loaded along the way if there was too much mail.

As though reminding the world of its existence, the first Short/Mayo composite crossing of the North Atlantic took place on 20 July, 1938. *Mercury* was flown by Don Bennett (later of Pathfinder fame) and *Maia* by Wilcockson, the two aircraft separated near Foynes and Bennett continued non-stop to Boucherville, doing 2,930 miles in 20 hours 20 minutes. The next day, he went on to Port Washington, New York. The return flight was on 25–27 July via Botwood, the Azores and Lisbon with a flight time of 25 hours. Mayo was so confident with these results that on 8 August he spoke of a fleet of landplane composites that would carry passengers as well as mail. By 1938, events and technology had overtaken the pick-a-back composite — although both the Allied and Axis air forces would use the idea again in the Second World War. Even with the writing on the wall, Imperial Airways continued to publicize the capabilities of the *Mercury-Maia* composite through 1938. On 6 October, assisted by *Maia* which lifted off from the River Tay, Bennett set a long-distance record for seaplanes by flying

Mercury non-stop from Dundee to Port Nolloth on the Orange River, South Africa covering 6,045 miles in 42 hours, 5 minutes, a seaplane record that remains today.[13]

In December, he would take *Mercury* on another record-breaking flight nonstop to Alexandria. No longer seeing any future in mail-only flights, the Air Ministry abandoned the scheme. It was also the end of an era for record breaking flights that had begun in the 1920s. After the bombing of the city of Guernica, the seat of Spain's Basque government in April, 1937, aviation had taken on a sinister aspect. *Maia* would be destroyed by bombing at Poole harbor on 11 May 1941 and *Mercury* scrapped for its aluminum on 9 August that year.

The inauguration ceremony of the EAMP to Australia, New Zealand, Tasmania and Fiji took place on 28 July, aboard the Red Funnel diesel ferry MV *Medina* on Southampton Water. It was a muted, very British ceremony — without fireworks, brass band or newsreel cameras. In attendance were the Secretary of State for Air, the Viscount Swinton, the Rt. Hon. G. C. Tyron MP, who had been a previous Under Secretary for Air and the postmaster general. On 2 August, the Qantas flying boat *Carpenteria* left Sydney with the airmail under the EAMP and on August 4, *Camilla* left Southampton with the first mail for Sydney. There were now eight weekly services from Southampton to Egypt, three to Central Africa, two to South Africa, five to India and three to Australia.

In preparation for the flying boats, Qantas captains had been trained in dinghy sailing and the Singapore Flying Club allowed them the use of their DH Moth floatplane. Despite local opposition, the Sydney harborside suburb of Rose Bay was selected as the site for the flying boat terminus, primarily because it was a large bay with calm water close to the city. Other sites considered were Rushcutters Bay and the historic Botany Bay. The latter had been a favored option due to its proximity to the airport at Mascot, but a seaplane terminal there would have required building a breakwater.

---

13   There is a commemorative plaque about this flight at Dundee on the Tay Estuary.

Rose Bay had seen a flying boat before — the first one to cross the Timor Sea and come to Australia from Europe. Marquis Francesco de Pinedo and Ernesto Campanelli arrived in Melbourne on 9 June 1925 in a single engine Savoia-Marchetti S-16 flying boat. They would continue on to Sydney, landing at Farm Cove in the harbor. The Savoia-Marchetti would later be beached at Rose Bay for repairs. On completion, Pinedo and Campanelli took off north for Brisbane on 6 August 1925, beginning their return to Italy via Asia.

In May 1938, Qantas moved its operations from Brisbane to the Shell Building in Sydney. The Rose Bay Flying Boat Base was opened on 4 August 1938, by Lord Huntingfield, the acting Governor-General of Australia. Following the cutting of a ribbon linking the aircraft to the shore, the Empire flying boat *Camilla*, under command of the Australian Captain Lester Brain, lifted

The Rose Bay flying boat base in Sydney, Australia. 1930s.

off for Britain with eight passengers, 265 lbs of freight and 207 lbs of mail. Brain would soon become a key figure in organizing the QEA ferry service that brought eighteen precious Catalinas from San Diego to Australia in 1941. He would pilot the first plane himself and his direct flight across the South Pacific was the third ever completed. In early 1942, he was put in charge of ground staff at the flying boat base in Broome, Western Australia. During the Japanese air raid on 3 March, he would be commended for rowing out to rescue survivors from the destroyed flying boats in the harbor.

The zoologist Richard Archbold used a Consolidated PBY Catalina flying boat he called *Guba II* in 1936–1937 for an expedition into the rugged and remote Snow Mountains of New Guinea. In 1939, with great foresight, the Australian and British governments chartered *Guba II* for a survey flight from Port Headland, north of Perth to Mombasa on the east coast of Africa. The object of the flight was to survey an airmail route to Africa in the event that Japan should block the Empire route at Singapore. After maintenance at Rose Bay, *Guba II* left Sydney on 3 June 1939 for Port Headland, arriving the next day, having covered 2,600 miles in 19 hours and 35 minutes. It was the first flight across Australia by a flying boat. Before arriving at Mombasa on 22 June, the Catalina refueled at Diego Garcia and Mahé,

Seychelles from where, in 1944, BOAC would operate a flying boat service to Durban.

The last flying boat that the Royal Australian Air Force (RAAF) would use, *Coolangatta*, was returned to Qantas in 1944. On 11 October, on take-off from Rose Bay, it would stall and hit the water. Its hull breached, the aircraft sank quickly. One passenger was killed and two crew seriously injured. Rose Bay would be the scene of a joyful event involving flying boats on 16 September, 1945. Two weeks after the Second World War had ended, nine RAAF Catalinas landed there, repatriating Australian prisoner of war survivors from Japanese camps. The returned POWs were greeted by 50,000 spectators and hundreds of small boats. Flying boat flights to London, using Sandringhams, resumed from Sydney on 18 May 1946. Unfortunately, a year later, Rose Bay would be the site for the scrapping of all remaining flying boats in Australia.[14]

The route to Australia by flying boat was from Southampton via Marseilles, Rome, Brindisi, Athens (overnight), Alexandria, Tiberias (Palestine), Habbaniyah (Iraq), Basra (overnight), Bahrein, Dubai, Karachi (India) (overnight), Raj Samand, Gwalior, Allahbad, Calcutta (overnight), Akyab (Burma), Rangoon, Bangkok (Siam) (overnight), Penang (Malaya), Singapore (overnight), Batavia (Netherlands East Indies), Sourabaya, Koepang, Darwin (Australia) (overnight), Karumba, Townsville (overnight), Gladstone, Brisbane and, finally, to Sydney.

The fares were more than twice as expensive as the cheapest steamship fare and nearly 60 percent more costly than the price of a first class berth. This put them out of reach of all except corporate executives, colonial officials, civil servants and high-ranking military officers. Even if it had the available leisure time, the British middle class would have been unable to afford the Empire flying boats — but then they couldn't afford the first class cabins on a Cunard liner either. These were "planes for the few". "It says something about British readiness for the war," wrote *The Guardian's* Giles Foden "and

---

14   A commemorative plaque at Lyne Park Sydney, reminds passers-by of the flying boat base that was once there. There is also a Sunderland Avenue and a Catalina restaurant.

for modernity in general, that we were building flying boats for colonial officials when Hitler was putting in orders for Panzers and the Volkswagen."

WHAT WAS TRAVEL ON AN EMPIRE FLYING BOAT LIKE?

Having chosen your destination and paid your fare, you receive confirmation of your flight in a gilt-edged card. Taking a flying boat in 1938 is something of an occasion. If news reached

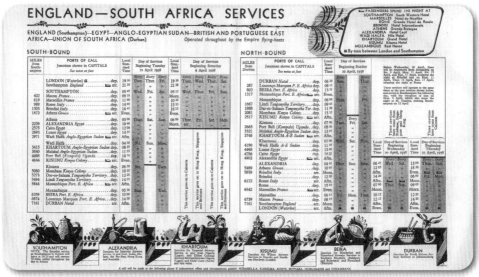

IMPERIAL AIRWAYS RETURN FARES FROM LONDON

PRICES ON APRIL 15, 1939

All accommodation and food en route was included

	FARE	EQUIVALENT IN 2020
ALEXANDRIA	£72	£4,868
CALCUTTA	£171	£11,585
SINGAPORE	£234	£15,854
SYDNEY	£274	£18,564
HONG KONG	£243	£16,463
PENANG	£225	£15,244

London that the weather at Southampton was inclement, Imperial Airways would lay on a tea dance in the *art deco* surroundings of Airways House. At Victoria Station, airline staff examine your passport, visas and inoculation certificate, taking charge of them to pass on to the flight clerk on the plane. Then you and your baggage are weighed — passengers were limited to 75–100 kilograms per person and 25 kilograms for the baggage. Those passengers over 85 kilograms in weight were limited to 15 kilograms of baggage.

You are then ushered to Platform 17 and walk to the rear of the waiting 19.30 Southampton and Portsmouth train. A year from now, these platforms will be overflowing with the British Expeditionary Force leaving for France and bewildered children being evacuated to the country. But this evening there are two Pullman coaches and a brake van with running boards lettered "EMPIRE SERVICE IMPERIAL AIRWAYS" and the R.M.A. name of the aircraft you were to fly on.

The evening before departure, The Captain and First Officer would call in to the Operations Office at Southampton to see the weather report and forecast. On the basis of the forecast and any other factors affecting the flight, the Captain would then decide which of the four routes across the mainland of France to Marseilles-Marignane would be flown the next day.

A uniformed member of Imperial's Traffic staff meets you at Southampton Station and transfers all the passengers by coach to the South Western Hotel for the first overnight of the journey. You receive a printed card of "arrangements" for the next few days — meals, stopovers etc. and this is repeated at every overnight stop. Now a block of expensive flats, at that time the South Western Hotel was known as "The Ritz of Southampton" as it served the prestigious liner trade. It is within sight of Dock Gate 4, which leads down to the new flying boat terminal and Berth 44 from where the *Titanic* departed on 10 April, 1912.

Guests at your hotel who boarded the *Titanic* included her designer, Thomas Andrews, who went down with the ship and the Managing Director of the White Star Line, Joseph Bruce Ismay, who didn't. You won't have much time to sleep as there will be an early morning call at 4:30 am.

A very short bus ride later, you (no doubt in a dazed bleary-eyed state) are at 108 Berth, waiting in the lounge. There is a light, early morning fog clinging to the surface of the harbor. Looking like a patient on life support, the flying boat is secured from the bollards with mooring lines and winched up to a pontoon. The launch from Calshot splashes in with the latest Air Ministry weather forecast. If it had been late, everyone would know there was nasty weather ahead. Thirty minutes before departure time, the flying boat's crew, less the Captain, assemble at the Operations Office near Dockyard Gate No. 8. They walk down to the pontoon to board the aircraft. Until a year ago, they and you would have been taken by a launch across the Water to where the flying boat was moored and, if it was raining, all of you would have been sodden by the time you got in. Today you notice that three of the crew are wearing white boiler suits over their uniforms and carrying small cases. The First Officer carries his personal tool kit (screwdriver, pliers, torch and cotton waste) the Radio Officer his radio bag and the Flight Clerk his typewriter and document case. The First Officer, approaching the aircraft, checks that the tail line locking nut has been removed from the slip release hook and that the tail line is secure. Unlike the other two, he boards through the aft "hatch" that you will also use, to inspect the lower deck, before going up to the cockpit by the ladder in the pantry.

The Steward (the one not in a boiler suit) also boards through the aft hatch and inspects the passenger cabins before supervising the loading of the pantry stores. The stores, which for a sector which include a meal could weigh as much as 140 kg., are in hampers and are loaded through the inward-opening loading hatch above the pantry sink on the starboard side. The steward sets about unpacking and stowing the food before he greets the passengers.

Your baggage has been collected — its weight known since the night before and entered into the calculations for fuel and route. On any aircraft but particularly a flying boat, the weight, stowage and securing of the freight and baggage is of the greatest importance. Flying below the weather could get turbulent, so the flying boat has to be balanced with great skill and the Flight Clerk is the load master. He has to know, to the pound, the exact weight of everything and everyone onboard: the bullion, the letter and parcel mail, the passengers and their baggage, the company mail, the contents of the pantry, the freight and even the weight of the crew and their baggage.

With the aid of a small crane, three stevedores have already loaded the baggage and mail bags from the starboard side but sometimes the Flight Clerk does it himself (hence the boiler suit). Freight and stores are stowed aft, your baggage and intermediate mail in the forward hold, and the main mail load (first in, last out) in the upper mail room and over the Center Cabin. The Flight Clerk supervises the strapping down of all of the "dead load" and calculates the position of the aircraft's center of gravity, which is required to lie between the limits defined by the Certificate of Airworthiness.

After checking that they are ready to receive you, the traffic officer leads you down the ramp to the swaying pontoon (Southampton is the only place in the Imperial network that has Braby pontoons — at every other stop you will be in a launch) to the aft hatch. Its "C" name underneath the cockpit windows with "Imperial Airways London" by the forward hatch, the flying boat portrays the solidity of a battleship but the aerodynamics of a whale. A youthful memory of the wire and wood biplanes of Alan Cobham's flying circuses comes to mind. That this metal ship with wings will fly 624 miles to Marseilles by lunch time is the culmination of what began on a lake in upstate New York twenty-seven years before. The hatches are open, all lights — wingtip, tail and interior — ablaze in the dawn. In the huge portholes shadowy figures move about in the cabin and cockpit.

You notice two flags hanging limp behind the aerial, giving the aircraft a nautical air. Considered to be ships while on the water (what aircraft has a bilge?), the Empire flying boats are required to fly flags, pennants and ensigns as a merchant ship would. It is the Flight Clerk's job to ensure that at appropriate times, the Civil Air Ensign, the Imperial Airways House Flag (later the BOAC House Flag), the Royal Mail Pennant, the national flag of the country they are currently in (and a set of semaphore flags, if needed) were flown.

If you are alert enough, you may notice that the leading edges of the flying boat's wings, rudder and struts are smeared with a thick yellow substance. It looks to you like railway grease — and that exactly what it is. Airframe and airscrew icing create problems on the overland sectors across France where the aircraft climbs to get over the clouds carrying a threat of ice. Icing may have been the cause of *Capricornus* (the first Empire flying boat to be lost), crashing in France on 24 March 1937. To combat this, Imperial Airways considered three remedies — the Goodrich pulsating boot which is now standard equipment on North American airliners, the Dunlop porous leather sleeve which contained a glycol/ethyl solution and last, "Kilfrost" grease, a compound developed by the railways to stop points freezing in the cold weather. Because the Southern Railway was a major shareholder in the company, this was chosen, the yellow substance liberally applied to flying boats on the Southampton to Marseilles run. As with all sailors who like things shipshape, Imperial's pilots were said to hold "Kilfrost" in low esteem.

As the water laps against it, you apprehensively clamber into your home for the next few days, stepping down into what you will later learn is the promenade cabin. The first sensations you have are smells: the tang of sea air, the whiff of engine oil, (a hint of coffee?) and the smell of leather. Then the cold hits you — the vaguely green cabin is freezing as only a metal box that has been moored in the Southampton Water can be. The heating (you are told by the traffic officer who hears this question maybe three times a week) does not come on until the starboard inner engine has started — and even then takes about thirty minutes to warm the plane's interior

Passengers dining with the captain on an Imperial Airways flying boat.

to a comfortable temperature. Two staff in navy blue uniforms with white shirt, dark tie and polished shoes meet you. The Steward greets you by name or as "Sir" or "Madam", and as he is wearing his uniform cap, salutes and shows you to your seat which has a little table in front. The Flight Clerk with the pad, checks your name against the passenger list and, dashing your hopes of photographing the Parthenon and Pyramids from the air, asks for all cameras, placing them in the special camera box which he says is sealed. He reminds us that he has our passports and inoculation booklets before disappearing to his "office" at the fore of the aircraft.

You now have an opportunity to examine your fellow travelers. Contrary to expectations, those who most took advantage of the Empire flying boats to Africa, Asia and Australia were rarely big game hunters, honeymooners, movie stars or famous authors. When the voyage by ship to Kenya took 19 days, the flying boats (like all commercial aviation) offered speed. In June

Capricornus was the first Empire flying boat to be lost, crashing in Ouroux, France, on 24 March 1937, with five fatalities.

1938, an Air Ministry survey found that business not leisure dominated air travel. Forty percent of the passengers checked-in at the Southampton flying boat base were businessmen. Thirty percent were government officials and army officers. Not all these people traveled in the course of doing their duties; however, some were starting and finishing their home leave. Those who paid their own way were the intriguing twenty percent who were travelling for pleasure. Five percent were making urgent (presumably non-leisure) private journeys, and five percent were unaccounted.[15]

As all six of us are seated in the promenade saloon — (better than the forward cabin to prevent airsickness, we are later told) the Steward standing at the midships archway welcomes us. He first points to our individual wall lights above the seats and demonstrates their control switch. The button to summon him is indicated next as are the locations of the toilets — male and female. As you attempt to get used to the pitching of the flying boat, he explains how our green leather seats recline — (warning us not do so during take-off and landing) and how

---

15   Gordon Pirie, *Incidental Tourism: British Imperial Air Travel in the 1930s.* Journal of Tourism History, 19 March 2009 pg 53.

the seat belts work. Apologizing for the cold and saying that he has closed the louvres, he offers muffs and blankets. You wisely keep your hat and coat on, staying well wrapped up until the heating makes itself felt. But where can you put your coat within easy reach — and your book? As if reading your mind, the steward indicates the luggage rack above your head, hung by chords, as on a train. Your overnight bag with your toiletries is deposited in the recessed metal compartment. Meanwhile the Flight Clerk is busy going through the whole plane — we hear his footsteps above us, checking the baggage compartment behind us and even the lavatories for stowaways (on a flying boat it is not only a criminal offense but a weight problem as well). Then he checks outside the aircraft to ensure that the engineering staff have left. Satisfied, he withdraws the fenders, putting them in the mooring compartment and re-enters.

Although the first sector of the flight is, except for the Channel, overland, the steward goes through the emergency procedures in event of ditching, about the lifebelts and how to use them and points at which windows could be opened if required. He warns us that a complete emergency drill with all occupants in the life rafts will be carried out at sometime before the flying boat reaches Alexandria.

The nervous amongst us are reassured that the green spray of water that will submerge our windows at take-off is normal and the high-pitched whine we are about to hear is the flap motor that moves the flaps out for take-off. Additionally, that the flames we might see shooting across the top of the engines are also normal — that the Pegasus (he refers to the engines as if they were winged horses) are not on fire. Is there a "Smoking Cabin?" a passenger asks. Indicating the "No Smoking" sign above the doorway, the steward says (putting on a rueful grin) there used to be, but now because of the amount of mail that we carry, it is the Flight Clerk's office. We accept that with pride, having heard often enough in the press that the mail bags are the sinews that today hold the Empire together, much as trade and the telegraph did in our grandparents' time. The mail has absolute priority and we are fortunate to get seats at all. That the contents of the sacks above and around us will be read within a week in Karumba and Karachi, Akyab and Darwin is, in this age of steamships, nothing short of incredible. Can we see the bunks that we have heard so much about is another question? Again, the apologetic grin — the bunks are not fitted for a daytime flight. The steward doesn't tell us that with the flexing of the fuselage in flight they are impossible to set up and the airline has abandoned the idea of passengers using them.

But, he says, tea, coffee or Bovril will be served as soon as we have reached cruising altitude, with lunch after Rome and tea and snacks after Brindisi. Menus will distributed as well as the latest newspapers, magazines and playing cards. The steward ends his presentation with our arrival this evening in Athens (which at almost two thousand miles away from Southampton sounds like science fiction to you). Dinner and a good night's sleep at the chosen hotel will end our day.

We glimpse the Captain boarding the aircraft through the forward hatch and going up to the Control Deck. There are snatches of conversation with the Flight Clerk that the fog may delay our departure. The latter follows him soon after to report "All passengers seated and hatches fast, Sir" and presents the load sheet for signature. The Captain checks it and signs the "Pilots Certificate of General Fitness of Aircraft".

The Transport officer makes his exit and we hear shouts, a whistle being blown — the Captain blasts an "L" in Morse and the thump of lines disconnected. The outer engines are started first throwing a spray against the windows, followed by the inner. Peering through the doorway ahead, you might see someone (it is the Radio Officer) standing in the open mooring hatch at the aircraft's nose hauling the line in and fastening the hatch shut after. The launch tows us out and, once freed, speeds ahead, ruffling the water for us, its crew looking for debris. A flashing green light somewhere no doubt clears us to taxi. We become aware of movement on the water, the slap of waves and see the floats shudder in the wind. Because this flying boat is fully-loaded, it swings into the wind on the starboard side when taxiing due to airscrew rotation. Without brakes, other than the drogues — which could only slow a flying boat down but not stop it — the crew has to anticipate continually to avoid difficult situations.

Interspersed with lights, the dull grey shore moves slowly past and the flying boat turns, presenting us with another shoreline. The captain (it seems to us) can't make up his mind and moves about erratically, this way and that. We follow the effects by looking at the float outside the window, which is sometimes submerged, sometimes free up in the air. The water surface is not too flat to get airborne and, having created the required swell, the captain accelerates the aircraft towards it. No matter the noise of the engines, they now feel hopelessly underpowered and are sure to lose the battle to get this dreadnaught into the air. All engines now surging, a green wave covers our portholes, making the cabin dark around us. This goes on for a while — it seems to us — until the flying boat breaks the suction that holds our hull tight. Then the cabin begins to lift and the green curtain drops away. We are airborne in the grey Southampton dawn.

The captain holds the flying boat close to the water, allowing us the view of the miniature houses and streets below slowly coming alive. We are blissfully unaware that with the war a year from now, the same wide portholes will be blacked out. When the necessary speed is reached (it is 95 knots) the aircraft begins to climb to a cruising altitude, cutting through the white clouds and roaring towards the English Channel.

We now take the opportunity to explore our home — its vastness grows when we walk to the toilets passing through a small center cabin. This, as we later see, is where the Captain and First Officer dine and where passengers are sometimes invited to join them. We peek into the former smoking room where the clerk is at his desk, typing away on a portable typewriter with one hand and, because of the bumpy movement of the flying boat, holding it down with the other. The crew member we never see is the Radio Officer as he can't leave his station and the Steward brings his meals to him on a tray, balancing it up the ladder from the pantry to the control deck.

As there can be no night flying, all dinners and breakfasts are taken at hotels and lunch is the only meal served onboard. Depending where they were, sometimes even lunch was from a hotel en route. If that hotel was Raffles out of Singapore, fortunate passengers opened their individual wicker baskets to tuck into cold chicken, fruit salads, sandwiches, lobster salads and cheese selections.

No cooking was done on the Empire flying boats as the 2 kW. electrical generating capacity did not allow for heating food or for refrigeration. Meals prepared by caterers are put into vacuum flasks and stowed in either the hot box, or the ice chest. The preparations in the pantry depend on the meal being served. Most lunch menus started with fruit, so this would be prepared first. Fruit juices were decanted from the vacuum flasks into serving jugs and the bread rolls and RyVita placed in baskets. Preserves and butter were put on plates and covered with doilies. Hot food was served either from the hot box or from vacuum jars. The vacuum jugs for tea and coffee were positioned ready for use. Stewards soon mastered the techniques needed to get items of food, hot or cold, out of the vacuum flasks intact.

The steward distributes the lunch menus and disappears to see to the needs of the crew. When he returns to our cabin, he carries trays laid with white linen table cloths, serviettes, side plates, cruets and metal cutlery. All food is served on ceramic plates and all drinks in glasses. The Imperial Airways Gazette for September, 1937 gave a typical lunch menu:

LUNCH:

Iced Melon
Roast Chicken, York ham, Veal Galantine
Tomatoes and Asparagus Tips
Fresh Fruit Salad and Cream
Cheese — Cheshire, Cheddar, Cream Cheese
Toast, Imperial Assorted Biscuits
Crystallised Fruit
Coffee and Liqueurs

There is a wine list together with the usual range of spirits. Cocktails are available, including the famous "Airways Special" (composition unknown). On sale are alcoholic and soft drinks. Free of charge items included such drinks as tea, cocoa, coffee, chocolate, Bovril, OXO, Horlicks and such items as sandwiches, cocktail snacks, biscuits, fresh fruit, aspirin, smelling salts, *eau de Cologne*, fruit salts, cotton wool for the ears, barley sugar, saccharine, Glucose-D, air-sickness tablets, soap and towels, pencils, notepaper engraved with the aircraft's name, badge and a related quotation, postcards and descriptive booklets of the route and night stops. On loan for the flight are playing cards, crossword puzzles, jigsaw puzzles, books, children's magazines, games and sunglasses. This standard of cabin service was maintained until the entry of Italy into the war in 1940.

The galley of an Imperial Airways flying boat.

Although the country's "chosen instrument", the Imperial Airways London office was in a shabby former furniture depository behind Victoria Station. The site for the new headquarters was chosen because it was between the coach and train terminals and backed on to the Southern Railway station where passengers would have direct access to Platform 17 (now 19). London was going through its Portland stone phase (the Shell-Mex building on the Embankment and BBC's Broadcasting House are contemporaries) and the architect Albert Lakeman also used white Portland stone for the terminal. "Airways House" opened on 5 June 1939, its *art deco/streamline* exterior receiving the accolades it deserved. Deceptively only 80 feet deep, but 500 feet wide, the 5-story concave building has a symmetrical facade with a 10-story central clock tower and wings curving forward to form a crescent shape. As well as the central location for checking in passengers, the building was also the airline's Head Office, the very top of the tower affording the directors of Imperial Airways impressive views of the city.

By late 1937, Imperial's dated and disorderly state could no longer be ignored. The government appointed a special committee of investigation under Lord John Cadman, Chairman of the Anglo-Persian Oil Company who was credited with introducing 87-octane fuel to Britain. As a petroleum engineer in the Middle East, Cadman knew the value of aviation, having used a Junkers F.13 to fly from Baghdad to Tehran for meetings with the Shah and his ministers. By road, the journey would have taken up to five days, crossing three mountain ranges, but by air it was ordinarily completed in four hours.[16]

Cadman reversed the recommendations of the Hambling Report of fifteen years before. Published in March, 1938, the Report emphasized Imperial Airways' failings — that the pilots were not allowed to bargain collectively, that the planes had

---

16   When his company was testing a new pipeline running from its oilfield at Maidan-i-Naftun to a new refinery at Abadan, they employed local people. Such was their enthusiasm for the work that they loosened the bolts on the pipeline at night so that they would be hired to tighten them up the next day. An aircraft was bought to patrol the pipeline as drones do today.

Airways House, which opened in 1939, is today
used by the National Audit Office.

no deicing equipment, and that the "Buy British" restraint had crippled its operations. It should be noted that Cadman did not recommend the formation of a joint airline overall, nor did he propose any form of public ownership.

Sir Eric Geddes had died in June and Sir George Beharrell who had been with him at Dunlop was made temporary chairman of Imperial Airways. Having kept the balls in the air since 1925, Woods Humphery fully expected to be Imperial's new chairman. But the Cadman Report made him a scapegoat, saying that he had taken "a commercial view of his responsibilities that was too narrow", and warning any immediate improvement in the situation was likely to "involve some change in directing personnel."

Facing a lack of confidence in the House on his rearmament policy (or lack of), Prime Minister Neville Chamberlain did not want another on civil aviation.[17] He summoned Sir John Reith the Director General of the BBC and appointed him Geddes's successor. The dour, 6-foot 6-inch Scot, known as the authoritarian ruler of the BBC (he was nicknamed "Wuthering Heights") thought the job beneath him. But as the quintessential *mandarin*, Reith accepted, hoping that as a reward he would be given a position in the War Cabinet. Reith held that Imperial Airways and British Airways should be amalgamated into one worldwide company and that such a company would be free of any private shareholding to be run, like the BBC, as a public Corporation with service to the public. One can imagine how he must have felt on July 4, 1938 leaving the grandeur of BBC House with its *art deco* architecture and works of art for the former furniture depository. His first act was to have the ceiling of his office lowered to enhance his height.

Woods Humphery had been a friend of Reith's since their boyhood days as apprentice engineers, but Reith wanted no power-sharing with him. He felt that the Cadman Report had effectively tarred and feathered him and, embittered, Woods Humphery resigned and went into self-exile in the United States. As the new broom, Reith warned that he was going to buy aircraft from outside Britain for Imperial (as British Airways had done) and asked for the loan of RAF bombers to cope with the Christmas mail load. Share values and government approval went up — which left Reith free to orchestrate the merger of Imperial Airways and British Airways Limited into a single chosen instrument — British Overseas Airways Corporation (BOAC). The Bill received Royal Assent

---

17   In 1937, when Juan Trippe arrived in Britain to visit Shorts, after seeing German rearmament, he couldn't get over the complacency. "Don't they know?" he is supposed to have said.

on 4 August 1939, just prior to the commencement of the war. Clive Pearson, the Managing Director of Whitehall Securities who had helped form British Airways in 1935, was appointed Chairman of BOAC. Chamberlain did reward Reith by making him Minister of Information. However, there was no love lost between Reith and the new prime minister, Winston Churchill, who elevated him to the Lords where he could do no harm.[18]

With the creation of BOAC on 24 November 1939 "Airways House" would be renamed the more prosaic "BOAC Terminal". During the Second World War, to escape the bombing, airline staff were evacuated to Bristol and housed in the Grand Spa Hotel, Clifton with offices in Lower High Street. Neither Lower High Street nor the BOAC Terminal escaped the Luftwaffe, the latter badly damaged when an unexploded bomb went off nearby. When the airline was renamed in 1974, the building became the "British Airways Terminal", closing to passenger use on 14 November 1980. Now a government warren filled with those who audit one's taxes, the only clue as to its original use is Eric Raymond Broadbent's sculpture *Speed Wings Over The World* above the entrance.

But history wasn't finished with Woods Humphery yet. In early 1940, the Air Transport Auxiliary (ATA), an organization under the aegis of the Ministry for Aircraft Production (MAP), was set up to ferry aircraft from factories to squadrons. Churchill's Canadian Minister of Aircraft Production Lord Beaverbrook asked for Woods Humphery's help in organizing the Atlantic Ferry Organization (ATFERO) to fly U.S. made aircraft directly from North America to Britain.[19] No one knew whether an Atlantic bomber ferry was practical — Lindbergh had only flown across it 13 years before.[20] The alternative was dismantling the aircraft to ship to Speke Airport, Liverpool

18   https://www.bbc.com/historyofthebbc/research/john-reith/reith-in-wartime

19   Pigott, Peter, *Wingwalkers: A History of Canadian Airlines International.* Harbour Publishing, 1998. pg.112.

20   One who made the Atlantic flights possible for Ferry Command was Patrick McTaggart-Cowan, the Rhodes Scholar meteorologist at Gander. With the U-boats sinking ships that would have provided him with weather conditions, his forecasts were invaluable. The Americans called him "McFogg" and helped by stationing weather ships in mid Atlantic, armed to the teeth.

but with marauding U-boats, there was no guarantee that they would ever get there. Imperial Airways captains with Atlantic experience were seconded to ferry the aircraft over. They included Bennett, Wilcockson and Griffith James "Taffy" Powell who, in 1946, would begin Silver City Airways. They trained the volunteer pilots who were a mixture of bush pilots and American mercenaries in Montreal on what was to come.

On 10 November 1940, led by Bennett, the first flight of seven Hudson bombers prepared to take-off from Gander Airport for Aldergrove, Northern Ireland. It was the eve of Armistice (now Remembrance) Day and to wish them well, the local band formed up to play a rousing piece. But because of the winter darkness, the musicians couldn't read the sheet music and so struck up a tune they knew by heart from church parade. Facing the unknown, the Hudsons moved down the runway to the mournful strains of *Nearer My God to Thee*, the Titanic hymn. But keeping in sight of Bennett, all seven made it, the first of hundreds of aircraft to be flown across.

With the declaration of war, all flying boat operations were moved to Poole and Hamworthy in Dorset and operations offices were set up at Poole Pottery. Post-war, BOAC continued flying boat operations from Poole, incurring the displeasure of members of the Parkstone Yacht Club who had been banned from sailing and wanted a return to their pre-war status. The flying boats returned to Southampton on 14 April 1948 where the docks were now owned by British Railways which built a marine air terminal at 50 Berth in the Eastern Docks. This would close in September, 1958 when Aquila Airways ceased operations, ending Southampton's connection with flying boats.

Although 12 mid-air refuelings by the Harrows and *Cabot* and *Caribou* had successfully taken place between 5 August and 1 October, 1939, the war put an end to Cobham's air-to-air refueling. Even before that, the government and the public were wary of the whole procedure. The ignition of fuel vapor by a single spark might have been why the Pan American *Samoan Clipper* had exploded the year before. It didn't help that on 19 June, 1939, *Connemara,* one of the new S.30 flying boats, was destroyed while being refueled offshore at Hythe. The petrol barge had caught fire and it travelled up the hose to the aircraft. Dependent on weather and the skill of the pilots, inflight refuelling was too dangerous (or Heath Robinson-esque?) for commercial aviation. During the Second World, even as bombers struggled to get their bombloads to Berlin and Tokyo, it was never considered. Ultimately, what damned both Cobham's scheme and the Short/Mayo composite was the Pan American Boeing 314 *Yankee Clipper* taking off from New York on 20 May, 1939 and arriving at Lisbon on the 21st. The Future had arrived.

Imperial/BOAC knew it needed flying boats comparable to the Boeing 314 if it was to make the Atlantic crossing commercially viable. The S.23 and S.30 never had the range to do so and the airline pinned its hopes on the S.26 "G" Class, the last of the pre-war Shorts flying boats. With hostilities escalating, the RAF funded their development on the understanding that, should war be declared, they would enter military service. With their Bristol Hercules sleeve valve radial engines, the Short S.26s had a range of 3,200 miles at 180 mph, which would allow them to cross the Atlantic without refueling. Three were built: *Golden Hind, Golden Fleece* and *Golden Horn,* and by the time they were launched in 1939, they would serve in the RAF or BOAC.

Imperial Airways — romantic and old fashioned — had passed into history.

7   Hotels on the wing

Aerial goliaths were to be avoided — the Wanamaker Triplane (58 feet in length), the Zeppelin-Staaken R.XIV (73 feet in length) and the ultimate: the Caproni Transaero (77 feet in length) with three sets of wings — all spectacular to look at but with poor track records. Given the available technology, there was a limit to how big an aircraft could be and still fly.

The United States Army Air Corps (USAAC) didn't think so and neither did Boeing. General Douglas MacArthur, the Army Chief of Staff decided in 1931 that the USAAC should have a heavy bomber with the range to protect Alaska and Hawaii from Japanese incursion. Bill Boeing's Seattle company was known for military aircraft like the F4B-4, Y1-B9 monoplane bomber and the P-26A "Peashooter". Its ventures into commercial aviation had been costly failures. Most recently, the overbuilt, cramped Boeing 247 had lost out to Donald Douglas's DC-2. When Boeing was invited to submit a proposal to the USAAC, one of its engineers, Claire Egtvedt, challenged Boeing to hire more engineers to design bigger aircraft. "We are building airplanes, not cement sidewalks." he said. The company began work on the XB-15 in 1934 — called the "Gran' Pappy", it was destined to be just that to a family of large airplanes including the Boeing Clipper, the B-29, the B-52 and the 707 and 747.

At 87 foot, 7 in length and with a 149 foot wingspan, until the B-29, the XB-15 was the largest landplane ever built in the United States. Its flight deck the size of a living room, the behemoth had a range of 5,000 miles and featured an autopilot and deicing equipment. Underpowered by four Pratt & Whitney 1830 engines, it was slow and cumbersome. Boeing understood that the "one-off" was a test bed, its purpose to learn how to build an aircraft of that size. It had a wing thick enough

The Caproni Ca.60 Transaero (above) was a nine-wing flying boat intended to become a 100-passenger transatlantic airliner. It had eight engines and three sets of triple wings.

The Wanamaker Triplane (below), was a large, experimental triplane flying boat — the first four-engined aircraft to be built in the United States.

for a passageway to get to the engines in flight, a flight deck instead of a cockpit, stations for a flight engineer, navigator, radio operator, sleeping quarters for the relief crew, even a galley with hot plates. The XB-15 greatly expanded Boeing's technical capabilities but, combined with the failure of the 247, building it almost bankrupted the company. Boeing laid off half its workforce and brought in drastic economy measures — the most memorable a sign in the washrooms over the paper dispenser that said: "Why use two when one will do?"[1]

Wellwood Beall was a Boeing salesman but also, having graduated from the Guggenheim School for Aeronautics, an engineer. Sent to Shanghai to sell Peashooter fighter planes to the Nationalist Chinese, he was recalled to Seattle in 1934 and assigned to the engineering department. While in China, Beall heard that Pan American was going to operate flying boats across the Pacific, all the way to Hong Kong. His initial reaction was disbelief — even with refueling bases, it would never work. "It will be 10 to 15 years" he said, "before that sort of thing is commercially practical." On the ship home, his wife remarked that she could not understand how anyone who loved planes as much as he did could be so negative about their future. Before they landed in Seattle, Beall had worked out the plans for a giant flying boat.

With the three Martin Clippers assigned to the Pacific, Trippe had yet to find a flying boat for the Atlantic. In 1936, Trippe invited proposals from aircraft manufacturers for a long-range flying boat able to carry enough payload to make it economical. It had to be capable of flying for 2,400 miles at an altitude of 10,000 feet. Lindbergh had warned him that there were no islands like Midway, Wake and Guam islands in this ocean. Trippe even threw in an added inducement of a $50,000 bonus to the winner. "I believe in tying the bag of oats out front." he said. In mid-Depression United States, was there a market for such an aircraft? As he would later do with the Boeing 707 and 747, for Trippe, it was always "Build it and they will come."

---

1   The next day there was an engineer's response: "Why use one when the job is only half-done?"

Twenty years later, he would be in the same situation — this time looking for a jet airliner that had the range to cross the Atlantic. Boeing's Dash 80, with its Pratt & Whitney J57 turbojet engines, didn't have the power to get an airliner to Europe. But Pratt & Whitney had just tested the J75 for the numerous Cold War fighter aircraft then coming online, among them the Canadian-built Avro Arrow. Trippe called on Bill Allen, the president of Boeing, and asked him to substitute engines. Allen refused — the Dash 80 was Boeing's return to the commercial market after the Stratocruiser failure and he was not about to jeopardize it with an engine designed for fighter aircraft. Trippe persisted — saying if he couldn't get in through the front door, he would try the back. He began on Fred Rentschler of Pratt & Whitney. Rentschler was an aviation icon — in 1926 he had bought a small tool company and led it to create the seminal Pratt & Whitney Wasp — the only engine today designated a historic landmark. He told Trippe to forget it — the J75 was classified. Trippe had enough political clout to have it declassified as the civilian JT4A and continued to hound Rentschler for weeks after. When nothing came of this, with typical Trippe flamboyance, he bought 120 JT4As for $40 million. Pan American's bankers were aghast — the engine was still on its test bed. Now needing a plane to go with the engines, Trippe played Bill Allen off against Donald Douglas, whose DC-8, then on paper, could be adapted for either the J57 or J75. On 13 October 1955, at a party thrown for airline executives, Trippe announced that Pan American would be operating a jet across the Atlantic by 1958. In that instant, every piston engine airliner was made obsolete. The Jet Age had arrived, and no airline wanted to be left behind. As Trippe expected, Allen called.[2] Could he buy those 120 engines off Trippe and adapt the Dash 80 (soon to be called the Boeing 707) to use them? His persistence had paid off. It was vintage Juan Trippe.

---

2   Bill Allen would be awarded the Collier Trophy in 1955 for the B-52 — not the Dash 80 which, as the Boeing 707, would revolutionize commercial aviation.

Sikorsky, Pan American's customary source for flying boats, responded to Trippe with a design that would eventually be the VS-44A. Powered by four Pratt & Whitney Twin-Wasp radial engines, it had a wingspan of 124 foot, an overall length of about 80 foot and a gross weight of 57,500 lbs. Its range, depending on load and the quantity of fuel, was approximately 4,000 miles. The VS-44A met Pan American's requirements for speed and range but was rejected as too small for what Trippe had in mind. Consolidated Aircraft proposed a four-engine flying boat that would later become the PB2Y "Coronado" but its design was also rejected. Irascible as always, Glenn L. Martin refused to bid — swearing that Trippe had ruined him by ordering only three M-130s.

Using the lessons learned from the XB-15 and the 247, Boeing put its resources into two parallel four-engine aircraft — a bomber (Model 299) and a commercial airliner (Model 307), both sharing the wings, tail, rudder, landing gear, and engines. Its directors allocated $275,000 for development of both but the designs went $150,000 over budget. Shown to the media on a warm July day in 1935, Model 299 was so impressive that an awed Seattle reporter said, "She's a flying fortress".[3] (Like jeep and Kleenex, the name became a generic term for the bomber). Then the prototype Model 299 crashed. The pilots had forgotten to disengage the elevator locks. The military were not impressed and chose the cheaper Douglas B-18 Bolo instead, ordering 350 of them and awarding Boeing the consolation prize for 13 Model 299s, now called the B-17. Company engineers redeveloped the bomber, but it would not be until 1938 that the military, still not convinced, would reluctantly order 39 B-17Bs.

Licking its wounds, bathed in red ink and moving to Plant 2, Boeing initially declined to compete for the design of a giant flying boat for Pan American. Boeing had not built a flying boat since the HS-2Ls in 1918 and large flying boats like the Dornier Do X had been commercial failures. Clairemont Egtvedt had succeeded Bill Boeing as president and put his best engineers,

---

3   Boeing trademarked the name.

E. Gifford Emery and Edward Curtis Wells, into planning the Model 307.[4]

Nothing happened to Beall's idea at first as the company put his engineering talents to work re-developing the B-17. But, using his dining room table, he worked on the nucleus of a flying boat at home. He planned to suspend a cavernous metal hull under the wing of the XB-15. Empty, the flying boat would weigh 40,000 lbs and with a payload of 42,500 lbs, it would be an 82,500-lb aircraft! For a generation that had grown up in the era of sputtering canvas biplanes, this must have been a mind-blowing experience. Beall shared the concept with Chief Engineer Robert Minshall. They submitted the design to Egtvedt who saw the potential. He is supposed to have said in his soft-spoken Scandinavian accent: "Our business is manufacturing big airplanes. We opened up this field; we should stay with it." With the blueprints in hand, Egtvedt traveled across the country to the Chrysler building and on 9 May 1936 showed them to Trippe and André Priester. To safeguard their design, Beall and Minshall applied for a patent at the U.S. Patent office on 1 June, for having invented the B-314, a "new, original flying boat".[5]

Lindbergh, who kept in touch with Trippe from exile, warned him about choosing Boeing with its poor reputation for commercial aircraft. The Lone Eagle's increasingly anti-interventionist stance was beginning to embarrass Trippe and disappoint Americans. When he was awarded a medal by Hermann Göring in 1938, Lindbergh's name was taken off all Pan American literature.

As there were no other entries, Boeing won the competition by default. Pan American contracted for six B-314s on 21 July 1936, with an option for six more. At $512,000 each, the airline would be financially responsible for $4.8 million including spares. The contract specified that the first deliveries would begin 17 months after signing (January 1938) and failure to

4   Trippe, who would also consider the DC-4E, bought the first two 307s in 1937 and briefly considered using them on the Atlantic instead of flying boats.

5   Robert J. Minshall was a pioneer in aircraft design and would be awarded the Ed Musick Trophy Memorial Trophy for 1940.

meet that date would incur heavy penalties. The first delivery did not happen until March 1939 but Trippe was so taken with this whale on wings that he never exercised the penalty clause. He even ordered six B-314As on 1 October 1939 which would be ready by 1941.

Structurally, the 314A was identical to the 314. Changes were relatively minor. While the engines were essentially the same, fuel capacity was increased by 1,190 gallons to 5,448, passenger capacity was increased from 82 to 85, and gross weight was increased from 82,500 lbs to 84,000 lbs. Speed was also increased from 193 to 199 mph. and the range to 5,200 miles with required reserves. The first B-314A was launched in March 1941, and all six had flown by July. Two were slated for the Pacific and four for the Atlantic but, with the war, all that changed.

The B-314 was to be the last aircraft built at Plant 1 on the Duwamish River, next to the Red Barn where Bill Boeing had begun the company in 1916. Beall was named project engineer and given a team of 11 engineers. By its completion, 6,000 engineering drawings, 11.5 miles of electrical wiring, millions of rivets and 15,200 bolts were used. The 152 foot cantilever wing had to lift a cavernous body that needed to be deep enough for a double-deck configuration. Except for a few parts, the structure was entirely of metal with the two fuel tanks and mail cargo sections built into each side of the wing mid-section. Instead of the struts that the M-130 used to keep the engines high enough away from water, the Boeing engineers copied the Sikorsky XPBS-1 patrol bomber and the Consolidated XPB2Y, both of which relied on a streamlined hull to put the wing directly into the upper fuselage. The Wright 2600-3 Twin Cyclone radial engines chosen had been designed for fighter aircraft and this was the first time they would be used in a commercial plane. Another precedent was the use of 100-octane fuel in a commercial aircraft — which Capt. Robert Ford would discover was in short supply elsewhere when he took the *Pacific Clipper* the long way around the world in 1941. As with the XB-15, the B-314's thick wing chord allowed access

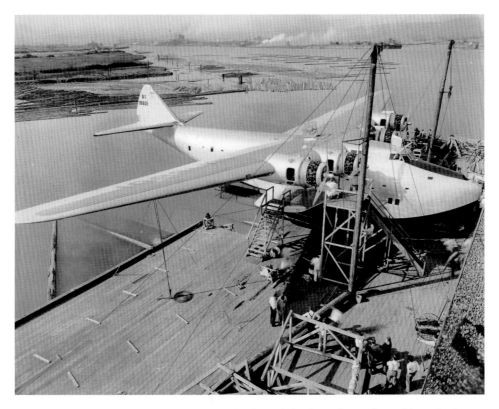

The Boeing 314 prototype, NX18601, in the original configuration with a single tail. (Boeing Airplane Company)

to the engines during flight and, between June 1939 and June 1941, 431 in-flight engine repairs were performed by B-314 engineers in this way.

An engine failure in mid-ocean is the nightmare of every pilot, more so as the now windmilling propeller increases the drag of an already stricken aircraft. Priester, head of the Pan American team sent to Seattle, insisted on Hamilton Standard fully feathering propellers for the B-314 which allowed the blades to turn edgewise in the air stream, stop rotating and eliminate much of the drag. Unlike it's contemporaries, the Short's S.23 and the Consolidated Catalina with their wingtip floats that reduced drag and increased range, the B-314 had sponsons like the M-130 — (except that Boeing was forced to call them "hydrostabilizers and fuel reservoirs" because Martin

The flight engineer of a Boeing 314 could access the engines while in flight to carry out repairs.

had copyrighted "sea wings"). Heat and power were taken from the manifolds around the engine exhaust stacks. Per hour, they delivered 360,000 BTUs and a volume of 170,000 cubic feet of air. All electric power was provided through a 12/24-volt Direct Current system of 15-volt generators and two 12-volt batteries. Its hull would have a double bottom from where pumps forced gasoline, stored in the hydrostabilizers, up to the wing tanks and engines.

When completed, the first Boeing 314 (NX18601) was moved down the slipway with the launching scheduled for 31 May 1938. According to the tide tables, the deadline was to be 5 pm for the ship to enter the water for sufficient depth and exit out of the shallows. For the trip down the Duwamish River and into Elliot Bay, the Clippers were lashed to a barge, which was then towed down the river past the Spokane Street drawbridge and into Elliott Bay by a small tugboat at either end.

A national radio network had its microphones set up on the dock for the event. When 5 pm arrived and the flying boat began to move, the radio announcer began: "This mighty triumph of American enterprise, this great Flying Clipper ship that will span the Atlantic and the Pacific carrying the flag of the United States to world supremacy in the air, is being lowered majestically into the water here at the plant of Boeing Airplane Company in Seattle."

There were also reporters from the East who were covering the launch. One of them was Jim Piersol of *The New York Times* who was also an aeronautical engineer. "The tail is too small for all that airplane," Piersol warned. "Quit worrying," said Beall. "It's been tested. It's based on the XB-15 and that's doing all right." On 4 June, the flying boat was towed to Elliott Bay where in 2002, the only remaining Boeing 307 ditched during a test flight from Boeing Field to Everett.[6] Test pilot Edmund T. "Eddie" Allen began the taxiing tests, the press following along, hoping to see the flying boat take-off. Having survived Post Office flights over the Rockies in DH.4s, Allen was a member of the Suicide Club and known as the best test pilot then. When he tried to taxi the Boeing in a crosswind, the aircraft tilted precariously, and the wing dipped so low that the outboard propeller bit into the water. John Borger, an engineer onboard remembered that there were times when water entered the cabin. Part of the trouble was quickly traced to the fuel loading — all of the fuel onboard was in the wing tanks and none was in the hydrostabilizers (sponsons), making for an extremely top-heavy condition. The engineers that accompanied Allen had doubts about the sponsons. Their dihedral — the angle at which they were attached to the fuselage — was too sharply tilted, making the flying boat unstable in turns.

The newsmen asked the watching Egtvedt what the trouble was. He attempted to soothe them over by replying that no one had operated a 'boat of this size before and that the co-pilot had probably "gunned" the engines on the wrong side by mistake. Priester was more sanguine. "Those troubles are trivial," he told the reporters. "The real news is in the high-speed runs. The spray curls back clean, under the sea wings. This is a real airplane — not one that covers itself with spray, so it can't get off well."[7]

When Allen took the B-314 on its first flight on 7 June, remaining airborne for barely 38 minutes, he found the Wright

6   Boeing restored it and the 307 is now on display at the National Air and Space Museum at Dulles International Airport.

7   Harold Mansfield was a Boeing company public relations director and author of, *Vision: A Saga of the Sky*. This is taken from his: *Boeing Enters the Aluminum Age*, Part 5: Giant Aircraft Need Better Testing, 1938–39.

Cyclones were too underpowered for so monstrous an aircraft.[8] And as Piersol had guessed, Allen had inadequate control — the single tail that engineers swore had worked in the wind tunnel — was too small to provide enough directional control for so large an aircraft. John Leslie, the Pan American divisional engineer, told Beall that the B-314 was unacceptable as it kept bouncing back into the air when touching down.

At the end of its first flight, the flying boat was hauled out of the water at the Sand Point Naval Air Station, a peninsula on the western shore of Lake Washington. There was no point in taking it back to Plant 1, the second flying boat was already in its place on the factory apron. The test program was conducted a little farther north, at the Pan American Matthews Beach facility, the Washington terminus for its flying boat service to Alaska.

All new aircraft have teething troubles and Egvedt understood that the B-314 (already six months behind its delivery date) had to be expensively rebuilt. The Clipper contract was going to be a financial loss — like the 247 and the Model 307. It would be two decades before Boeing would venture into the commercial market again.

Through the remainder of 1938 and well into the next year, company engineers worked hard to prove Lindbergh wrong. Two of them, Ed Wells and John Sanders designed the now familiar triple tail arrangement in one weekend, the sponson's angle was corrected and the Wright Cyclones improved. To prevent the bouncing, the flying boat hull was redesigned by adding 20 inches to the step position.

Finally, on 29 January 1939, NX-18601, the first Boeing Clipper, was ready to be passed on to Pan American. The airline would take delivery of the Clippers in Oregon to avoid paying tax in Washington State. Test pilot Earl Ferguson (soon to be killed in the Model 307 prototype crash on 18 March) took the flying boat from Lake Washington, Seattle to Astoria, Oregon. Onboard were Frank Gledhill (Yale Class of 1923)

---

8   The Douglas DC4 made its first flight the same day that the first Clipper flew, but the triple-tailed version was deemed too clumsy and Douglas had to redesign it.

A Pan American crew on the flight deck of a Boeing 314 Clipper.

with other Pan American officials to complete the transaction. Wellwood Beall accompanied them, having his day in the sun. It had been 5 years since he and his wife had stepped off that ship from China. They landed on the Columbia River opposite Astoria where a rowboat came out and took them to shore. There followed a scramble up a muddy slope at the river's edge from where a boy led them to a banker's office. The choreography of the sale was to take place by a conference telephone call with Pan American's New York office, a New York trust company and the Civil Aeronautics Authority (soon to be the Civil Aeronautics Board) in Washington. The lawyers — as lawyers do — had mimeographed a fifty-four-step routine. "Is the airplane at Astoria in fit and sound condition?" asked New York. Beall affirmed that it was. "Is Mr. Gledhill there to receive it?" Gledhill said "Yes." "Mr. Beall, have you the certificate of title?" A shock ran through Beall. He'd forgotten the certificate. It was in its metal frame on the wall of the stairway to the bridge, out there in the middle of the Columbia River. Gledhill waved a blank piece of paper and nodded vigorously to Beall. Beall stammered, "Yes, yes, I've got it here." "Will you sign it and pass it to Mr. Gledhill?" Beall signed the blank paper. "Civil Aeronautics Authority, will you record the transaction?" It was so recorded in Washington. The final payment cheque of $100,000 was handed to Beall. Phones clicked in three cities. That was when the Astoria banker must have seen the blank sheet. "What the hell have we done here?" he asked. "It's all right," said Gledhill. Then he grabbed Beall by the back of his coat collar. "Let's go get that damn piece of paper." Running back, Beall's feet sank ankle deep in the mud bank. What if the certificate wasn't there? What if the rowboat overturned in the choppy water? He got out to the flying boat. The certificate was there. The screwdriver shook in Beall's hand as he got it off the wall. He returned to the banker's office, handed it to Gledhill and sat down, limp but happy. "You need a vacation," sympathized Gledhill. "Better come along on the maiden flight to Hong Kong."[9]

From there, Capt. Harold Gray flew NX18601 to Alameda. The other five would be delivered at monthly intervals, the last on 16 June 1939. As delivered, the average cost of the first six Clippers was $668,908. An additional $756,450 covered spare engines and parts for all six. Although it would last barely a decade, the Boeing Clipper was the quintessential flying boat, evoking, more than any other, the Golden Age of Flying.

But, of all the aircraft's deficiencies, what passengers would have quickly noticed were the blocked toilets. Toilets on airliners then were holes in the rear of the fuselage — drafty and uncomfortable (the wind sometimes returned the effluent) and not to be used over populated areas. An actual flushable toilet on the B-314 was another of Beall's sales gimmicks, and he was justifiably proud of it. The flushing system was a rotating drum with a bucket inside and when a passenger put

---

9   Mansfield, ibid

Although it would last barely a decade, the Boeing Clipper was the quintessential flying boat, evoking, more than any other, the Golden Age of Flying.

the toilet lid down, the drum turned the bucket upside down and the contents were dumped out of a large vent into the ocean. Invited on the B-314's inaugural flight from Alameda to Hawaii on 23 February 1939, Beall was asleep in his berth when a furious Priester shook him awake. The two toilets were not flushing! The bleary-eyed Beall got them working but, on the flight, back, the same thing happened and this time he couldn't fix them. Priester's Dutch profanity at this didn't need translating. As soon as Beall returned to Seattle, the non-flushing flushable toilets were turned over to the Boeing engineers. They were mystified as the flushing mechanism had been tested for over a year. The solution (which made

---

The Boeing Clippers operated by Pan American Airways (PAA)

Model B-314

NC-18601 – Honolulu Clipper
NC-18602 – California Clipper (briefly Pacific Clipper in 1941)
NC-18603 – Yankee Clipper
NC-18604 – Atlantic Clipper
NC-18605 – Dixie Clipper
NC-18606 – American Clipper

Model B-314A

NC-18609 – Pacific Clipper (briefly California Clipper in 1941)
NC-18611 – Anzac Clipper
NC-18612 – Cape Town Clipper

Operated by British Overseas Airways Corporation (BOAC)

Model B-314A

NC-18607/G-AGBZ – Bristol
NC-18608/G-AGCA – Berwick
NC-18610/G-AGCB – Bangor

---

even Priester laugh) was the toilet paper. Pan American used ruffled, thicker, toilet paper than the paper Boeing used and that clogged up the drum and prevented it from turning.[10]

The Clipper required 2 ten-man crews, 6 each on the large flight deck — 3 pilots, navigator, a flight engineer and a radio operator and 4 stewards. The flight deck was 21 foot long and 9 foot wide with full headroom. It was lined in black to eliminate glare and two heavy maroon curtains were drawn behind the pilots at night, so light from the rest of the flight deck would not diminish their night vision. The crew rest area had seven bunks, three in the cargo area and four that folded into the wall of the bulkhead. In front of the cockpit, a ladder led to the bow compartment in the nose of the plane where the 91-lb anchor, 150 foot of rope and mooring post were. The boardroom, filled with the navigator's 7-foot long table, was directly behind the cockpit. Once airborne, with the aircraft on autopilot for much of the time, the navigator was the busiest of all crew. Using dead reckoning, celestial sightings and bearings from the radio operator, he kept constant track of the aircraft's position, altitude, course, speed and drift. He also frequented the two drift sight stations at the wing roots and the celestial observation dome at the aircraft's center of gravity from which their position could be checked against the sun, moon and stars. From the drift stations, the navigator would toss flares from the plane as drift indicators. He would line them up with the waves and they would tell him which way the waves were going in relation to the airplane, and that would give him the drift.

Across from the navigator sat the radio operator with his communications equipment and a direction finder. The B-314 had three transmitters and four receivers: redundancy assured safety. For the first 150 miles out, voice communication worked. After that, communication was on Continuous Wave (Morse code). Next to him was the oval hatch that led to the starboard wing crawlway. Seated just aft of the radio operator was the flight engineer, who monitored the engines, fuel flow,

---

10   Robert J. Serling, *Legend & Legacy: The Story of Boeing and Its People.* New York: St. Martin's Press, 1992. P.41.

(Above) the flight engineer's station. (Below) the radio operator's station (left) and flight engineer's station (right) on the Boeing 314 flying boat.

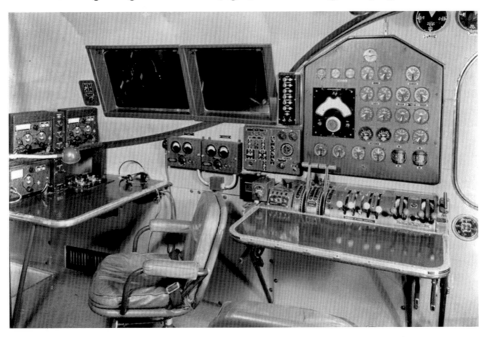

propeller control, air conditioning and engine cowl flap settings. If necessary, he could access the catwalks inside the wings to inspect and service the engines while in flight.[11]

Because of the losses of American and British seaplanes then due to ditching and fire, the B-314 had the highest standard for safety equipment on any aircraft. There were two emergency exit panels in every passenger compartment, except for the Deluxe which had one. All doors on the flying boat could be opened without structurally jeopardizing the aircraft. There were eight ten-man life rafts, four of which were accessible outside the aircraft. Every passenger seat had a life jacket with ring type life-preserver.

"They were quite a fabulous plane," Flight Officer Robert D. Fordyce reminisced of the B-314. "As a matter of fact, they were the only planes I've ever seen where somebody could walk out into the wing and change the generator on an engine. There were times during a flight when we used to do that, which was rather extraordinary. It wasn't at all dangerous." Flight Engineer Officer Stephen H. Kitchell explained how it was done. "You had two doors, one on each side, and you could go right out in the wing," he said. "We crawled out on a catwalk inside the wing and changed a magneto one time. Just stopped the engine and put a new magneto on. You were right inside the airplane; you could pull the fire wall off and there was the back of the engine."

Behind the cockpit on the starboard side, was the circular staircase that led down to the passenger deck. It was Beall's idea to put in a spiral staircase. The other engineers objected — it was a safety hazard. "Hell, that's easy to fix," Beall replied. "We'll put a railing on the staircase." A dapper portly little dynamo with a thin mustache, Boeing historian Robert J. Serling would write that Beall "had a flare for such swankiness — he was a lover of good food and wine — and his girth showed it. But it was that Beall-inspired luxury interior that made an impression on Trippe."[12]

---

11   Richard K. Schrader, *Bridging the Atlantic*. American History Illustrated 24, no. 3 (1989).
12   Robert J. Serling, *Legend & Legacy: The Story of Boeing and Its People.* New York: St. Martin's Press, 1992. P. 39.

The lower deck could seat 82 passengers by day and 40 in sleeping compartments by night. On transatlantic flights, passenger capacity was limited to 35 and on the California-Hawaii route to 30. The passenger deck was divided into eleven sections of compartments for sitting and sleeping at night, a dining salon, a galley, two lavatories for passengers and a special suite at the end of the plane. Directly under the cockpit was the first of the seven passenger cabins that stretched along the length of the flying boat. Behind it, on the starboard side, was the bar and galley with the men's dressing room/toilet opposite. Then the second passenger cabin followed and after it the 14-seat lounge that transformed into a dining room for meals. There were more passenger compartments after that and the bedroom with its curtained berths. Finally, there was the ladies dressing room/toilet and in the tail the Bridal or Deluxe Suite. This last was also Beall's idea — the marketer in him coming to the forefront.

The B-314s were finished with silver lacquer on all external metal surfaces and silver dope on fabric surfaces. The notable exception was black on the bottom of the hull and

hydrostabilizers and up the sides of the hull to the water line. For increased visibility from above, international orange was added to the top of the wing ahead of the rear spar. Registration numbers, Boeing trademarks, and airplane names were in black, and Pan American airline lettering was blue. For a while, prior to delivery and approximately a year thereafter, the first six

The ladies' dressing room/toilet on a Boeing 314 featured two turquoise leather-covered stools.

Boeing 314 — General Characteristics

Crew: 11, including 2 cabin stewards
Capacity: Daytime: 82 passengers, Nighttime: 40 passengers
Payload: 10,000 lb (4,500 kg) of mail and cargo
Length: 106 ft (32.33 m)
Wingspan: 152 ft (46.36 m)
Height: 20 ft 4½ in (6.22 m)
Empty weight: 48,400 lb (21,900 kg)
Loaded weight: 84,000 lb (38,000 kg)
Powerplant: 4 × Wright R-2600-3 radial engines, 1,600 hp (1,200 kW)

Performance

Maximum speed: 210 mph (180 knots, 340 km/h)
Cruise speed: 188 mph (163 knots, 302 km/h) at 11,000 ft (3,400 m)
Range: 3,685 mi (3,201 nm, 5,896 km) normal cruise
Service ceiling: 19,600 ft (5,980 m)

Clippers had the airline numbers from 17 to 22 painted on each side of the bow and the center fin.

Norman Bel Geddes was once more chosen to design the B-314's interior — and as with the M-130, his guiding principle seemed to be Oscar Wilde's "Moderation is a dangerous thing. Nothing succeeds like excess." This time he worked with Howard Ketcham, a New York color expert. Ketcham believed that color-controlled moods (during the war, the Office of Strategic Services [OSS] the predecessor to the Central Intelligence Agency, would employ him to design camouflage). On the Clippers' long flights, too subdued a color in a cabin interior led to boredom and claustrophobia and a too bright one would make passengers uneasy and nervous. Ketcham came up with combinations of what he called "skyline green, Miami-sand beige and Pan American blue."[13] The window blinds from

13   Gerald Clarke, *Pan Am's Clippers: The Revolutionary Planes that Transformed 1930s Travel.* Architectural Digest, May 2004.

A replica Boeing 314 at the Foynes Flying Boat & Maritime Museum
in Foynes, Ireland.

the Claude D. Carver Company, NY. were accordion-pleated shades on rollers, dyed to match Ketcham's colors.

The flying boat's lounges were in alternating color schemes — turquoise carpet with pale green walls or rust carpet with beige walls. Each stateroom could seat up to ten passengers on a daytime flight, but on overnight flights, when the couches were made into beds, each slept six. Every passenger seat had its own life jacket and every compartment had two emergency exit panels. The lounge was the social gathering spot for pre-dinner cocktails, cards and chat. Little tables pulled out to hold magazines and hors d'oeuvres and the chairs in light aluminum frames were cushioned with a newly developed "pillowy" substance made of horsehair impregnated with liquid rubber. Chair covers had stars on them for a sophisticated ambiance. The B-314 was also the first aircraft to have fireproof seats, upholstery and cabin linings. Both toilets had hot and cold running water — the men's with *art deco* light fixtures and square plate mirrors attached to the bulkheads, the ladies' with two turquoise leather-covered stools, a dressing table with a beige "Micarta" top and a mirror. There were also three smaller lavatories around the aircraft.

As one moved to the back of the plane, due to the curvature of the hull, there were steps up into the next compartment. The thick carpeting made of Australian horsehair mixed with latex, soft lighting, the comfortable upholstery in soothing colors and the soundproofing in the walls, all helped to create a special world set apart from the stormy weather and the world outside the windows. At night, the cabins became Pullman-like sleeping compartments, closed off by "Pan American Blue" curtains with stitched numbers. The airline logo in leather encircled each berth which was 6 foot 3 in long and 32 in wide with 35 in headroom, larger than Pullman beds on sleeping cars. Each berth had a window, reading light, ventilator, a steward call button and a clothes rack with hangers. The Deluxe Suite featured a love seat, coffee table, a combination dressing table and writing desk, and a davenport-style seat that converted into a bed. During the war, the Suite was enjoyed less by honeymooners than by senior military officers and VIPs like President Roosevelt and Prime Minister Winston Churchill.

The dining room which accommodated fourteen passengers at a sitting at five tables, had polished black walnut tables which were covered with Irish linen for meals. At the end of meal, the tables were hidden away to be replaced by the lounge furniture. Aware that its clientele expected this standard as they would on ocean liners, despite the weight, only the best bone china, silverware and European crystal were used.

When alcohol was allowed inflight, a favorite drink served on the Clippers was the "Clipper Cocktail." Supposedly enjoyed at bars that the crew frequented, its recipe varied according to route. In the Caribbean, it was golden rum, dry vermouth and a dash of grenadine. When the Pacific flights began, it was gin, orange juice and Curaçao and with the China Clipper it was amber rum, five-spice syrup and lemon juice. The original recipe from the early Key West days is below:

THE PAN AMERICAN CLIPPER COCKTAIL

This cocktail recipe is credited to world-traveler Charles H. Baker Jr., who settled into Coconut Grove, Florida — very close to where Pan American opened the first international airport. It was there that he might have started keeping company with the Pan Am pilots; he cites this drink as hailing "from the notebook of one of our pilot friends."

Serving: 1
1½ ounces apple brandy
1 dash absinthe
1 ounce lime juice
1 teaspoon grenadine
Combine all ingredients in a mixing tin and shake with cracked ice.
Strain into a chilled coupe or cocktail glass.

The B-314's tiny galley (4 x 4 foot) was Bel Geddes' masterpiece, incorporating plastic and lightweight metal to save as much weight as possible. This would continue well into the postwar era. In 1953, one Gerry Thomas, a food salesman visited a Pan American kitchen and was struck by the compartmentalized aluminum trays used. He returned to his company Swanson Foods and, adapting trays like that, television dinners were born. All kitchenware was designed so that on a bumpy flight, everything remained in place. The galley somehow fitted in a sink, ice box, stove and steamers as well as an aluminum cabinet for food, thermos jugs (with specially designed lips to prevent spills) and a two-tiered dish rack for 200 fine china plates. Below the sink was a 16-gauge aluminum ice box. The aluminum cabinet that contained the food was portable and removed at the stopover to be restocked. Although it was all about saving weight — there were 10 pairs of sterling silver salt and pepper shakers, 350 sterling silver flatware pieces in the "Modern" style and a sterling silver tea set. There were three steward lockers that kept all the passengers' passports and documentation.

Airborne cuisine began in 1783 when the Montgolfier brothers opened a bottle of champagne in the upper atmosphere to celebrate their achievement. Actual cooking of food while aloft originated with 19th century balloonists who recklessly attempted to do so while beneath explosive bags of hydrogen. Unremarkable to us today, but eating at altitude then was thought to be unnatural. It was said that Alberto Santos Dumont ate at a table suspended ten foot in the air to acclimatize himself to the experience. In the Paris of *La Belle Epoque*, the eccentric Brazilian aviator would, like Aladdin, float over the rooftops in his dirigible and tether it outside Maxim's, dropping in for the White Truffle and Duck Liver (Foie Gras) lunch.

In the 1930s, airline meals in the United States inevitably centered on fried chicken — one frequent flyer complained

The galley of a Boeing 314.

he had eaten so much of it that he could grow wings and not need the plane. From Pan American's birth, Trippe aimed for an exemplary culinary standard to attract the wealthy. Only Lufthansa, with its cuisine connections to the Zeppelins, came close. With the Boeing Clipper and its electrical output for freezers, ovens, steamers and fans, the airline could achieve the level of gustatory excellence that Santos Dumont would have enjoyed at Maxim's — Pan American even using that restaurant after the war for its catering in Europe. This was the summit of aviation luxury, perhaps never to be equaled until the advent of Boeing 747 and A380.

As far back as the Key West days, where other airlines relied on the disgruntled copilot to pass out sandwiches and passengers balanced their food on a pillow, Pan American put advertisements in the Miami newspapers, for young Cuban men born in the United States who were "alert and nimble " to become stewards. The applicants had to be boyishly small — the galley in the early Sikorskys could only be reached on hands and knees, while balancing a tray. In the 2 months of training the "boys" were put through, one week was spent in the equipment

shop to know all the parts of the flying boat and another with the beaching crew to learn seamanship. After graduation, they lived by the mantra "Service, Tact, Efficiency, Wisdom, Ability, Responsibility and Dependability."

When it was limited to operations in the Caribbean, all Pan American inflight meals were sourced from kitchens in Miami, but once the S-40s made South

Sleeping berths on a Boeing 314.

America possible, this changed to local caterers along the route. The steward's first job was to type up the menu, making a copy for each passenger. On the first leg of the flight, he would take their orders and radio ahead to the next station where the food was prepared. On arrival there, it was collected, reheated and served. This worked well as with the exact number of passengers, there was no wastage.

For an oceanic flight on the Boeing Clippers, an average of 250 lbs of fresh food was loaded on the plane before departure. Everything was fresh, and meals were not served until two hours after take-off as the meat had to be cooked and the potatoes peeled and put in pressure cookers. Pre-dinner drinks were served in the lounge after which the stewards converted it into a dining room with Irish linen tablecloths, serviettes and fresh flowers on the tables. The pillow, Pan American ads boasted, was now under the head of a sleeping passenger. In 1943, when President Roosevelt traveled to Casablanca to meet with Churchill and Charles De Gaulle, Pan American assigned both the *Dixie Clipper* and the *Atlantic Clipper* to carry him, his advisors, the Secret Service and communications equipment to Bathurst (now Banjul), in The Gambia. This would be the first flight of a president while in office and the *Dixie Clipper* the first Air Force One. Roosevelt was served a dinner that the Clipper passengers would have known: fresh melon, celery, olives, Jelly Rosa, Florida Salad, hot buttered rolls, Chateaubriand, parslied potatoes, string beans, a selection of various desserts which included peach melba and petit fours, mocha, fresh coffee and brandy. On the return flight, the president's 61st birthday was celebrated onboard and he was very touched by the surprise cake baked for him.

The Pan American standard for meals inflight was applied to United States military aircraft during the war, especially those on 24-hour patrols. In comparison with RAF aircrews on their flying boats, the Americans were pampered with diets that Pan American had pioneered. A lot of it might have been canned and frozen but, at the time, it was more appetizing and plentiful than the rationing at home. It also demonstrated the social difference between the two allies. While the Sunderland flying boat had a galley with a stove to keep its RAF crew of seven fed during long ocean patrols, such were the lack of cooking skills among Englishmen then, that it was almost impossible to recruit aircrew that liked to cook.[14]

But no matter how powerful the Clipper, weight limitations prevented the carriage of enough water for washing dishes and these were taken ashore and washed by the stewards in the customs buildings wherever the flying boat was. This took considerable negotiations in Canada, Newfoundland and Spain as it had never been done before. The weight problem also limited the carriage of sufficient drinking water and ice. The water for the toilets was recycled washbasin water.

No matter the amenities, it was still a long flight across the Atlantic. The Clipper lumbered along at a cruising speed of about 150 mph — not much faster than Lindbergh's *Spirit of St. Louis* in 1927 over the same ocean, and the complete flying time from New York to Southampton (depending on the winds aloft), was twenty-five hours. From Port Washington, it took five hours to reach Shediac, three more hours from there to Botwood, then fourteen hours to Foynes, and a final three hours to Southampton. But the plane also spent an hour refueling at Shediac, an hour and a half at Botwood, and an hour at Foynes. Still, a day and a half was faster than four days by ship.

In contrast with the more fortunate passengers on Empire flying boats, who were entertained by African wildlife, Buddhist temples and basking sharks below, the view over the Atlantic was hardly breathtaking — just the endless expanse of grey-blue featureless ocean. The Clippers would fly at about 8,000 feet but on occasion, though, they would be considerably lower.[15] Demonstrating that rank has its privileges, when Roosevelt took the *Dixie Clipper* across the Atlantic, he asked

14   My late father-in-law was a rear gunner on RAF Sunderlands during the war and his Canadian skipper made it a rule that the first crew member to criticize the cooking had to do it next. My father-in-law told the story of one of the crew looking at his effort and saying "This is shit ! But really good shit."

15   One captain used to fly very low and if a passenger asked how he checked the altitude, he would say, "Oh, I just open the window and put my finger out, and if I taste salt, I climb a hundred feet. "

that it fly over Haiti, so he could view the Henri Christophe citadel, the second largest masonry structure in the Western Hemisphere. He had explored it, on foot, as Assistant Secretary of the Navy in 1917 and, while the flying boat circled, enjoyed being a tour guide to all onboard.

It was only when the Clipper entered the cloud banks that the passenger could appreciate the grandeur of Nature — that among the towering mountains and valleys, turrets and blankets of cloud, how tiny this aircraft was. At night the sky over the ocean blazed with stars as if above the desert.

For servicing, the Clippers were put in and out of the water on special dollies built to fit their V-bottoms. At most bases, these were rolled down a ramp under restraint of a steel cable secured to a Caterpillar tractor. The tractor did the work on the haul-out after the flying boat had been floated into position over the submerged dolly. At some bases where the maintenance area was high above water level, as at San Francisco's Treasure Island, the dolly was put in the water on a marine railway. The dolly was rolled onto the level top of a special "car" that had its wheels angled to the slope of the track.

Despite its weight and because of its size, the Clipper was essentially a sailboat and, depending on the wind and tides, docking came with its own problems. Normal departures were made by starting the engines at the dock, after the passengers were aboard, and then taxiing out to the take-off area. This could not always be done, and it was sometimes necessary to tow the airplane out of narrow areas with a launch. Normally, after landing, the pilot would taxi to a buoy, then be towed into the dock by a boat or be winched in. But making a buoy in crosswind conditions in a narrow channel, like that at the La Guardia terminal, took more than half an hour of maneuvering with power, drifting backward to a new approach position with more maneuvering. Sometimes pilots would even cut the switches momentarily to reduce thrust when the engines were at idle speed. Reverse-thrust propellers, as an aid to water maneuvering, were still in the future and the water rudders had been eliminated from the B-314s as virtually useless.[16]

On 23 February 1939, the first Clipper NC18603 was flown from Alameda to Baltimore for its christening. The publicity about the impending Atlantic conquest notwithstanding, Pan American was in financial trouble, even before the bills for several commitments, both in Clippers and concrete, were due. The *Samoan Clipper* and the *Hawaii Clipper* had crashed within six months of each other, killing all onboard and for the first time Pan American experienced a loss of public confidence. As would happen after the Lockerbie tragedy in 1988, business plummeted, and institutional trust evaporated. Just as the French government approved Pan American flights to Marseilles on 20 January 1939 and the State Department ended the "Gentlemen's Agreement" on 2 February, the hostilities in Europe were concerning Americans enough to make them stay home — or at least venture only as far as the Caribbean and Bermuda. The two remaining M-130s were, by now, both in need of an overhaul and the company reduced its transpacific schedule by 60 percent. The U.S. Department of Commerce withdrew its authorization to use American Samoa as a refueling base, ending the New Zealand flights. To replace Pago Pago and return to the South Pacific, Pan American needed $200,000 for a base in French Noumea. Boeing was gearing up to begin building the B-314As in July and, at $800,00 each, Trippe had assumed a financial commitment of more than $5 million. With barely $300,000 in the bank, there was no use in asking for more.[17] The financial statement was so bad that in January 1939, the directors skipped the quarterly report. The airline had over-borrowed and was $6 million in debt.

Nor would Pan American have a monopoly on the its most lucrative route, the Atlantic. The new British airline, BOAC, was about to put its "G Class" S.26 in operation in June and

---

16   Much of the information on the Boeing Clippers has been taken from: Bowers, Peter M. *The Great Clippers, Part I.* Airpower, Volume 7, No. 6, November 1977., *The Great Clippers, Part II.* Wings, Volume 7, No. 6, December 1977.

17   Max Watson, *The Man Who Made Pan Am.* New Word City, Inc: 2011

The first Short S.26 "G" Class flying boat, *Golden Hind,*
on the River Medway at Rochester.

it could carry 3,700 lb across the Atlantic without refueling.
In 1938, Congress passed the Civil Aeronautics Act, creating
the Civil Aeronautics Board (CAB) which would, from now on,
approve all airline routes. Not since the days of the NYRBA had
Pan American coped with competition and it would no longer
be the nation's "Chosen Instrument". Another rival, closer
to home, was American Export Airlines (AEA). Owned by the
shipping lines American Export, it had been applying to fly
the Atlantic since 1937 but each time was stymied by Trippe.
President Roosevelt encouraged AEA's application, not only
because of his distaste for Trippe but because he wanted the
northern and southern Atlantic routes to be divided between
AEA and Pan American. Trippe succeeded in blocking this with
legal action but, given the impending war in Europe, Secretary
of State Cordell Hull supported Roosevelt in that Pan American
could no longer hold the monopoly on foreign operations.

On 15 June 1940, when Roosevelt approved a seven-year temporary certificate for AEA to serve Lisbon, the airline ordered three Vought-Sikorsky-44A's at a total cost of $2,100,000. Dubbed the "Flying Aces" by AEA, the three flying boats were named *Excalibur, Excambian* and *Exeter*. But thanks to Trippe, AEA would be kept out of the Atlantic until 1942 when it signed a contract with the Naval Air Transport Service to operate a wartime trans-Atlantic route. On 26 May the *Excalibur* would make the maiden nonstop flight from New York to Foynes, Ireland and on June 20 regular round trip service began.

Trippe's obsession about power, about new airplanes and about the concept of being the country's chosen instrument was by 1939 beginning to wear thin. Back from China, Bixby, now in the Chrysler Building, wrote to Lindbergh that "J.T.T. (Trippe) will never delegate authority and that he was partial to having 'yes men' around him." Only "Mummy" knew of the airline's expansion plans and the other board members were fed up of that.

American Export Airlines' Vought-Sikorsky-44A, *Excambian*, is preserved at the New England Air Museum.

First Lady Christens Yankee Clipper.

Washington, March 3, 1939 — *The Yankee Clipper*, 41-ton flagship of the Pan American Fleet which will carry America's colors in an international race of Transatlantic air supremacy, was christened today by Mrs. Franklin D. Roosevelt in a colorful ceremony at the Naval Air Station at Anacostia. Several thousand wide-eyed spectators watched the smiling First Lady crack a gold-trimmed bottle over the blunt nose of the all-metal, four-motored plane, largest of the world's heavier-than-air craft, and the first of six B-314s now being delivered for Pan American transoceanic services.

Water from the seven seas, rather than the customary champagne, filled the bottle. It splashed on Mrs. Roosevelt's face, white gloves, dark red suit and hat, but she and the officials on a barge in the river turned immediately to stand at attention for *The Star-Spangled Banner.*

From the *Pan Am Clipper* newsletter, March 1939.

The *Yankee Clipper* was then taken on a survey flight to Europe on March 11th Capt. Harold Gray, who would, in 1968, succeed Trippe as CEO of Pan American Airways, flew it from Port Washington to Horta, the Azores in 17 hours, 30 minutes. It would continue to Marseilles and Southampton, the CAB requiring five airmail-only proving flights as part of the process inherent with awarding the "Certificate of Convenience and Necessity" to Pan American.

Trippe had looked on as Eleanor Roosevelt christened the *Yankee Clipper* at the Naval Air Station. Did his thoughts return to 1929 when, at this very spot, he had upstaged Ralph O'Neill at the launch of the NYRBA *Rio de Janerio?* Little did he know that he was about to be upstaged himself, and by his own directors.

In a very Shakespearean way, his closest colleagues plotted to depose Trippe — almost on the Ides of March. Aircraft builder Grover Loening resigned from the airline's board, citing "the monopolistic aims of... one company in a tragic blunder of overexpansion, under-preparation and overworking..."[18] The board appealed to its chairman "Sonny" Whitney to lead a coup against Trippe. As the biggest stockholder in Pan American, he held 154,432 shares and his brother, Jock, another 56,400 shares. Both dabbled in several interests, their latest being Hollywood. Introduced to movies by former board member Merian C. Cooper of *King Kong* fame, "Sonny" had just co-financed an extravagant movie called *Gone with The Wind.* He used to joke that as he was too busy to run Pan American, he let Juan Trippe do it for him.

Reluctantly, "Sonny", who would much rather have been on his yacht, called a special meeting of the board on 14 March 1939.[19] Trippe was removed from office as chief executive officer but kept on in a powerless position as president. In keeping with his code of secrecy, no minutes of the meeting or of who voted against him, were kept. Scenting blood, the media collared Trippe after but he shrugged it off, saying he had voluntarily resigned. The headline "Trippe Tripped" was their response. Whitney disbanded his polo team to concentrate on running the airline and moved into Trippe's fortress of solitude on the 58th floor. He got rid of the three-foot globe and installed a captain's chair and cheerful curtains. Trippe was demoted to a small room at the end of the corridor. There he kept watch on which of his henchmen were now bending their knee to Whitney. He bided his time, knowing "Sonny's" other activities — polo, horse breeding, yachting or Hollywood, would win out and the other board members would have to ask him back.

Every Wednesday at 9 am Whitney called a weekly meeting and went around the table, asking each executive to report on his operation — something that had never happened before. Trippe continued to attend board meetings, sitting like Banquo's ghost, a silent hulk of fury. What infuriated him the most was that Whitney's signature was on the Boeing purchases. His biographers, Marilyn Bender and Selig Altschul, wrote that the other board members sensed he was rating them on their degree of cooperation with Whitney,

---

19   Even his ex-wives and mistresses didn't have a bad word to say about "Sonny"— except that he cheated on them.

storing their grades away for the day, when he would return to power and exact his revenge.[20]

Besides the imminent transatlantic expansion, Pan American also had two large real estate projects coming to fruition, the details of which were only in Trippe's head. To celebrate the completion of the Golden Gate and San Francisco-Oakland Bay bridges, San Francisco's Golden Gate International Exposition was then taking place. Integral to it was Pan American's flying boat terminal at Clipper Cove, Treasure Island — so called because the dirt used came from the former Gold Rush hills. Ever the publicist, Trippe visualized the Treasure Island terminal as he had at Dinner Keys, redolent with glamour and style. The reinforced concrete *art moderne* style building, topped by a glass control tower, beside large hangars, would be a fitting terminus for the world's first true transoceanic air route. At the close of the exposition, all the other buildings were to be torn down and, in their place, airport runways built for Pan American. Trippe had visions of future landplanes operating across the continent, connecting with flying boats on either side. Thus, Treasure Island would serve both seaplanes and landplanes.[21]

Closer to home, Pan American was moving its operations from Port Washington to the Marine Air Terminal (MAT) at La Guardia Field, scheduled to be opened by 31 March, 1940. Fed up with flights on which he was a passenger landing in Newark NJ, even though his ticket said "New York", New York's feisty mayor, Fiorello La Guardia, convinced New Yorkers to pay for an airport within their city limits. It helped that this was also to be federally sponsored and funded through the Works Progress Administration (WPA). At 558 acres and with nearly 4 miles of runways, the $40 million New York Municipal Airport — La Guardia Field was to be opened on 15 October 1939. Trippe knew the area as the North Beach Airport when, as a young

---

20   A. Mayo, N. Nohria, M. Rennella, *Entrepreneurs, Managers, and Leaders: What the Airline Industry Can Teach Us.* Palgrave Macmillan US. 2009

21   In 1940, the U.S. Navy took over Treasure Island and, as compensation, the city was given land on the San Mateo County mudflats, where the present airport is.

man, he used to fly his own plane to East Hampton. For $40 million, Pan American signed a lease for land at La Guardia to build a hangar and terminal. To design the terminal building, Trippe chose Delano & Aldrich (the first a distant cousin of President Roosevelt) the same architects that had done the Terminal Building at Dinner Key. In 1939, the future Idlewild Airport (now John F. Kennedy International) was a golf course next to a swamp and MATS was the only place all overseas flights left from. That it neighbored the 1939/40 New York World's Fair with its theme "The World of Tomorrow" fitted in with the building's architecture. When it was dedicated, in March 1940, Pan American employees could not help but notice similarities with the Dinner Key terminal, especially the mural *Flight* depicting the history of man's involvement with aviation from Icarus to Da Vinci to the Wright brothers. Measuring 12 foot in height and 237 foot in length; *Flight* was the largest mural created as part of the WPA. James Brooks, the social realist artist would complete it in 1942, leaving to serve in the military.[22]

A central circular core of two stories from which a rectangular entrance pavilion and two symmetrically opposed one-story wings project, the building is an architectural gem — the frieze of golden flying fish on the terminal roof line look vaguely like Clippers. Inside, above a bust of La Guardia, a silver Clipper hangs from the ceiling, suspended in perpetual flight. The 'Flight' mural extends to the men's room where the stall doors have propellers on them. On March 31, 1940, the first flight from the Marine Air Terminal by a Clipper would occur. The flying boats (like his airline) long gone, the former Pan American terminals at Dinner Key, Alameda and La Guardia remain Trippe's legacy. The first transatlantic mail-only flight by a Boeing Clipper

---

22   During the 1950s, many WPA artists were thought to be in collusion with Communists. The muscular men and women they had depicted building America were seen as too proletarian and several works of art that had been created for the Rockefeller Center, post offices and other public facilities were destroyed. *Flight* was completely painted over by the Port Authority of New York & New Jersey, because some saw left-wing symbolism in it. In the late 1970s, aviation historian Geoffrey Arend, a La Guardia Airport employee, rescued the mural and raised the funds — with donations from *Reader's Digest*, DeWitt Wallace and Laurance Rockefeller — to re-enlist Jim Brooks to restore it to its original condition. The mural was rededicated on 18 September, 1980 and designated a New York Interior Landmark.

The James Brooks *Flight* mural, at LaGuardia's Maritime Air Terminal, was completed in 1942 and restored in 1980, having been painted over during the McCarthy era. It traces the history of aviation from Icarus to Pan American's Boeing 314s.

took place on 20 May, twelve years, to the day, after Charles Lindbergh took off to cross the Atlantic in his *Spirit of St. Louis*, Capt. Laporte flew the *Yankee Clipper* to Marseilles with 112,574 pieces of mail, mainly first day covers. Also carried were four dozen California marigolds for Britain's *Queen Mary* and 16 employees to teach locals about refueling the Clippers. Stewards were sent out as well to find the best hotels and restaurants at stopovers to restock the galley.

When the Clipper flew over the New York World's Fair, there was a radio hook-up between the plane and ground. With a crowd of thousands listening in, Capt. Laporte exchanged words with the dignitaries below, while the Boeing circled. When the brief exchange ended, the crowd cheered wildly as the plane flew off towards Europe.

The airline announced that it would be operating twice-weekly services to Europe, with one flight each route — the *Yankee Clipper* on the northern route via Botwood and Foynes and the *Dixie Clipper* on the southern via Horta and Marseilles. Because the Spanish Civil War was still in progress, it was not allowed to fly over Spain and would take a curving path around the Portuguese and Spanish coasts to Marseilles. When the airline announced that transatlantic passenger service to Marseilles would begin at the end of June 1939, it immediately received 500 requests for tickets.

Port Washington on Manhasset Bay, Long Island, was where Glenn Curtiss first piloted his *Golden Flyer* in 1909. The flying boat inventor had chosen Port Washington because of its proximity to New York but also because Peter McLaughlin, his father-in-law, owned the hotel in Mineola, NY.[23] A monument on the town dock also commemorates the first commercial survey flights across the Atlantic when Capt. Harold Gray left from here in the Pan American S-42B for Foynes and Capt. Arthur C. Wilcockson brought the *Caledonia* in on 9 July, 1937.

It was early afternoon on 28 June 1939, when the crowd began to gather along the shore of Manhasset Bay. The town declared a semi-holiday in honor of the record-setting flight that was about to take place and the local high school band serenaded the swell of people moving to the shoreline. By 1:30, several thousand New Yorkers were straining to catch a glimpse of the gray leviathan bobbing gently on the waves. The giant flying boat, the words *Dixie Clipper* painted on her bow and "Pan American Airways System" on her fuselage, was about to take to the air on a journey into history. For the first time, ordinary people, not professional aviators, would cross the ocean by a flying boat. The one-way fare from New York to Lisbon was $309 ($5,671.78 in 2020) and $375 ($6,883.23) to Marseilles. The crew comprised:

Capt. Robert Oliver Daniel Sullivan.
Flight Officer Gilbert B. Blackmore.
Flight Officer Robert D. Fordyce.
Flight Officer Benjamin B. Harrell.

---

23   Once the "Golden Flyer" proved successful and attracted the press, McLaughlin changed the hotel's name to "The Gold Bug".

Engineering Officer John A. Fiske.
Assistant Engineering Officer Melvin C. Anderson.
Assistant Flight Engineer Officer Stephen H. Kitchell.
Radio Officer Harold G. Lambert.
Radio Officer Harry L. Drake.
Steward Bruno Candotti
Steward John Salmini.

Half a century later, Blackmore, Fordyce and Kitchell were interviewed about the flight and, although in their 80s then, remembered it clearly.

As with all such events, there were the ceremonies to get out of the way first. Flashbulbs popped as photographers busily snapped shots of crew and passengers alike; speeches were read; the passengers bid excited farewells to friends and relatives and, on the water, yachtsmen positioned themselves to see the take-off better. At 1:30 pm, a bell rang the signal for the passengers to queue up, show their tickets, and have their luggage weighed. According to Pan American's historical accounts, 5,000 spectators cheered,

Passengers board the *Dixie Clipper,* on 28th June 1939, for the first commercial flight across the Atlantic Ocean

and a brass band played a Sousa march as the *Dixie Clipper*'s passengers — the women wearing corsages, hats and gloves, the men in suits and ties, walked down a floating pier and ducked into the aircraft's doorway.

The *Dixie Clipper*'s four giant engines coughed into life at 1:59 pm. and the culmination of what Curtiss had begun in this very bay started to taxi across it. As the band played on and the crowd cheered, the plane surged forward, churning a white wake behind it, before breaking the surface and climbing into the clear afternoon sky. The roar of its engines drowned out the gun salutes from four yacht clubs and the whistles from the craft in the harbor. Exactly 42 hours and 10 minutes later, at 1:21 pm local time, June 30, the aircraft was expected to land at Marseilles — after two refueling stops, the passenger to spend one night aboard the plane and the second at a hotel in Lisbon. Until this flight, the fastest way across the Atlantic was aboard the RMS *Queen Mary*, which had made the sea voyage in 1938 in a record 3 days, 20 hours, 42 minutes. Compared to that, 42 hours was a breeze.

In *The New York Times* the next morning, the Associated Press described the scene this way: "With the ship's departure at 2:12 p.m. on a 4,650-mile flight, aviation's long-cherished dream of regular transatlantic passenger service by plane became a reality." The first commercial flight marked the beginning of the end for passenger ships, until then the only way to cross.

Twenty-five minutes after the *Dixie Clipper* took off from Port Washington, the *Yankee Clipper* landed at Southampton, thereby inaugurating regular mail service between the United States and Great Britain.

Most of the 22 passengers were wealthy, well-known or both. They included C. V. "Sonny" Whitney and his wife, John M. Franklin, President of the United States Lines, Roger Lapham, President of the American Hawaiian Steamship Company, the railroad executive W. J. Eck, (who had applied eight years earlier to be on the first transatlantic passenger flight), and Louis Gimbel of Gimbel's department store. The crew had good reason to remember him. "Pan American gave all the passengers a silver cigarette case (embossed) with a facsimile of the ticket," Kitchell said. "Mr. Gimbel was showing us his and he said, 'What do yours look like?' and we said, 'Well, we didn't get any.' And he had them made up for each of the crew. I've still got mine. It has (the words) 'First Transatlantic Passenger Flight' and my name on it."

Passengers mingled freely with the crew when they were off duty. "Everybody was so excited, even the passengers, that I don't think they slept much," Kitchell remembered. In a letter he wrote on the flight, passenger Russell Sabor agreed: "Life aboard the plane has settled down as much as one would settle down on the *Normandie* or the *Queen Mary*, and people are getting acquainted. Menus and passenger lists are being passed around for various autographs."

Someone who probably didn't mingle much on that flight was Colonel William Donovan. A classmate of Roosevelt's in law school, Donovan had won the Medal of Honor in the First World War, leading an infantry charge and earning the nickname "Wild Bill". The year after this flight, his exploits would be told in the James Cagney movie *The Fighting 69th*. Roosevelt would select Donovan to be America's first modern-day spymaster and (presumably) he was going to Britain to learn the dark arts of espionage from British intelligence.[24] As the founder of the OSS, there is a statue of Donovan at CIA Headquarters, Langley, as there is of Nathan Hale, George Washington's spymaster who was caught and hanged by the British. "Wild Bill" was hugely controversial and, instead of Donovan, President Eisenhower would wisely put Allen Welsh Dulles (who despite covert affairs both sexual and state) was said to be "the most boring man in America" at its head.

Because of the occasion, Pan American had "pushed out the boat." Months before, the airline had asked the Waldorf-Astoria Hotel to plan, prepare and serve meals appropriate for the event. Each passenger had a formal place setting, with dinnerware displaying Pan American's monogram. The menu included shrimp cocktail, turtle soup, steak or chicken, mashed

---

24   Jock Whitney was one of Donovan's agents and parachuted into occupied Europe. To his family's relief, when captured, he would escape.

potatoes, asparagus, ice cream and coffee or tea. A selection of champagnes, wines and liqueurs also was available.

Then to bed, which Sabor described thus: "Of course, the beds, bedrooms and berths are about as fine as the best hotels could afford, complete with linens." He described the berths as "white, fluffy, soft down" and the dressing rooms "the envy of many a fine hotel."

The next morning, the passengers were treated to a breakfast of strawberries and cream, fresh juices, dry cereals, poached eggs with bacon and sausage, rolls and coffee, tea or milk. Among the 22 passengers, there were six women, including, according to the Associated Press, "Mrs. Clara Adams of Maspeth, N.Y., a veteran of history-making flights (who) planned to keep on going after she reached Europe and to circle the world on regular passenger planes. She expected to arrive home in 16 days."

Betty Trippe was also a passenger and she wrote in her diary: "There are many at home who think us either fools or pioneers to make this trip, but with the great advances in scientific knowledge, we are neither. Actually, it is a much less hazardous trip than those made in the old sailing clippers years ago, when one is at the complete mercy of the elements and out of touch with the rest of the world for weeks on end."

The first leg of the flight ended with an ocean landing in the Azores between the islands of Faial and Pico. Sometimes the waves here caused difficulties, but not on the inaugural trip. "A lot of times the swells were so big that it was real bad," Kitchell said. "But the captain on that trip, Sullivan, was an expert in taking off and landing in swells. He had a knack of just riding those swells until all of a sudden, he'd call back to us, 'Give us the power,' and we'd give him full power and off we'd go. But he had a knack, a sixth sense of feeling the swells as we came in." Sullivan had been First Officer on the China Clipper flight on 22 November 1935, from San Francisco to Honolulu with the late Capt. Ed Musick, and the vanished navigator Fred Noonan. After a flight of 15 hours, 55 minutes, the *Dixie Clipper* taxied into Horta where it spent one hour, 24 minutes being refueled. It took off again at 12:30 pm local time, flying another six hours, 44 minutes before landing on the Tagus at Lisbon at 7:14 p.m. local time. Wrapped in overcoats to ward off the evening's chill, the *Dixie Clipper*'s passengers left the aircraft at Lisbon to spend the night in a hotel before taking off for Marseilles. At 1:21 p.m. on June 30, the *Dixie Clipper* landed at Marignane, Marseilles, its place in history assured.

Ironically, it would be in Lisbon that Capt. Sullivan (who had the sixth sense about water landings), would crash the *Yankee Clipper* on 22 February 1943. The Clipper would strike the water at 6:47 pm with sufficient force to cause damage to the hull and the left wing was completely sheared off. The probable cause of this accident, concluded the CAB, was "an inadvertent contact of the left-wing tip of the aircraft with the water while making a descending turn preparatory to landing." The report concluded that Sullivan had erred in his judgement of the position of the aircraft in relation to the water. *Time Magazine* which covered the enquiry held in New York was more succinct: "Last week the crash report of the Civil Aeronautics Board marked 'Official' what airmen already knew: the Atlantic's chief pilot, 50-year-old Captain R.O.D. Sullivan, was responsible for the crash. Stocky, weather-beaten Robert Oliver Daniel Sullivan had more than 14,000 hours in his logbook, more than 3,200 of them in Pan Am's great Boeing clippers. But, despite his long experience of sea and sky, he could not explain later what happened."

There were fatal injuries to 19 passengers and 5 crew. Among those passengers rescued was the singer and actress Jane Froman, whose battle to recover from her injuries later became the subject of the 1952 film *With a Song in My Heart*.

"Sonny" Whitney appeared in the historic photographs officiating at the first regular transatlantic service on May 20, 1939 and, accompanied by his wife, savored the 28 June first passenger flight to Marseilles. But he soon began regretting his courage. He knew little of what was happening and discovered there was no use asking the other board members for help. Unfortunately for Whitney, in January 1940, the company posted a record year-end profit of $1.98 million which was attributed to Trippe's unwavering vision.

With the start of hostilities in Europe, Pan American's close cooperation with the White House and the U.S. Navy put the airline on a wartime footing in both the Atlantic and Pacific. That summer, Pan American returned to the South Pacific on 18 July,1940 when the *American Clipper* arrived at Auckland, the first scheduled service from San Francisco via Honolulu, Canton Island and Noumea. President Roosevelt and the British government wanted its cooperation in establishing air transport services and bases worldwide — and only one man could do this. The State Department, which had condemned Trippe over the AOA, blithely acknowledged that he might be a dictator "but he was our dictator."

Trippe's secrecy had paid off — in January 1940, the board ate crow and offered Whitney up as a sacrifice. "Sonny" stepped down, selling off his shares and leaving the airline that he, Hambleton and Trippe had founded in 1927. Good-natured to the end, Whitney said that he never had any ambition to run Pan American and had only done so to keep one of Trippe's more ruthless enemies on the Board from taking over. On the plus side, in February, the movie he had co-financed, *Gone With The Wind* swept the Oscars that year.

For a long time after, Trippe refused to pardon Whitney, or anyone else who had opposed him, and the collateral damage include some of the old stalwarts from the Dinner Key days. At one point, he agreed to meet Whitney for lunch for a reconciliation but changed his mind and turned around shortly after. Until his retirement in 1968, no one dared oppose Trippe ever again. Intriguingly, when he moved back to his old office, the beloved globe was put into storage. Trippe no longer needed it — he had conquered the world.

Although the Battle of the River Plate in December 1939 had been fought in the south Atlantic, it demonstrated to the United States that the war was closer than Americans wished and the Clippers on the northern route flew almost empty. In any case, with Britain as a belligerent, the U.S. Neutrality

Act prevented Pan American from using Shediac and Botwood and the northern route was suspended. The southern route, however, did a booming business as refugees made their way first to Marseilles and then to Lisbon. The first Clipper to arrive in New York after Nazi Germany invaded Poland carried passengers with harrowing tales of their travels. "I've never seen a prettier sight than the Clipper" said Justin D. Bowersock, the aviation editor for the *Kansas City Star*. "And when I stepped aboard, I felt just as if I were home".[25]

The *Lisbon Clipper* was immortalized in the movie *Casablanca* (1942). As the whine of a small plane is heard overhead, the police chief, Captain Louis Renault (Claude Rains) turns to Rick Blaine (Humphrey Bogart) saying "Plane for Lisbon. You would like to be on it, wouldn't you?" Bogey asks, "What's in Lisbon?" Comes the reply, "Clipper to America". You must remember this.

---

25   *Glamourous Crossing: How Pan Am Dominated International Travel in the 1930s.* Meredith Hindley, Longreads, February 2015.

8   Flying boats at war

I n the last summer before the war, about to disappear
into history, Imperial Airways could take pride in its
achievements. These were the airline's halcyon days,
its Indian summer before it was subsumed into BOAC.
Conceived by the Hambling Committee, in 1924, to eliminate
unprofitable competition, it had almost been stillborn by a
pilots' strike. In fifteen years, Imperial Airways had fulfilled its
mandate of "uniting the scattered colonies of the Empire and
Commonwealth" as Sir Sefton Brancker had wanted.

First by landplane from Croydon and now flying boat from
Southampton, Imperial had carried thousands of passengers
and, with the Empire Airmail Scheme, tons of mail, especially
at Christmas. Its fleet had evolved from war-surplus HP W.8
biplanes to Arthur Gouge's graceful Empire series. Its flying
boats now flew twice a week from Southampton to Africa and
down to Durban in 5 days, three times a week across Asia to
Singapore in 5½ days and across the Dutch East Indies to
Sydney in 10 days. In a world of escalating tensions, Imperial
Airways was a *Pax Britannica* of the skies.

As expected, an enterprise of this scale had casualties.
Of the 25 original S.23 flying boats, by August 1939, eight
had crashed, either through icing, crew error, wind shear,
porpoising or hull failures. Attempts to conquer the Atlantic
by ingenious schemes such as the Short/Mayo composite and
inflight refueling had been brave but over-adventurous. More
hopeful, for the North Atlantic route, were the S.26 "G-class"
flying boats, the first of which had flown that July.

While the British company would rather have operated the
services to Australia and New Zealand itself, thus completing
an "All-Red Route", those Dominions had formed their own
flying boat airlines QEA and the Tasman Empire Airways Ltd
(TEAL) to fly the same routes.

Like Imperial Airways, flying boats today are a remnant of romantic colonial nostalgia, but in the 1930s, they gripped the imagination of a public mired in the Depression. Advertisements of the day touted the "absence of that chained-to-a-seat feeling" and contrasted the flying boat experience to that of "bored passengers sitting in serried rows" in land-based aircraft. Here was justifiable British pride in knowing that the routes which held the Empire together, bringing "air mindedness" to Africans, Arabs and Australians alike, did so with great panache. In 1938, when his flight to Alexandria was called, one passenger recalled that he felt "every inch an Empire builder."

The war began for Imperial on 29 August 1939, when the London-Paris service — the one that had begun the airline — was suspended. On 1 September, all flights from Britain to the Continent followed suite. There was to be no flying between sunset and sunrise and, by 3 September, private flying was forbidden. All of Imperial's landplanes were moved to Whitchurch airport, near Bristol, and its flying boats to Poole Harbor, although their maintenance would continue at Hythe.

That Italy might soon be a belligerent had been considered, as it would shut off the entire Mediterranean, especially the essential refueling stops at Rome and Brindisi and both the British and French governments attempted to woo Mussolini to remain neutral by promising him territorial concessions in Africa. If Portugal joined the Axis, the critical refueling stops at the Azores and Lisbon would no longer be available, either to BOAC or Pan American — nor would its colonies in Africa. In the Far East, Japanese military expansion would isolate India, Ceylon, Burma, the Malay States, Hong Kong and Australia. But a war with Germany would be especially catastrophic as it would put the Short's works at Rochester, and Imperial's at Southampton, within easy reach of the Luftwaffe.

Imperial Airways and the Air Ministry had been preparing for war since the Munich Crisis of 1938. With its railway connections, Poole had been chosen as a wartime base for the flying boats. Like Southampton, Alameda, Durban and

Rose Bay, flying boats will always be at that city's heart. Poole harbor was fortified with block ships in readiness for sealing and devices called "spiders" (which protruded just above the water) were secured into the harbor bed to deter paratroop landings. When "the little ships" left Poole to collect the stranded troops at Dunkirk, the townspeople gathered at viewpoints like Constitution Hill to watch them go.

Through the war some 650 BOAC staff were employed at Poole on the flying boat services. At first, the Imperial Airways/ BOAC office was in the billiard room at the Antelope Hotel in the High Street. In mid-1942, the staff were moved to better quarters at the Poole Pottery, where there were four cubicles suited to Immigration examination and the main showroom for the Customs Hall.[1]

In 1942, the flying boats were returned to Hythe temporarily — to give the Navy use of Poole Harbor to launch a diversionary attack on the Normandy coast, in case the North African landings failed. Customs were put in a hotel half a mile away from Hythe with Immigration officials in its greenhouse. On 23 March 1943, a BOAC PBY Catalina, G-AGDA, crashed on landing outside Poole during a training flight, killing 3 of the 6 onboard. During the build-up for "Operation Overlord" and D-Day, in May 1944, the flying boats were again removed from Poole, this time to the RAF flying boat base at Pembroke Dock, returning in September. Beginning 18 September 1945, RAF Sunderlands brought to Poole Harbor the prisoners of war held by the Japanese — those that would not have survived the journey home by ship. Through the coming months, the mercy flights from the Far East were to arrive at Poole almost daily.

The "phony war" from September 1939 to April 1940 allowed for some respite. The airline continued with flights to Rome, Brindisi, Athens and Alexandria while Italy was still neutral. With wartime requirements, the flying boats were given red, white and blue recognition stripes and now as part of BOAC on

---

1   On 10 March 2016, a Blue Plaque was unveiled at Harbor Heights Hotel, Poole, where passengers and crew would have stayed before embarking on an Imperial Airways/BOAC flying boat.

A BOAC Boeing 314A in Poole Harbor during the Second World War.
The girls are wearing pre-war British Airways uniforms.

1 April 1940, Lee-Elliott's "Speedbird" would be added under the aircraft's name.

The government of Australia was more precipitate about the war — it stipulated that the six Qantas flying boats — *Coogee, Corio, Coorong, Carpentaria, Coolangatta* and *Cooee* — should be kept south of Singapore and made available for Royal Australian Air Force (RAAF) use. With a frontline that extended from New Guinea to the New Hebrides, a few flying boats were to be impressed into service with the RAAF's 11 Squadron. After negotiations with London, the BOAC flying boats *Centaurus* and *Calypso* that were at Rose Bay were commandeered and *Coorong* and *Corio* given in exchange. *Centaurus* was designated A18-10.6 in the RAAF and armed with under wing bomb racks capable of carrying 500-lb bombs, together with two former World War One Lewis guns mounted each side of the rear freight compartment, and a machine gun on top of the hull. Initially put on patrol, as the Catalinas became more plentiful, *Centaurus* and *Calypso* were used more as passenger carriers, assisting in evacuations.

In contrast, in 1940, with the German surface raiders *Orion* and *Komet* sinking shipping in the South Pacific, the government of New Zealand would use TEAL's two S.30 flying boats *Aotearoa* and *Awarua* for military purposes. On loan to Imperial Airways since March 1939, they were flown to New Zealand to begin a scheduled service across the Tasman Sea, between Auckland and Sydney. Having sent its own small air force to Britain, New Zealand relied heavily on the two TEAL flying boats for maritime reconnaissance, putting one on an hour's standby, even while continuing to maintain the scheduled air service to Sydney. Crews of both aircraft were part of the Royal New Zealand Air Reserve; gun mounts and bomb racks were installed on both aircraft as was the early use of radar. When the Pan American Clipper flights resumed in July 1940, with the number of Americans transiting through Auckland to Australia, this impacted on the TEAL flights.

The British government's priority was an air service to the United States, its lifeline for influence and military purchases and with Pan American about to close its northern route through Botwood, it considered alternatives.[2] The Empire flying boats barely had the range to make the Lisbon-Bathurst (Banjul) route to cross the Atlantic to Natal, and while Spain did grudgingly allow refueling at Las Palmas in the Canary Islands in 1940, given the strong fascist influence in its government, this could not be relied on.

The S.30 flying boats *Cabot* and *Caribou,* with their inflight refueling capability on Atlantic crossings, were chosen until the S.26 "G-class" became operational. But before this could happen, in an ill-conceived decision, the military impressed both into RAF service, arming them with machine gun posts. The three "G-class" flying boats were also taken over and equipped with power-assisted rear gun turrets.

---

2   One of the last passengers to transit through Botwood was Lester B. Pearson, the future Canadian prime minister. Then First Secretary at the Canadian High Commission in London, Pearson had been in Ottawa to arrange for the evacuation of British children to Canada. He would be awarded the Nobel Prize in 1957.

Aotearoa, one of TEAL's two Short S.30 flying boats.

In the first instance of military service, the BOAC pilots Captains Store and Long were commissioned as RAF flight lieutenants and ordered to fly *Cabot* and *Caribou* to Norway with radar equipment and operating staff. They would leave for Norway on 4 May, both arriving at the harbor in Bodø, north of the Arctic Circle. In keeping with the fiasco that was the Norwegian campaign — poorly equipped troops and an inadequate air cover of Gloster Gladiators — the Luftwaffe would efficiently locate and destroy *Cabot* and *Caribou* so that by 7 May they were at the bottom of fiords and their crews evacuated by a destroyer. For sheltering them, the town of Bodø, fared little better. On 27 May, in retaliation, the Luftwaffe would launch a heavy air raid on it, killing 13 locals and 2 British soldiers. The loss of the only two aircraft that had the potential to cross the Atlantic was a serious blow — and not only to BOAC.

The fall of France in June 1940 led Mussolini to declare war on Britain and BOAC staff from Brindisi were evacuated on *Caledonia*. Cut off from home, *Caledonia* continued through Africa to Durban. In a 'Scarlet Pimpernel' operation on 20 June, Bennett and Bill Morgan were tasked with flying the Polish

General Wladyslaw Sikorski to France to evacuate his staff. They flew *Cathay* to Lac de Biscarosse and waited through the night for them. With the enemy closing in, Bennett might have left except Churchill himself had promised Sikorski this would be done. Hearing German tanks in the area, the pilots hid the flying boat under some large trees. The Poles arrived at 4:47 am and *Cathay* took off, flying over approaching tanks, evading the Luftwaffe and arriving back at Poole at 9:32 am — the only shots fired at them were from a British cruiser. Don Bennett would leave the airline after this and go to Canada to work for the Atlantic Ferry Organisation, later transferring to the RAFVR.

The closure of the Mediterranean meant that airmail that had been in transit from Britain to the Far East and Australia was sent by ship to South Africa. Seventeen flying boats had been orphaned from Poole, which included some of the original S.23s, the Qantas flying boats and the S.33s. Durban was chosen as the BOAC wartime overseas headquarters and airline employees were sent to South Africa on the *Capetown Castle* where until 1945, they stubbornly continued to wear their Imperial Airways insignia.

The Horseshoe Route that circumscribed the Indian Ocean and bridged the Empire was born of necessity. Mail and VIP passengers arriving by ship from Britain were now flown from Durban via Lourenço Marques, then Beira-Lumbo-Mozambique (overnight stop)-Lindi-Dar es Salaam-Mombasa-Kisumu-Port Bell (overnight stop) on the Nile, and onward to Laropi-Juba-Malakal-Khartoum (overnight stop)-Wadi Halfa-Luxor-Cairo (overnight stop)-Habbaniyah-Basra-Bahrain (overnight stop)-Sharjah-Jiwani-Karachi (overnight stop)-Calcutta-Rangoon-Bangkok (overnight stop)-Singapore. From here Qantas and TEAL took over to Sourabaya-Darwin-Sydney and Auckland. In the summer of 1941, when the demands of the war in the Mediterranean overstretched BOAC's share, QEA took over the route from Singapore to Karachi and opened its own engine overhaul facility at Rose Bay.

The first flights on the Horseshoe Route from Durban to Sydney and from Sydney to Durban, both left on 19 June and arrived at their destinations on 1 July. The first dispatch of mail from London was on the *Arundel Castle* on 19 June. It connected at Durban with a flying boat which left on 10 July and arrived in Sydney on 24 July. Going the opposite way, the first Horseshoe mail left Cape Town on the *Winchester Castle* and arrived on the Clyde on 21 July. From there, as all mail had to pass scrupulous examination by the Censor, it took a week to get to London. In addition, mail from New Zealand continued to be flown across the Pacific to the United States by Clipper and then by air and ship to Britain.

While the generous EAMS postage rates were canceled, and surcharges reinstated to reduce mail loads, this had little effect on the letter-writing public. Cut off from family and friends and with troop mobilizations, they continued to write, sending large amounts of mail and overwhelming the capacity of the flying boats. After 19 August, flights on the Horseshoe service were increased to twice a week.

Through the war years, as the global war waxed and waned, the BOAC/Qantas flying boat crews adapted to changing geopolitical situations, always avoiding the attentions of the Luftwaffe, or pro-German Vichy governments in Syria and Africa and increasing Japanese encroachment in Asia. With their wartime duties, the S.23s were converted to "Austerity Standard" with the pantry removed and bench seats that allowed for 30 or more passengers installed. More powerful Pegasus engines and extra fuel tanks were added.

Though the United States and Pan American Airways were neutral, both aided the Allies whenever and wherever possible. Clipper crews on the Atlantic and Caribbean runs looked out for U-boats and lifeboats, reporting locations of oil slicks and debris where Allied ships had been sunk. The Pan American pilots were cautioned about getting involved as U-boats sometimes floated emergency flares on the ocean surface to trick pilots into flying low for a closer look — and then shooting them down. Even before the United States was in the war, Pan American crews sought the cloak of darkness in mid-Atlantic to avoid the Focke Wulf 200 Condors hunting for convoys. Clipper captains planned their flights to arrive at Foynes at sunrise. The crew slept during the day in the quiet village of Adare and took off at sunset, either on to Lisbon or returning to Botwood. The Foynes-Lisbon flights, within range of the Luftwaffe, were especially dangerous — as the BOAC DC-3 carrying the actor Leslie Howard, shot down in 1943 proved — and the Clippers flew within the clouds as much as possible.

With *Cabot* and *Caribou* gone, the two S.30 flying boats *Clyde* and *Clare* (which as *Australia* had run aground at Basra on 9 August 1939) were assigned to the Atlantic run. Amidst Britain preparing for invasion and the government considering evacuating the Royal Family,[3] on 3 August 1940, *Clare* took three passengers, one of whom was C. R. Fairey, the head of the British Purchasing Mission, to the United States. Flown by Capt. Kelly Rogers, although it left in great secrecy, the first BOAC transatlantic flight was seen off by Clive Pearson, Chairman of BOAC, Sir Archibald Sinclair, Secretary of State for Air and Sir Francis Shelmerdine Director General of Civil Aviation. *Clare* arrived at Botwood in 16 hours and six minutes and then proceeded to Boucherville and New York. With many Americans against involvement in a European war, the flight was as much a promotional victory as an aviation one. It demonstrated to the American public that despite their Ambassador Joseph Kennedy's predictions, Britain was not about to surrender. *Clare* had flown unescorted and brought with her the latest British newspapers for delivery to Roosevelt and Wendell Wilkie, both of whom would soon support the "Lend-Lease" Act. On its return flight, Mayor La Guardia sent a goodwill message to William George Coxen, the Lord Mayor of London, whose city was at the time being devastated in the Blitz. On its return flight, *Clare* carried Billy Bishop,

3   Plans had been made that if the Germans invaded to have a flying boat land at the Welsh Harp (a London reservoir) or a lake in Wales, to evacuate His Majesty and one of the S.30s was on standby through August and September.

BOAC's S.30 flying boat, *Clare*, photographed by *LIFE Magazine* at La Guardia.

the Canadian First World War air ace to London to meet with Churchill and set up the Commonwealth Air Training Plan.[4]

The degree of desperation was captured on the next Atlantic flight on 14 August. Flown by Captains J.T. Kirton and Joe Shakespeare, *Clare* took four passengers to New York. Chief among them were Sir Henry Tizard, Scientific Advisor to the Chief of Air Staff and Capt. Harold H. Balfour, the Permanent Under Secretary of State for Air. After what had happened in the countries overrun by the Germans, the British scientific community wanted to establish a technical exchange with the

---

4　　Both men enjoyed their Scotch and when Churchill was in Ottawa dining with the Canadian prime minister W. L. Mackenzie King, who was a teetotaler, Churchill would escape to Bishop's home, which was a block away.

United States, both as a means of preventing their efforts from falling into enemy hands, but also in the hopes of shoring up a potential ally. Churchill was initially against "giving away the shop", but the retreat at Dunkirk from 26 May to 4 June convinced him otherwise.

They were airborne at 14.00 and skirting the balloon barrage, this time were protected by a fighter escort as far as the Irish coast. Fighting gale force winds, it was to be an uncomfortable crossing, the passengers sitting on seats lashed to the floor between fuel tanks. The four passed the time playing hands of bridge under a single lightbulb and in contrast with the pre-war cuisine, dined on coffee, sandwiches, Bovril and biscuits for breakfast. Before landing at Botwood, the flying boat flew over Tizard Harbor, Newfoundland, named for Sir Henry's father in recognition of his exploratory work in the previous century. They landed at New York, taxied to the new Marine Terminal, berthing next to the *Yankee Clipper*.

The Tizard Mission was to hand over to the United States British scientific secrets that ranged from the cavity magnetron (the core technology for microwave radar that had been developed a few months earlier by scientists at the University of Birmingham), the plans for Frank Whittle's jet engine, the feasibility of an atomic bomb, rocket design, gyroscopic gunsights, self-sealing fuel tanks, plastic explosive and advanced submarine detection. While much of the papers came later by ship, Tizard's suitcase — later called by historians "the suitcase that saved the world" was the most valuable cargo a flying boat would ever carry.[5] The degree of urgency in the mission was such that it was later revealed Tizard had bet his colleagues that Britain would fall before they could return from the United States.[6]

---

5   The rest of the team left Liverpool aboard the Canadian Pacific ship *Duchess of Richmond*. All the classified material was kept in a locked metal box. Should the ship be attacked, it was to be thrown overboard — small holes had been drilled in its sides to keep it from floating.

6   The exchange did not go smoothly. The RAF needed the Norden bombsight for its raids on Germany but, on the advice of his generals, Roosevelt refused to give it, in case it fell into enemy hands. After the war, U.S. intelligence experts were shocked when they interrogated Luftwaffe personnel: the Germans had known the bombsight's secrets even before the war, thanks to a spy at Norden.

Capt. Harold Balfour had been a RFC pilot in the First World War with seven enemy aircraft to his credit. He knew the value of aviation in wartime and, without Treasury approval, took the initiative to approach Juan Trippe and buy three of the Boeing 314As from Pan American. With Washington's agreement, the sale took place on 22 August 1940, each Clipper selling for $1,035,400 (they had cost Trippe $800,000 each), with 12 Wright Cyclone GR-2600-A2An engines at $16,753 each and six Hamilton Standard propellers totaling $21,750. It was a tidy profit for Pan American which agreed to train the BOAC crews.[7]

The first, NC18607, was ferried to the new BOAC base at Baltimore by a Pan American crew. It was given the British registration G-AGBZ and named RMA (Royal Mail Aircraft) *Bristol*. It was followed by NC18608, which became G-AGCA *Berwick*, and NC18610 which became G-AGCB *Bangor*. The black paint on the Boeing hulls was replaced with a silver lacquered coating. On either side, the aircraft's names were painted in blue, on the bow, above a "Speedbird" with a large Union Jack just below the cockpit panels. Between the wing and the tail, the British registration was emblazoned in large letters. Balfour caught Churchill's disapproval for this — only the prime minister could be impetuous — and even while the Battle of Britain raged above it, there was a lengthy debate in the House of Commons about Balfour's misuse of power. The Boeings were maintained at the BOAC base in Baltimore and began service in August 1941 between Poole, Lagos and Baltimore, giving the British a reliable lifeline to the United States.

Between 3 August and 11 October 1940, *Clare* and *Clyde* would make five round trips to New York — the propaganda value of them was incalculable. The *New York Post* would write: "Bombs are dropping in or near Fleet Street every night... but this copy (of a British newspaper) reached New York yesterday aboard the flying boat *Clare*, only three days after it had rolled off the presses around the corner of Fleet Street." Tizard, however, would take the *Yankee Clipper* back.

---

7   Little known then was that in 1939 Japan had attempted to buy three B-314s and Boeing, then in financial straits, might have considered it, except President Roosevelt prevented the sale.

The publicity that the flying boats and the Tizard Mission garnered would play their parts on 10 January 1941, when Roosevelt, now re-elected, introduced the Lend-Lease program to Congress. It gave the president the power to lend arms to Britain with the understanding that, after the war, America would be paid back in kind. Congress accepted the plan and the chairman of U.S. Steel, Edward Reilly Stettinius Jr. was appointed to administer it. He was Trippe's brother-in-law and Roosevelt would wait for him to leave the room before discussing Pan American's monopoly on international air routes.

To connect with the vital Pan American Clippers, BOAC's *Cathay, Clare, Champion* and *Clyde* were put on the Poole-Foynes-Lisbon shuttle. The invasion of Greece by Italian and German forces in October 1940, meant that Athens was lost as a refueling stopover, and Alexandria and Cairo were now within range of enemy bombers. The BOAC flying boats were moved to Rod-el-Farang on the Nile which, with the feluccas, house boats and the old bridge, was difficult for taxiing and take-offs. When the British regained some control over the Mediterranean, the flying boats began a Lisbon-Gibraltar-Malta-Cairo run. This was essential for Malta, bringing medicine and food to its besieged garrison and evacuating the seriously ill. *Clare*, sheltering at the RAF seaplane base at Kalafrana, Malta, was too tempting a target for a Junkers Ju.88, which bombed her. Although the fire was extinguished, it was a warning to BOAC and the flying boats were replaced by Liberators and transferred to the West African route.

The British government looked for a safer air route to the Middle East and India through mid-Africa using a combination of flying boats and landplanes. With Bathurst, Lagos, Freetown and much of the Belgian Congo on rivers, flying boats operating from Lisbon were ideal to connect with landplanes at those ports. Avoiding Vichy-held African colonies, the faithful *Clyde* and *Clare* were the first Empire flying boats to stage through the area. After Khartoum, they flew west to Stanleyville (Kisangari) Leopoldville (Kinshasa), Libreville, Gabon and Lagos, Nigeria.

Sadly, having served so well both in Africa and Atlantic, on 14–15 February 1941, *Clyde* was blown upside down in a storm on the Tagus and, while her engines and propellers were retrieved, remnants were sold for scrap. *Clare's* fate was destined to be another maritime mystery. On 14 September 1942, carrying 13 passengers and 5 crew, she disappeared into the darkness, just outside Bathurst. A search the next day revealed some wreckage and six bodies. There was a theory that, with an engine failure, Capt. Musson was jettisoning fuel and may have fired a Very pistol to illuminate the ocean below and this exploded the aircraft. Uncannily, the Lufthansa Dornier 18 mail plane, *Pampero,* had also vanished a few miles out of Bathurst on 1 October 1938. After that, the Lagos-Freetown-Bathurst-Lisbon-Foynes route was left to the three BOAC Boeing 314s and the "G-class" flying boats *Golden Hind* and *Golden Horn*, both now shorn of their dorsal turrets.

When the forces of pro-German Iraqi politician, Raschid Ali-al Gaylani, laid siege to the British bases at Ramadi and Habbaniyah in April 1941, BOAC flights through Iraq were suspended. British women and children were evacuated by one of the last flying boats going through, but the BOAC staff were captured and incarcerated in Bagdad.

Ordered by RAF Middle East Command to evacuate air force personnel from Souda Bay, Greece, on 21 April *Coorong* and *Cambria* were pulled off the Horseshoe Route and camouflaged in green and brown above the waterline — in the hope of duping Luftwaffe fighter aircraft that they were Sunderlands. Hiding next to a tanker in Suda Bay, the pair awaited the daily load of exhausted men — sometimes fifty at a time, to fly them out. Greece surrendered on 24 April and Suda Bay came under continual air attack. The last evacuation flight was on 5 May and, dodging Stukas, the two BOAC flying boats had accomplished 13 roundtrips carrying 469 passengers, an average of 36 a trip. As usual, they were fired upon only by the Royal Navy.

Eugene Esmonde had served with the Fleet Air Arm in the Mediterranean in the 1920s and at the end of his commission, in 1934, joined Imperial Airways as a First Officer. He was put on the routes to the Middle East, India and Burma and in

1935 survived a serious accident when his heavily overloaded aircraft crashed into the Irrawaddy River. Promoted to Captain on 3 July 1937, he flew the Empire flying boats to Australia. With the coming war, Esmonde resigned from Imperial Airways in May 1939, to take up a commission as a Lieutenant-Commander in the Fleet Air Arm.

On the night of the 24th May 1941, he led a squadron of nine Swordfish aircraft (affectionately called "Stringbags" by their crews), armed with torpedoes, to make a 120-mile flight in foul weather and into headwinds to find the German battleship, *Bismarck*. Esmonde attacked through intense anti-aircraft fire from the battleship and scored one hit, amidships on the starboard side. He was awarded the Distinguished Service Order for this action and was to go to Buckingham Palace to receive it when the German battlecruisers *Scharnhorst* and *Gneisenau,* with the cruiser *Prinz Eugen*, made their "Channel dash" from Brest back to Germany. On 12 February 1942, Esmonde led six Swordfish aircraft to attack them. Without fighter cover, the airmen knew that their chances of success and survival were slim but pressed on regardless. They encountered a hail of fire from the ships and Luftwaffe in their desperate attempt to damage the enemy vessels. Just after he had fired its torpedo, Esmonde's Swordfish sustained a direct hit. But he continued the run-in towards his target until his plane burst into flames and crashed into the sea. Three of the other Swordfish were also shot down and their crews killed. Esmonde's body, still in his lifejacket, was washed ashore in the Thames Estuary near the River Medway.[8] He was awarded a posthumous Victoria Cross for his actions. All who remembered him in Imperial Airways mourned.

One of the first air travelers in the history of British aviation was W. H. Pilkington who, in 1919, had taken passage in an Airco DH.9 from Hounslow Heath to Le Bourget. In 1940–2, with a considerable amount of influence in high places, the glass manufacturer made three trips by air to the United States. His account of air travel in wartime is a trial of fortitude, courage

---

8   There is a memorial to Eugene Esmonde at Woodlands Cemetery, Gillingham, Kent.

and spartan accommodations — the opposite of what it would have been a few years before. After three months of waiting, he was finally booked on the KLM DC-3 from Whitchurch to Lisbon from where he was to take the Clipper. Pilkington left his Bristol hotel at 6 am and proceeded to the airport. There he met the tedium and tyranny of bureaucracy — when everyone leaving or entering Britain was automatically viewed as a suspicious character and procedures were known to last hours. "It took two hours for the eight of us (five passengers and three crew)" he wrote, "to be taken carefully through all the important formalities of customs, immigration, censorship, currency permits and so on... During all this, we were kept in a cold little room about ten feet square with a military guard..."[9] They finally took off but after 40 minutes were back again at Whitchurch — the weather in Portugal was so bad that there was no chance of landing at Lisbon. For seven successive days after, Pilkington and his companions left their hotel at 6 am and went through the same formalities before the same officials at the airport. On his eighth attempt, the pilot made it into Lisbon.

Once there, Pilkington had great trouble finding a hotel room, "...there were thousands of refugees from all parts of Europe, mostly waiting to get to America" he wrote, and trying to get a seat on a Clipper was impossible. After days of trying, the indefatigable Pilkington gave up the attempt and this time went to America very uncomfortably, by ship. On return by Clipper, he would make it as far as Bermuda with one of his travelling companions, the author H. G. Wells. More successful (and prophetic of commercial aviation's future) was another wartime flight when Pilkington flew from Montreal to Prestwick, Scotland in a freezing BOAC Liberator, the passengers sleeping on bags of folded parachutes, some in the bomb bay.

Wartime Lisbon was what Shanghai had been in the 1920s and Berlin in the 1930s. On August 4, 1940, a young man boarded the *Dixie Clipper* at La Guardia for Lisbon. Compared with the other passengers, he looked like an unassuming

---

9   Kenneth Hudson and Julian Pettifer: *Diamonds In the Sky*. Ibid, p.117

schoolteacher — except he had $3,000 wrapped around one of his legs and a list of 200 Jews — artists, scientists, doctors and authors, who were trapped in Nazi-occupied France. Varian Fry had been able to get a seat on the Clipper through the influence of the Unitarian Service Committee in New York. As a member of their Rescue Committee, once in Lisbon, he would manage an escape network that smuggled hundreds of refugees from Nazi Europe to Lisbon — there providing them with false papers to get on a ship.[10]

Portuguese ground crews warned the Pan American airmen to watch out for desperate refugees who might try to stow away on a Clipper to freedom in America. Locals whispered warnings about German spies plotting sabotage from the city's cavernous wine cellars. Clipper Capt. James McLeod remembered hearing the rumors, then keeping a low profile in Lisbon. "You sort of drew your horns in after the war began," he said. "You automatically didn't do a lot of talking."[11] It did not help the Americans that Donovan's OSS staged a raid on the Japanese Embassy in Lisbon to steal the codes — only to discover that U.S. naval intelligence had already "cracked" them. Understandably, Pan American put its crews up at the ornate Estoril Palace at Cascais beach outside Lisbon — where they took up skeet shooting.

Inevitably, with so much flying boat traffic, Lisbon was the scene of disasters — the first on 9 January 1943, caused by well-meant intentions. Capt. John H. Lock was an experienced Imperial Airways pilot and had flown the DH.86 *Dorado* on the first scheduled flight into Hong Kong on 24 March 1936. Now commander of the S.26 "G-Class" *Golden Horn*, when his aircraft needed an air test after an engine change at Lisbon, he offered to treat the local staff to a flight over the harbor. He was warned not do to so, both by the BOAC staff in Lisbon

---

10   Fry was so good at what he did that he became an embarrassment to both the Portuguese government and U.S. Embassy in Lisbon, which did not renew his passport in 1941, and he had to return home. Called the American Schindler, he rescued 2,000 people, among them Hannah Arendt, Marc Chagall, Max Ernst, André Breton and Arthur Koestler.

11   Antonio Finns, *Sky Kings*. Sun Sentinel, Sept. 24, 2000.

and London. Locke ignored the orders and packed the *Golden Horn* with a local VIP plus marine staff, customs officials, and some wives. Because the flight was unauthorized, there was no passenger list or how many there were. Once he got the flying boat airborne, Number Three engine caught fire — the "G-Class" like all British flying boats then, did not have fire extinguishers or fully feathering propellers. The smoke from the burning engine flowed from inside the wing, forward to the flight deck and out through the windscreen side panels.

Blinded, Locke attempted to land — when the aircraft porpoised and crashed into the Tagus. There were two survivors, the radio officer and a Portuguese operations officer. That neutral Portuguese citizens were killed in a British military aircraft strained bilateral relations. Soon after, on 22 February, the *Yankee Clipper* would also crash at Lisbon, also flown by an experienced captain.

Now courted by both the American and British governments (and all supplicants on the Pan American board), in June 1941, Juan Trippe was in London. He was to be the keynote speaker at the Royal Aeronautical Society's annual Wright Brothers dinner. (One wonders, did he ask to see the Wright Flyer — the aircraft that began it all — which was also in London?)[12] The city had been undergoing sustained bombing since September 1940 and Trippe and General "Hap" Arnold were on the roof of the Dorchester Hotel watching the panorama of searchlights and anti-aircraft fire. An aide from 10 Downing Street joined them to say that the prime minster wished to speak with him. Trippe met with Churchill in the bomb shelter under Downing Street, the two men with much in common — in egos and vision.

The prime minister must have been at his lowest ebb. Crete had fallen that month, the sea lanes in the Mediterranean were shut down and Rommel had driven the British out of Libya. At

---

12   Angered by the Smithsonian Institute's early treatment of them, Orville Wright had given the *Wright Flyer* to the London Science Museum, in 1925. During World War II, the airplane was safely stored in an underground chamber outside London. After the war, Orville agreed to leave the Flyer at the Science Museum until they could make a copy of it for permanent display. A national treasure, it was returned to the United States in 1948.

that moment, *Ceres* was stationed at Khartoum to evacuate BOAC staff from Cairo when Rommel entered the city. And as if highlighting the dire situation, on 20 June, BOAC lost its prized "G-Class" *Golden Fleece* off Cape Finisterre, Spain, to enemy action.[13]

Communication with North Africa and east of Suez was in jeopardy. Would Pan American be interested in operating a trans-Africa overland route to the Middle East? The prime minister's request must have been music to Trippe's ears. He excelled at ambitious, complex projects that required heavy financial investment. Pan American had already completed projects like the trans-African route in South America and the Pacific. In 1965, when everyone thought they would soon be careening around on supersonic transports, Trippe would coerce Bill Allen into building the original people-mover, the Boeing 747. He is supposed to have said, "If you build it, I'll buy it." Allen replied, "If you buy it, I'll build it."[14] Trippe jump started the program, somehow raising $550 million to order 25 Boeing 747s. As with the Sikorsky S-42, the Boeing 314 and the 707, yet again he had provided the impetus for a new aircraft — and this time with the Boeing 747, one that would define commercial aviation for the next fifty years.

His country may not have been at war in June 1941, but the Pan American president was nothing if not prescient and patriotic. He had just used his majority interest in SCADTA, the German-run airline in Latin America that operated routes adjacent to the Panama Canal, to stage a management takeover. All German personnel were purged to quell concerns about possible sabotage attempts on the canal.

---

13   Not known at the time, but the *Golden Fleece* had an engine failure and made a rough landing which caused the hull to cave in. The captain and first officer were the only survivors and endured 3 ½ days on a life raft until rescued by a U-boat. The pair spent the remainder of the war in a POW camp.

14   When Allen balked — Boeing did not have a plant large enough to build the 747 — Trippe hedged his bets and told him that he was in discussion with Lockheed for a commercial version of its C-5A. Lockheed never had any intention of building a commercial version but Boeing couldn't take that chance.

Without consulting the White House, Trippe assured Churchill that his airline had the experience and skilled workers to construct a chain of airfields and supply depots that would stretch from west African ports up through Sudan to Egypt so that supplies could be flown not only to the embattled British Eighth Army but as far as Tehran for the Soviet Union which that month had entered the war. As it had been in the Pacific, Pan American was once more the proxy for the U.S. government. This was an undeclared war, one that Roosevelt believed Britain was about to lose unless his country came to its aid. *LIFE* Magazine subtitled its October 1941 profile of Trippe: "Pan American Airways Young Chief Helps Run a Branch of U.S. Defense." Although he usually preferred to remain in the background, letting Pan American's planes and accomplishments generate excitement, this time the article focused on Trippe as its subject.[15]

Run by Frank Gledhill, Pan American Airways-Africa Ltd came into being and contracts with the American and the British governments were signed on 12 August. Despite a challenge from American Export Airlines, the CAB awarded the contract to Pan American's Atlantic Airways Ltd to ferry aircraft from Natal, Brazil to Takoradi, Ghana and onward to Cairo. The "Takoradi Route", Pan American pilots used to say, separated "the men from the boys."[16] Using the two remaining Martin M-130s, Pan American was to operate a service from New York via San Juan-Port au Prince-Belem-Natal to ports in Africa. Stripped of their opulent interiors, the *China Clipper* and *Philippine Clipper* ferried men and materials to Liberia, the Gold Coast (now Ghana) and Lagos, Nigeria.

Permission was negotiated with the Belgian government in exile for a New York-Leopoldville service and the Boeing *Cape Town Clipper* arrived at Leopoldville on a proving flight on 16 November 1941. It would be the longest proving flight — a route

---

15   Meredith Hindley, Longreads, February 2015.
16   The former Pan American airfields can still be seen in Darfur, their runways reinforced with the steel strips that Trippe got from Fiorello La Guardia when the mayor demolished the old New York, Sixth Avenue, elevated line, in 1940.

of more than 19,000 miles from La Guardia to Leopoldville and return. As the United States was neutral, the welcome at Leopoldville was muted. Capt. Gray and crew were met by the U.S. Consul Patrick Mallon and a reception for them was held at the consulate. This was in contrast with the next flight on 12 December, 5 days after the Japanese attack on Pearl Harbor. Although the Clipper had been delayed 24 hours, the turnout at the Leopoldville ferry landing was overwhelming with crowds of Europeans and Africans, flags and bunting, a military band and girls presenting Gray with flowers — all welcoming the new ally.

Cut off from London, Paris and Brussels, colonial Africa was revitalized with the flying boat air links by BOAC and Pan American which announced that, starting 11 December, fortnightly flights from Lisbon to Dakar, Senegal, Bolama, Portuguese Guinea-Bissau and Fisherman's Lake, Monrovia, would begin.

Europeans had been in Africa since the 15th century — but not so Americans and the following is taken from the Pan American Airways-Africa Newsletter of the day:

THINGS WE'LL REMEMBER ABOUT AFRICA
by James Corcoran

How we appreciated our bananas and peanut butter... the beach, its foamy, spraying surf... the cocoanuts on shore at "thruppence" each... native women carrying everything from wine bottles to five-gallon cans filled with water atop their heads... fish laid out on the sidewalk to dry, the prairie vista on our way to work — tall grass bent by the strong westerly winds and the clouds bumping against the low hills in the distance... the mahogany trees we saw on bush trips, with their fin-like "buttress" roots, South Africans who look like Hoosiers and speak like English profs, playing croquet... the everchanging tropical cloud formations... local restaurants, with dusky, sloe-eyed waitresses... *Alexander's Ragtime Band* as played by an African on a broken down piano...the eternal cry in the street from urchins "Masta Penny! I beg you, Penny..." the stench from the native market place where everybody sells but no one seems to buy. Finally, the ride to carve a sprawling, growing Yankee city... Yep, we will remember all these things when we get home and look at the ivory elephant, we toted back to put on the mantlepiece. But more important —

inside us will be the feeling that we were in on a typical "slambang" American enterprise, the speed and extent of which the natives will never comprehend, and the enemy will prefer not to.

The Americans introduced baseball, chewing gum and ice cubes to Africa — the locals were fascinated by the last. At Fisherman's Lake, Pan American maintenance crews kept a mini zoo with leopards, gazelles and giraffes. At the base's closure they didn't bring any of the animals home with them, unlike their colleagues in South America. Capt. Steve Bancroft former All-American football player and married to the movie actress Mae Clark, once dove off a Clipper's bow into Brazil's Rio Negro to wrestle an anaconda hiding in weeds along the riverbank. Bancroft captured the serpent and brought his new pet home to Miami. Another reptile enthusiast was Flight Engineer William Haast. He began the Miami Serpentarium, a Dade County tourist attraction — easily spotted along the highway thanks to its towering 35-foot concrete cobra. On layovers near jungles, Haast would arm himself with a gun, a hooked pole and canvas bags and venture into the jungles in search of snakes. Customs in Miami knew better than to check his luggage.

The "88" was the most famous and feared German artillery weapon of the war. It could propel a 20.25 lb high-explosive shell to altitudes beyond 30,000 feet at a rate of about 15 projectiles per minute. No matter how high the Allied bombers flew, the 88 mm guns could decimate their formations. Examining one was a high priority with the U.S. military and the first 88mm captured in North Africa was picked up by a Clipper at Fisherman's Lake. It was only the barrel and the Pan American maintenance men made cradles for it at each bulkhead to distribute the load and bolt it down in the flying boat's passageway. Local labor had been used to shoulder it into the flying boat at Fisherman's Lake but, at La Guardia, removing the barrel by cranes was less successful.

Like their Imperial Airways colleagues, Pan American pilots in Africa would sometimes depart from their flight plans to overfly the waterfalls and savannah and watch the flying boat's shadow stampede the herds below. But in mid-December 1944, the Clipper pilots were told to keep on a tight schedule and return promptly to the United States on every flight. Years later, Flight Officer J. J. Donahue recalled he was too focused on his duties to pay attention to the technicians and Christian missionaries boarding, or to the boxes being loaded onto the flying boat.

No one could have known that the dark, glittery dirt in those boxes would soon incinerate whole cities, killing thousands of Japanese. The Congo had always been a source of mineral wealth but, with the war, it was even more so. When European explorers first hacked their way to the central Congo, they saw BaTeke warriors smear fluorescent clay on their bodies to frighten their enemies. The U.S. government wanted the pitchblende for a similar reason: it contained uranium for an atomic bomb. As early as 1939 Albert Einstein had warned Roosevelt that the world's supply of high-quality uranium ore — the key ingredient for the atomic bomb — could be found in Czechoslovakia (now under the Nazis) and the Shinkolobwe Mine in the Congolese province of Katanga. At first the uranium was transported by rail to Lobito in Portuguese-neutral Angola (which the OSS said was infested with Nazi spies), and later to Matadi, on the mouth of the Congo river. Pan American Clippers brought it out from there, their pilots ignorant of what the shipments were for until after the war.

By the summer of 1941, Japanese military expansion in the Pacific, encouraged by the war in Europe, alarmed Roosevelt enough to send a Marine battalion to Wake Island and have a landing field for B-17s built. As the Clippers were the only aircraft with the range to operate in the Pacific, Pan American captains were given an envelope prior to their flights to open if the military situation in the Far East started to deteriorate. Marked "PLAN A, TOP SECRET, FOR CAPTAIN'S EYES ONLY" it contained contingency plans that were to be opened if war should break out while they were away. Instructions for each leg of the journey were provided in case communications with Alameda should break down. At 7:55 am, on 7 December 1941 the code "Climb Mount Niitaka" signaled the start of the attack on Battleship Row, Pearl Harbor. The first Allied and flying boat casualty of the Pacific War had occurred a few hours before the attack on Pearl Harbor. Beyond the international date line, it was early morning on 8 December in Asia. An RAF Catalina of 205 Squadron, piloted by Pilot Officer P.E. Bedell, on patrol off Singapore spotted the Japanese invasion fleet approaching Northern Malaya. No one heard from it again. After the war, Japanese records revealed that Bedell had been

attacked by a "Jake" a Japanese catapult-launched float plane which must have damaged his radio. Five Nakajima Ki-27 fighters were directed to his location and the Catalina was shot down with the loss of all its crew.

In Hong Kong, Capt. Fred S. Ralph and his crew had been told it would be an early departure from Kai Tak. They were at the slipway watching

The *China Clipper* over Hong Kong Harbor.

the ground crew refuel the S-42B *Hong Kong Clipper* (formerly called the *Bermuda Clipper*, it was nicknamed *Myrtle*) they had brought from Manilla the day before. Beside it, "Sampan Annie" in her black suit and basket-like coolie hat was ready to begin her job. She was Pan American's "water man" and although 56-years old, her skill at getting her sampan around a Clipper, passing a line to the officer in the bow, getting all

295

lines into place and warping the aircraft up to the dock, was known to be amazing. In the early days of the CNAC Sikorskys, Annie also did the beaching but, to her disappointment, the larger Martins and still larger Boeings did not require that at Hong Kong. Annie's real name was Chin Yun Gi and her proudest possession was the PAA Flight Engineer's button which had been presented to her by Vic Wright. She always wore it, sometimes upside down, when she appeared at Kai Tak for an arrival or departure.[17]

How Capt. Ralph heard that Japan had declared war on Britain and the United States, and that Manilla was already under attack is unknown, but by 7:44 am he had. He planned to get the Clipper out immediately and fly to a lake in Kunming before the Japanese arrived. Fortunately, he did not have to worry about boarding the passengers. The bus from the Peninsula Hotel was late that morning — a businessman had overslept — and that saved the passengers' lives.

But it was too late for the Pan American crew — the Zeroes were already wheeling over Kowloon. They bombed Kai Tak Airport, strafing the CNAC aircraft on the field and then made for the Clipper at the water's edge with incendiary bullets. It took seven attacks before the flying boat, heavy with fuel, burst into flames and burned to the waterline. Ralph and his crew would escape from Hong Kong on a surviving CNAC DC-3 and eventually return to New York via Asia and Europe. *Myrtle* would be the only Clipper casualty of the war due to enemy action. As to "Sampan Annie" — she and her family would fade into the Japanese occupied British colony. On 11 January 1970, the first Pan American Boeing 747 landed at Kai Tak and the next morning the *South China Morning Post* published a photograph of its captain accepting a welcome scroll from the diminutive 86-year-old and yes, "Sampan Annie" was wearing her Flight Engineer's button.

The *Anzac Clipper* commanded by Capt. Lanier Turner, with 17 passengers onboard, was then nearing Hawaii. It had

17   *New Horizons*, September 1941. Written by W.B. (Shorty) Greenough — Pan American Airways Chief Mechanic — Hong Kong.

been an uneventful flight except the B-314 had left Treasure Island almost an hour late due to mechanical problems. On 6 December, Turner had watched his daughter's piano recital and, on the way home, stopped at the office. There he was given a briefing and sealed orders that were to be opened if Japan and the United States were at war.

At about 8 am, First Radio Officer W.H. Bell on the *Anzac Clipper* picked up an announcement from a Honolulu radio station. The passengers were stretching their legs, getting ready for their arrival in Honolulu and Turner had come down the spiral staircase for coffee when Bell rushed down to say that Pearl Harbor was under attack. Had the *Anzac Clipper* been on time, it would have been caught in the attack!

Turner broke the news to the crew and passengers, and without fuel to go anywhere else, made for the Hawaiian island of Hilo, hiding in the clouds as he did. It took two hours to get there and, before the plane alighted, they checked the beaches to make sure it was safe to land. They were afraid that the locals might think, in the confusion of the day, that the Clipper was an enemy aircraft. They were met by a launch carrying the military and FBI who checked their identity. Turner called the Pan American control tower at Honolulu and was briefed on the destruction there. Told to return to California, he and his crew pushed the Clipper into the foliage on the shoreline, camouflaging it with buttermilk and lampblack, a trick from Turner's barnstorming days. All refueling was done by hand and that night the *Anzac Clipper* left for San Francisco, its crew and passengers exhausted by the events.

The M-130 *Philippine Clipper* had just taken off from Wake Island for Guam on 8 December when Capt. John Hamilton, who was a lieutenant in the Naval Air Reserve, got the news about Pearl Harbor. He returned to Wake where the military asked if he could do a reconnaissance of the area, escorted by the Grumman Wildcat fighters. Ground crew refueled the Clipper — just as the Japanese attacked. The entire base, including the Pan American hotel, was bombed and although a line of bullet holes showed that the Clipper had been hit, the damage was negligible in comparison. Hamilton decided to take off immediately — they stripped the plane of all non-essentials, loaded the Pan American employees onboard and taxied out. It took three attempts before the now overloaded flying boat lifted off. Left behind were the Marines and civilian construction workers — all of whom fought the Japanese until surrendering to brutal captivity and when the island was bombed by the United States — the remaining survivors were executed.

Midway was 1,185 miles away and blacked-out. On approach, Hamilton saw two warships leaving the atoll and heard that it had been shelled that afternoon. He was able to bring the Clipper into the debris filled lagoon where it was refueled and the next day, they made for Pearl Harbor, which although still coping with the damage of the day before was safe for landing. On 10 December, Hamilton flew the *Philippine Clipper*, under radio silence, to Treasure Island.

But the most iconic of all flying boat endeavors was to come. On 1 December, the Boeing 314 *Pacific Clipper* left Treasure Island for Auckland. Its scheduled stops were Honolulu, Canton Island, Suva and Noumea. The replacement for Kingman Reef, Canton Island, had been named for the whaler that had been wrecked there in 1854 — its crew took to their lifeboats and sailed/rowed 3,200 miles to the Marianas. Claimed by both the British and Americans, Canton was deserted until the Pan American chartered ship *North Haven* brought a construction crew to it on 18 May 1939. A radio station was built and the coral heads dynamited so that it was ready for the Clippers going on to Auckland. As it was close to Tarawa, in 1941 the U.S. Army built an airfield which, post-war, was used by Pan American Boeing 377s and Qantas Constellations. It is now part of Kiribati.

The routine flight would keep the crew away from home for two weeks. On 8 December, two hours before landing at Auckland, First Radio Operator John D. Poindexter, taking down Morse code dispatches, heard the first reports about the attack on

Pearl Harbor. Then came a cryptic two-word message: "Plan A." This was a prearranged signal that meant all Pan American aircraft in flight were to maintain radio silence, land at their next scheduled destination and await instructions.

Capt. Robert Ford reached into his flight bag for the emergency orders. He briefed the crew and passengers that the airline would now be operating on a wartime basis and they would continue to Auckland, New Zealand. When they landed in the Auckland harbor, in the confusion of what was happening in Hawaii, it was thought the California coast could be bombed next and the Pan American base at Alameda a prime target. At the chaotic U.S. consulate, a clerk thrust a piece of paper into Ford's hand:

> Security: Top Secret
> To: Captain Robert Ford
> From: Chief, Flight Operations Pan American Airways System Chrysler Building New York City, NY
> Subject: Diversion plans for NC18602
> Normal return route cancelled. Proceed as follows:
> Strip all company markings, registration numbers, and identifiable insignia from exterior surfaces. Proceed westbound soonest your discretion to avoid hostilities and deliver NC18602 to Marine Terminal LaGuardia Field New York.
>
> Good Luck.

Told that it was no longer safe to return the way he had come, Ford was to chart his own course to get home by going west via Asia, Africa and the Atlantic — until he saw LaGuardia, New York. His crew had to determine a route suitable for a giant flying boat, finding harbors, lagoons and rivers large enough to set down on, avoiding the enemy and scrounging 100-octane aviation fuel along the way. There were no aviation maps available, but the librarian at the Auckland Public Library found some school geography textbooks and old marine charts. Essentially, the crew of the *Pacific Clipper* were on their own.

After camouflaging the aircraft as best they could, hiding all company markings, they set off, returning to Noumea. "We elected to start by returning to Noumea to pick up station personnel and spares, a crated engine and a barrel of engine oil, on 16 December," wrote Capt. Ford. There, they evacuated all 22 Pan American personnel including two company mechanics and a radio technician who were asked to join the crew. With Ford, it now consisted of: First Officer John Henry Mack, Second Officer Roderick Norman Brown, Third Officer James G. Henriksen, Fourth Officer John Delmer Steers, First Engineer Homans "Swede" Rothe, Second Engineer John Bertrand Parish, First Radio Officer Jack Poindexter, Second Radio Officer Oscar Henderickson, Flight Stewards Barney Sawicki and Verne Edwards. Those who joined the flight at Noumea were radio technician Eugene Leach, and mechanics Joe Moran and Bill Valdez.

They flew to Gladstone, Australia just above Brisbane where the airline personnel were dropped off to get back to the United States. Ford recounted, "I was wondering how we were going to pay for everything we were going to need on this trip. We had money enough for a trip to Auckland and back to San Francisco, but this was a different story. In Gladstone, a young man who was a banker came up to me and out of the blue said, "How are you fixed for money?" "Well, we're broke!" I said. He said, "I'll probably be shot for this." but he went down to his bank on a Saturday morning, opened the vault and handed me five hundred American dollars. Since Rod Brown, our navigator, was the only one with a lock box and a key we put him in charge of the money. That $500 financed the rest of the trip all the way to New York."

The *Pacific Clipper*'s first leg to Darwin was completely overland, a hazardous situation for a flying boat as any emergency would force them to belly land on the desert. They spent the night in Darwin, the town expected to be bombed at any moment and most of the civilian population had been evacuated. The Americans were given a place to shower and change; much to their amusement their "locker room" turned out to be a deserted Australian Army brothel.[18]

---

18   John A. Marshall, *The Round The World Saga of the* Pacific Clipper.
https://www.panam.org/pan-am-inspirations/634-saga-of-the-pacific-clipper

Then it was on to Surabaya in the Dutch East Indies. The second largest city on the island of Java, Surabaya was protected by a British garrison and a squadron of RAF Brewster F2A Buffalo fighter aircraft. As it was in the war zone, the plan was to refuel and get away as quickly as possible.

The Dutch were notified to expect the *Pacific Clipper*, but they never received the message. Instead, they scrambled the Buffalos to meet what looked very much like a Japanese flying boat. In the fever of the times, any unidentified aircraft was an enemy one and they were ready to shoot the Clipper down — until the remnants of the American flag on the wing were seen.

With the RAF pilots still shadowing them, Ford got the flying boat safely into Surabaya harbor — which he was later told had been mined. On landing, the crew members were given inoculations against typhus and cholera, and several of them became quite ill.

Back home, because of wartime secrecy, none of their families knew where the crew were — or even if they were still alive. It would be a long six weeks for their wives and families.

At Surabaya, there was no 100-octane aviation fuel and they made do with 76-octane automobile fuel, filling the Boeing's 4,000-plus gallon tank laboriously from five-gallon tins. The flight engineers transferred all remaining aviation fuel to the two fuselage tanks and filled the wing tanks with the lower octane automobile gas. "We took off from Surabaya on the 100-octane, climbed a couple of thousand feet, and pulled back the power to cool off the engines," said Ford. "Then we switched to the automobile gas and held our breaths. The engines almost jumped out of their mounts, but they ran. We figured it was either that or leave the airplane..." From Surabaya, they flew visually, crossing the Indian Ocean, while keeping an eye out for Zeroes.

"We were now faced with the task of trying to locate the coast of Ceylon (Sri Lanka)." wrote Capt. Ford. "We had to fly on dead reckoning alone, for we had had an overcast all night, which prevented our getting celestial fixes, and we had to estimate what the wind allowance should be... we lacked charts, especially with regard to elevation."

Descending into the Indian port of Trincomalee, the *Pacific Clipper* surprised a Japanese submarine that had surfaced. It would be difficult to determine who was the more surprised, the Japanese submarine commander or the crew of the Clipper. The plane was low enough for the crew to watch the submarine's men scurrying to aim deck guns at the aircraft. They climbed quickly through the clouds and out of sight but saw a flash of gunfire under them through the haze.

At Trincomalee, 100-octane aviation fuel was found, as were some maps and charts of the Near East and Africa. The Clipper's crew were invited to a Christmas Eve dinner at the governor's residence. The guests included Lady Edwina Mountbatten, the wife of Lord Louis Mountbatten, chief of operations in the Southeast Asia theater, who wanted to hear all about their adventures. "I fell sound asleep several times during the meal." wrote Capt. Ford.

One of Number Three engine's eighteen cylinders had failed, wrenching itself loose from its mount and Christmas Day was spent repairing it. Carols were sung and thoughts were of loved ones back home, it was a sad event for all. Finally, early in the morning of 26 December, they took off from Trincomalee.

The route took the plane along the coast of India to Karachi. There they were again forced to use 76-octane fuel before heading to the island of Bahrain. From here, they would fly across the great land mass of Saudi Arabian desert to Khartoum. The plan had been to fly straight across the Arabian Peninsula and the Red Sea into Africa. "When we were preparing to leave Bahrain, we were warned by the British authorities not to fly across Arabia," wrote Ford. "The Saudis had apparently already caught some British fliers who had been forced down there. The natives had dug a hole, buried them in it up to their necks, and just left them."

"We crossed the Arabian desert at 10,000 feet, then across the Red Sea — from the Red Sea into the Anglo Egyptian Sudan. Reached the Nile late in the afternoon and followed it to where the Blue Nile and the White Nile meet. Spent New Year's Eve onboard the ship in the middle of the Nile. Millions of small gnats inside and out." Ford wanted to refuel quickly and leave but he received a "vital military affairs" message asking him to wait for unidentified VIP passengers from Cairo.

"We waited for two days," Fourth Officer Steers reported. "The VIPs were the publisher of a Chicago newspaper, his wife and sister-in-law." Because of engine trouble, the BOAC aircraft flying them made a forced landing and the passengers did not show up and Ford was authorized to continue without them.

After a three-mile length of the Nile was checked to make sure no bathing hippos impeded take-off, the plane left Khartoum for Leopoldville. Once more, they would be flying across desert and, later, dense jungles, with no hope of a safe landing if the engines — spluttering on automobile fuel, overheated and failed. Ten and a half hours later, they touched down on the Congo River. From the air, Ford had thought the current was much slower than it really was. Once down, he attempted to minimize the forward thrust by "blimping" all four engines i.e. an intermittent interruption of all ignition on them.

Leopoldville was a new Pan American base and facilities and spare parts were limited. A pleasant surprise awaited them however, when two familiar faces greeted them at the dock. A Pan American Airport Manager and a Radio Officer had been dispatched to meet them, and Ford was handed a cold beer. "That was one of the high points of the whole trip," he said. Also welcome was 100-octane aviation fuel for the 3,100-nautical mile flight over open seas to Natal, Brazil. Heavy with fuel, the B-314 took off the next day, taking nearly three minutes to become airborne. Because the weight of the fuel in the wings was pressing on the ailerons, control was difficult, and they narrowly missed crashing into a canyon.

To navigate across the Atlantic, Second Officer Roderick N. Brown constructed a Mercator projection of 10 degrees of latitude on a strip of paper. "This served as our chart from Leopoldville to Natal," he explained. "At night over water, we dropped flares and with our drift sight we checked drift and ground speed. During daylight we dropped smoke bombs."

Some 23½ hours later, they saw the coast of Brazil. They landed in the harbor at Natal just before noon. While they were waiting for the necessary immigration formalities to be completed, the Brazilian authorities insisted that the crew disembark while the interior of the airplane was sprayed for yellow fever. Two men in rubber suits and masks boarded and fumigated the airplane. They spent four hours in Natal, refueling and repairing an engine exhaust stack that had blown off at Khartoum. A part taken from a Navy Catalina was put on it with a tin can wrapped around, it was held with bailing wire. It was not until after they had departed that the crew discovered that most of their personal papers and money were missing, along with a military chart that had been entrusted to Navigator Rod Brown by the US military attaché in Leopoldville, all stolen by the Brazilian "fumigators."

Anxious to be back in U.S. territory, they headed for Port of Spain. The following day would be the final leg of the journey. On 5 January 1942, the Clipper left Port of Spain for New York. The next morning, just before 6 am, LaGuardia tower received this message:

"LAGUARDIA TOWER, PAN AMERICAN CLIPPER NC1602, INBOUND FROM AUCKLAND, NEW ZEALAND, CAPT. FORD REPORTING, DUE ARRIVE PAN AMERICAN MARINE TERMINAL, LAGUARDIA, SEVEN MINUTES."

The tower control operator, sleepy after the night shift, incredulous because of the flight's origin and that no such flight was expected, asked Ford to repeat the message. Then he told him that the seaplane base was closed until after sunrise. After more than a month and 31,500 miles flying, the *Pacific Clipper* had to circle over New York for another hour before it could land.

"In the offices of the Immigration officials" Steers later wrote. "we explained that we had no passports, no contraband; had our pictures taken, a cup of coffee, questioned by the Army and the reporters, and then were told that we were transferred to the Atlantic Division." To the relief of the crews' families, it did make the front page of the *New York Times* the next day: "Pacific Clipper, Racing War, Circles Globe, Lands Here."

Although the flight of the *Pacific Clipper* was unparalleled in aviation history, (they had crossed the Equator four times), no one was given citations or awards. The crew was debriefed, given two weeks off, then returned to flight duty. The country was still reeling from the shock of Pearl Harbor and the story was forgotten until many years later.[19] One can only imagine how Trippe, the ultimate publicist, could have milked this saga. Ford himself called the whole trip "completely routine." Like his crew, he spent the war flying contract missions for the military. He continued flying for Pan American, leaving the airline in 1952 to "retire" to his 880-acre ranch at Penn Valley, CA. Ford would die of pancreatic cancer in 1988.

A flying boat would star in another historic drama a week later. Prime Minister Churchill would fly home from Washington on *Berwick* on 14 January 1942 after forging the Grand Alliance with President Roosevelt. It had been planned that he was to take it from Norfolk to Bermuda where the battleship HMS *Duke of York*, on which he had met Roosevelt in December, was waiting. However, having been away for three weeks with the war situation deteriorating in North Africa and the Far East, the prime minister was eager to return home. Once in Bermuda, he asked Capt. Kelly Rogers if the Boeing could fly directly to Britain and was assured it could. His staff worried that this was a rash move and with Sir Charles Portal the Chief of Air Staff and Sir Dudley Pound First Sea Lord also onboard, it was putting too many eggs in one basket. Lord Beaverbrook, who was on the plane, even said: "If we lose Churchill, we lose the war." The safety of the *Duke of York,* and escorting destroyers outside the reef, was infinitely more reassuring.

Churchill's own account was as a passenger appreciating all that the Clipper had to offer – Wellwood Beall would have been pleased — and it was later published in *LIFE* Magazine.

"There was really no danger; we were in sure hands. The flying boat lifted ponderously a quarter of a mile from the reef, and we had several hundred feet of height to spare. There is no doubt about the comfort of these great flying boats. I had a good broad bed in the bridal suite at the stern with large windows on either side. It was quite a long walk, thirty or forty feet, downhill through the various compartments to the saloon

19   The only remnant of the *Pacific Clipper* is a tattered piece of fabric with the NC number on it, pinned to the wall of the Pan American display, at Boeing's Museum of Flight in Seattle.

and dining-room, where nothing was lacking in food or drink. The motion was smooth, the vibration not unpleasant, and we passed an agreeable afternoon and had a merry dinner. I went to bed and slept soundly for several hours."

Waking up to autograph bulletins from the flight deck about their position, height and speed, Churchill saw the flight as a "photo op". In a first for prime ministers, he piloted the flying boat, at least long enough for photos to be taken of him doing so, with a Corona clamped firmly in his mouth. He had not flown an aircraft since 1919 when a crash had almost killed him, and, because he had had a heart attack while at the White House, his doctor Charles Wilson stood beside him on the flight deck. At one point, Churchill turned to him and said: "Do you realize we are fifteen hundred miles from anywhere?" Wilson reminded him, "Heaven is as near by sea as by land." "Who said that?" Churchill asked. "I think it was the sixteenth century captain Sir Humphrey Gilbert searching for the Northwest Passage." Wilson replied.

They flew on into the dawn with a fog hiding the British coast. To their horror, the navigator reported that at one point *Berwick* was over German-occupied France. The prime minister strained to see the enemy below, but Kelly Rogers put them back over Britain and began the descent into Plymouth harbor. On landing, a prepared press release was handed out about the Atlantic flight — the first for a prime minister. With his flair for the dramatic, Churchill later added that the BOAC flying boat had been regarded as a "hostile" and that Fighter Command had sent six Hurricanes to shoot it down. In his official report, Kelly Rogers wrote that this was untrue and that "the flight had gone very well in all respects."

With the war, Pan American, as with all other airlines in the United States, came under military management and the B-314s were taken over — four going to the Army and five to the Navy. No longer "Clippers", they were given standard military designations in the C-for-Cargo category as C-98s. They continued to be flown by Pan American crews under their original civil registrations. Pan American's Pacific routes

Winston Churchill, at the controls of the BOAC Boeing 314 flying boat,
Berwick, in 1942.

were reduced to the single San Francisco to Hawaii leg. The
airline would keep the two M-130s, two Sikorsky S-42s, and
one Boeing. In 1943, with more landplanes available, the Army
transferred its four C-98s to the Navy which retained title to all
nine until after the war.

As with the M-130s, the two Sikorsky S-42 Clippers did
not survive the war. On 22 July 1943, the *Bermuda Clipper*
(once the *Pan American Clipper III*) was on the Negro River
at Manuas, Brazil preparing for a flight. When No. 1 engine
caught fire, the pilot directed the mechanic to pull the fire
extinguisher handle. By mistake, he pulled the fuel dump
handle and fuel poured out, to be ignited by flames from the
engine. All escaped in time, but the aircraft burned itself to
the waterline and sank into the river. The *West Indies Clipper*

(the original *Hong Kong Clipper* that been used on the Pacific survey flights) crashed on take-off at Antilla, Cuba on 7 August 1944, killing 17 passengers.[20]

Manpower shortages in wartime forced Pan American to hire Madeline Cuniff, the first stewardess on the Clippers.[21] The New York-Bermuda run took 5½ hours, Cuniff remembered, and she was the only cabin staff onboard. When she worked the full transatlantic crossing at war's end, the flight was a ponderous 21 hours. Because of this, passengers got to know each other very well and Cuniff hosted bridge tournaments onboard. The only help she had were the State Department's diplomatic couriers who regularly flew the Atlantic and were always happy to do the washing up and putting down the sleeping berths.

With the Clipper fleet in military use, Pan American and all other airlines in the United States used the profits from their government contracts to equip themselves with the latest landplanes. Chief among them was Howard Hughes' Trans World Airlines (TWA) which bought Boeing Stratoliners and Lockheed Constellations. With the Chicago Convention in 1944, TWA now wanted to fly overseas.

Hughes is better known today for his mammoth flying boat the *Spruce Goose*. The concept of a giant flying boat was born in 1942, at a time when U-boats were sinking hundreds of Allied ships, many of them built by Henry Kaiser. The steel magnate conceived the idea of a ship that would have wings and asked Hughes to design and build it. The maverick Hughes took on the task, made impossible by the government's restrictions on steel and aluminum which were critical to the war effort. An aircraft

---

20   What did survive the war was the *Brazilian Clipper*, the first S-42 Pan American had bought in 1934. It was flown by Charles Lindbergh and Ed Musick on the inaugural flight to Rio. In 1945, unable to find a home for his family in Miami, one. Lemuel Stewart saw the S-42 at Dinner Keys awaiting the scrap yard. He bought it for $750, took the wings and engines off, jacked up the 70 ft. fuselage, loaded it onto a trailer, and towed it to a nearby canal. He re-caulked the hull, painted it, launched it in a Florida waterway and moved his family into it. Its present whereabouts are unknown.

21   Madeline Cuniff was also a pilot. The author Ken Follett would interview her for his book *Night Over the Water* about a flight on a Pan American flying boat at the outbreak of World War II.

Howard Hughes' gigantic eight-engined H-4 Hercules, the *Spruce Goose*, flew only once and for just one mile.

made entirely of wood was possible — Geoffrey de Havilland had been phenomenally successful with his all-wood Mosquito fighter-bomber. Designated HK-1 for "Hughes-Kaiser", the flying boat was designed to carry 750 fully equipped troops or two Sherman tanks over long distances. It had a single hull, eight radial engines, a single vertical tail, fixed wingtip floats, and full cantilever wing and tail surfaces. The entire airframe and surface structures were composed of laminated wood (birch not spruce) and all primary control surfaces, except the flaps, were fabric covered. When Kaiser withdrew from the project in 1944, the monster was re-designated H-4. It had not flown by 1945 when the need for flying boats had ended. Finally, on 2 November 1947, Hughes and a small crew started the eight radial engines for taxi tests. He lifted the aircraft 33 feet off the surface of Long Beach Harbor, CA., and flew it for one mile for less than a minute, remaining airborne 70 feet off the water, before landing. The H-4 Hercules never flew again, and the world's largest flying boat can be marveled at the Evergreen Aviation & Space Museum, McMinnville, OR.

Ironically, the former Hughes Aircraft buildings in Los Angeles, including Building 15 where the *Spruce Goose* was built, were converted into movie sound stages and scenes from two movies were shot there — *The Aviator* and *Titanic.*

In both world wars, the great ocean liners — the *Lusitania,* the *Lancastria,* the *Empress of Canada* and the *Wilhelm Gustloff* proved easy targets for the enemy. Unarmed, crowded with civilians and without escorts, the flying boats in the Pacific suffered similarly.

As the Allies attempted to stem the relentless Japanese advance through South East Asia, the BOAC/Qantas flying boats shuttled food, ammunition and aviation fuel to various outposts and brought out European women and children. Flights to Bangkok were terminated as the Thai government threw their lot in with the enemy. One by one, the BOAC/Qantas staging posts in the Malay States, Sumatra, Batavia and Surabaya fell to the Japanese in frightening succession. *Calypso* evacuated 42 adults and nine children from Rabaul on 26 December. Capt. Carlos Madge flew *Cassiopeia* from Cairo to Singapore with ammunition in December. On the return flight, he evacuated the wives and children of BOAC staff. Taking off after refueling at Sabang on the northern tip of Sumatra on 28 December, *Cassiopeia* hit a heavy swell or debris. The flying boat broke in two and, while the crew rescued as many of the women and children as they could, four died in the darkness, including a 17-day old baby. The next flying boat through Sabang picked up the survivors.

The year of 1942 promised to be even worse for the flying boats. Designed in 1936 for the wealthy few, Arthur Gouge's creations were now the crowded lifeboats from a rapidly sinking British Empire. On 17 January *Coolangatta* ferried women and children from Kupang and Ambon to Darwin. On 4 February Capt. W.H. Crowther took *Coriolanus,* the last flying boat out of Singapore, overfilled with 40 passengers onboard, and when that city fell on 15 February, *Calypso* and *Coogee* picked up escapers offshore. *Coolangatta* landed at Ambon which was already occupied by the Japanese to rescue stragglers on 12

February. Company personnel were evacuated from Rangoon by *Coorong* on 21 February and flown to Basra.

The flying boat captains knew that the cat and mouse games with the Zeroes would eventually catch up with them. Unlucky *Corio* with 13 passengers onboard was caught near Kupang on 30 January, the Zeroes raking its fuselage, killing all passengers huddling in what had been the promenade deck while its captain attempted to evade them by beaching the flying boat.

Sometimes crashes were not caused by the enemy but pilot error. *Coogee* flown by the RAAF, crashed at Cleveland Bay, Townsville on 27 February. Overloaded with air force personnel, its center of gravity may have shifted on landing, causing the aircraft to plough deeper and deeper into the water until the hull caved in. Eight occupants drowned; it took two days before the mangled bodies could be retrieved from the wreckage.

Sent to pick up Dutch consular staff from Tjilatap, the last port in Java that was still free, on 28 February *Circe* disappeared on the return flight with all aboard. A search by *Corinna* proved fruitless and it was thought she had met her fate by meeting up with the Mitsubishi A6Ms returning from attacking the aircraft carrier USS *Langley*.

The only defenses that the flying boat pilots had against the Japanese were stealth — i.e. radio silence and operating under cover of darkness — neither ideal for flying boats — and diverting to "funk holes." It was noticed that raids were predictable and timed according to a schedule. By listening to the radio, the pilots could avoid them by hiding out in a sheltered cove they called a "funk hole."

The Horseshoe Route via Singapore and Surabaya was now broken and the flying boats were routed through Port Blair, the Andaman & Nicobar Islands to Calcutta. Darwin was bombed on 19 February – with *Camilla* escaping in time thanks to Capt. Bert Hussey and his crew. A landing of Japanese troops was imminently expected, and the port was closed to further traffic. In desperation, Broome, a small pearl fishing town on the east coast of the Indian Ocean, was chosen as its replacement. With its deep-water anchorage only accessible after wading through a half mile of mud, it was not ideal for flying boats. Its location also made for a longer flight across the Timor Sea and payload was reduced — crews improvised by lashing fuel tanks from Wirraway aircraft to the flying boat cabins for extra mileage.

With thousands of refugees fleeing the Japanese advance, Broome soon became a chaos of frightened locals (many of the workers in the pearling industry were Japanese) and raging fever. Without accommodation onshore, evacuees, many of them women and children, remained onboard the flying boats that brought them, living in a cramped and overcrowded situation. When Java was overrun, Dutch naval Dorniers and Catalinas packed with the families of the crews kept arriving and, by 3 March, there were 13 at Broome. The plan was for them to refuel and move on to Perth. As only three could enter the harbor at any one time, the others were kept out in the bay until the *Nichol Bay*, the port's only fuel barge could reach them. But as the tide receded, all outside were caught fast in the mud.

Coast watchers warned of a Japanese reconnaissance plane hovering over Broome on 2 March, as did the incoming Dutch crews. The raid began at 9.30 am the next day with six fighters pouncing on the harbor. *Corinna's* crew were refueling from *Nichol Bay* when it was set ablaze. Within minutes, all the stranded flying boats were on fire, the screams from within them drowned out by cannon fire. The RAAF's A18-10, formerly *Centaurus,* caught fire immediately — it had already been refueled and with 1,400 gallons of fuel, it burned down to the waterline. There were many individual acts of heroism that day: Corporal Andrew Ireland rushed to the A18-10's flight deck and, in the face of enemy fire, released its dinghy. The remainder of the crew (except the captain and second pilot who were ashore) dived through the hatches into the sea. Dutch evacuees and aircrew who had survived the attack were hauled into the dinghy which, built to hold five persons, eventually reached a larger rescue craft with 13 aboard.

Some flying boat hulls exploded, others just sank according to the order in which the water entered their hulls, drowning all within. Locals dived into the water to rescue the women and children, despite the fear that the bleeding wounded had attracted sharks. A Qantas staff member saw his wife being machine-gunned and his three children drowned. A USAAC Liberator which had just taken off from Broome airfield, moments before the raid started, cartwheeled into the sea in flames — the only survivor walked ashore after thirty-six hours in the water.

The Japanese departed as swiftly as they had come but not before they shot down an incoming KLM DC-3 carrying refugees (and supposedly a parcel of diamonds) which crashed north of Broome. The fires on the flying boats were only extinguished by the incoming tide and many of the bodies have never been found. *Camilla* which had been at Port Hedland began ferry flights, taking the severely wounded to Perth. In all, 24 aircraft had been destroyed. Fifteen were flying boats — in addition to the RAAF's A18-10, the Dutch lost 5 Dorniers and 4 Catalinas, the RAF 2 Catalinas, the US Navy Patrol Squadron 2 Catalinas and Qantas the *Corinna*. Historians have called 3 March 1942 "Australia's Pearl Harbor". A more accurate and poignant name would be "The Massacre of the Innocents."[22]

With the Clipper flights to Auckland ended after Pearl Harbor, the government of New Zealand felt especially isolated. It was imperative that the Honorable Walter Nash, the country's Resident Minister to the United States, be flown to Honolulu to continue to Washington. The veteran of many inaugural fights, Capt. Burgess was asked to take Nash and his wife in *Awarua*. They left Auckland on 18 January 1942 and using former Pan American radio and accommodation facilities at Suva and Canton, arrived at Pearl Harbor on 21 January — the first Empire air service in Hawaii.

On the return home, because the *Awarua* had no markings, the pilot of a Dauntless fighter aircraft from the USS *Enterprise* fired upon it. Burgess had the Civil Air Ensign flown from the observation hatch to identify them and there seemed no damage had been done. Back in Auckland on 27 January, a

22   M. McCarthy, J. Green, S. Jung and C. Souter: *The Broome Flying Boats Report —* Department of Maritime Archaeology, Western Australian Maritime Museum. No. 170. 2002.

hole in the fuselage was fixed. As a souvenir, the maintenance staff gave Burgess a "hole" in a piece of scrap metal.

When the RNZAF got its Catalinas in mid-1943, *Awarua* and *Aotearoa* were taken off their military duties. Both flying boats survived the war, the first scrapped at Auckland in 1947, the second to become a tourist attraction at Walsh Brothers Flying School at Mission Bay until also scrapped in the early 1950s.

With increased demand for transporting personnel, the RAF continued to impose upon BOAC, which had suffered the loss of so many Empire flying boats. Now in Belfast, Shorts was nationalized in 1943 and Arthur Gouge was dismissed. To cope with the RAF's demands, BOAC was given six ex RAF Sunderland IIIs. Put in civil markings, they were stripped of their armament and fitted with bench-type seats. Six more were converted for the airline in 1943, with a further 12 in 1944. Called the *Hythe* Class they were named for places beginning with "H" — *Hatfield, Hampshire, Hamble* etc. These were followed by 12 Sandringhams in the *Plymouth* Class which were named *Penzance, Poole, Perth* etc. The bench seats were replaced with 16 and later 24 passenger seats and the Pegasus engines with more powerful (and reliable) Pratt & Whitney engines. The Hythes would be put on the Poole-Lagos route and later flights to Cairo and India.

As so many of their troops were in the Middle East and Europe, in early 1943, the Australian and New Zealand governments prioritized the setting up of a mail flight across the Indian Ocean that would join up with the remnant of the Horseshoe Route. The Australian government asked Qantas to set up a service from Australia to Ceylon (now Sri Lanka), landing at the RAF base at Lake Koggala, 80 miles from Colombo.

Qantas had pilots who were experienced in pre-war flying boat operations, the RAAF had navigators and the British Government made available five Catalinas stripped of all defensive weapons, deicing equipment, oxygen systems and cabin insulation to save weight. As the Cocos Islands were within range of Japanese aircraft, they were deemed unsuitable as a refueling stop. This was to be a non-stop 5,451-mile flight which became known as the "Double Sunrise" flights because the crew and passengers often saw two sunrises during the 30

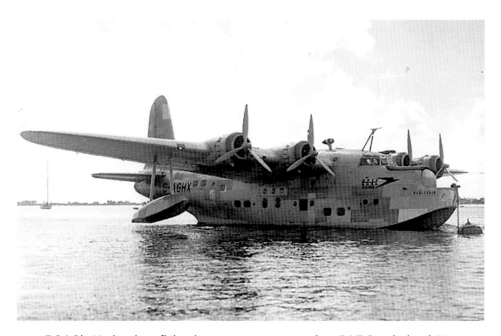

BOAC's *Hythe* class flying boats were converted ex-RAF Sunderland IIIs.
Pictured is G-AGHX, *Harlequin*, in Poole Harbor.

hours plus spent in the air. Additional fuel tanks were fitted in the Catalina fuselage and, when full, the aircraft's take-off weight was 35,000 lbs, 6,000 lbs above normal and the Catalina payload was limited to only 1,000 lbs. A maximum of three passengers could be carried, all of whom were awarded a certificate of membership to "The Rare and Secret Order of the Double Sunrise".

The Swan River in Perth with its smooth water allowed for take-offs with the heavy weight, the Catalinas barely clearing the bridge at Fremantle. Qantas built a hangar and jetty at Nedlands and Captain Crowther set up the office in Yorkshire House on St. Georges Terrace with the aircrew put up at a hotel on the Perth Esplanade. All wore civilian clothes — Hudson Fysh who visited Nedlands ensured that even with the use of RAAF navigators, this was a Qantas operation. Sometimes this caused the crews to be handed white feathers by members of the public for not joining up.

The first Double Sunrise flight left Perth at 4 am. on 29 June 1943. It was flown by Capt. Russell Tapp who had on

25 April 1931 flown the first airmail from Brisbane to Darwin. To prevent interception by Japanese aircraft, the mid-ocean part of the route was flown at night and the whole flight was in radio silence. For the Qantas crews this was like venturing into Outer Space, with no hope of being found or rescued if an engine failed.

To know their position over the featureless ocean, the RAAF navigators used either dead reckoning or sextant reading of the stars.[23] To find the aircraft's drift, flame flares in metal tubes were dropped from the aircraft which burst on impact with the water into either smoke during the day or flame at night. The drift was measured with a bearing compass. In September, the route was even extended by 1,400 nautical miles, to Karachi, where BOAC would take over.

As the average trip was about 28 hours, wicker hampers with cold chicken, sandwiches and small cakes were carried with tea or coffee in a thermos and soft drinks. Two bunks for the off-duty crew and three chairs were installed in the blister compartment to provide passenger accommodation. There was a small toilet at the rear wall. Without heating or oxygen and flying at 10,000 to 12,000 feet, it was an uncomfortable flight, and everyone kept their thick suits and fur lined flying boots on at night.

Beginning in June 1944, Qantas augmented the Catalinas with two converted Liberators. They flew a shorter 3,077-mile route from Learmouth to Ratmalana airfield outside Colombo, making the journey in 17 hours with 5,500 pounds of payload. Christened the "Kangaroo Service", this was the first time that the now-famous Kangaroo logo was used on a Qantas plane. With more Liberators, the Catalina's days on the Double Sunrise flights ended on 17 July 1945 when the last Qantas Catalina took off from Lake Koggala for Perth. After 271 crossings of the Indian Ocean, without loss, and delivering 648 passengers and 18 tons of mail, the era of the Double Sunrise flights

---

23   Navigating on this route meant that it was necessary to know the stars of both hemispheres, as they flew across the Equator.

ended.[24] As war's end, the five Catalinas were scrapped as per the Lend-Lease Agreement.

The year of 1943 was the beginning of the end for flying boats. With more landplanes and airports available, they lost their air supremacy. The RAAF gave up their Empire flying boats on 13 July 1943 and *Coolangatta* was returned to Qantas. Camouflage paint was removed from the Empire boats in August and, with North Africa retaken, they could once more operate through the Mediterranean (albeit hugging the Libyan coast) rendering the African part of the Horseshoe Route to second place. For all future RAF transport duties, Air Transport Command was established on 25 March 1943. The fear (and accompanying intrigue at Whitehall) that it might also take over BOAC, caused Pearson to resign. That the Command was composed entirely of Douglas Dakotas, Liberators (from the Atlantic Ferry Service) and Avro Yorks, all landplanes for use on the hundreds of wartime airfields around the globe, was an omen. So too were the advent of two aircraft that year: the Avro Lancastrian that the Canadian Government Trans-Atlantic Air Service operated on scheduled flights from Montreal to Prestwick and the first flight of the Lockheed 049 Constellation on 9 January. Both aircraft were proof that, with refueling at Gander and Shannon, the Atlantic Ocean could be crossed — above the weather and soon in pressurized comfort, rendering the commercial flying boat to history.

American Export Airlines (AEA) would continue to use its 2 remaining Vought Sikorsky VS-44s supplementing them with DC-4s in 1944. On 15 August 1947, *Exeter*, bought by a South American airline, crashed on the River Plate off Montevideo. *Excambian* went through several airlines until it was left to rot on a Peruvian beach. For a while, it ignominiously served as a hot dog stand in the U.S. Virgin Islands. Eventually, the VS-44 was restored in 1983 by some of the same men who built it and is now at the New England Air Museum in Windsor Locks, Connecticut.

---

24   The Qantas Catalina Memorial to the Double Sunrise flights at Abrahams Park, Nedlands, Perth, was dedicated in June 1983.

The last year of the war was a tragic time for Pan American. On 8 January, it lost the *China Clipper* the last M-130 with 23 of its occupants killed. On 3 November, the *Honolulu Clipper* was on "Operation Magic Carpet" bringing 26 military personnel home from the Pacific, when it lost power in both starboard engines. The pilots landed it 650 miles east of Oahu shortly before midnight. The tanker *Englewood Hills* found the aircraft and took the passengers off on the morning of 4 November. The passing escort carrier *Manila Bay* sent aircraft engineers to restart the engines but they failed to do so. The carrier then began towing the Clipper but the line broke in heavy seas. The seaplane tender *San Pablo* took over and the tow proceeded slowly until 7 November when the *Honolulu Clipper* hit the side of the *San Pablo*. The collision crushed the airplane's bow and sheared off the starboard wingtip. With salvage proving impossible, the *Honolulu Clipper* was sunk by shelling from the *San Pablo* on 14 November.

As Pan American, now an all landplane airline, did not want the Clippers back, they were turned over to the War Assets Administration. Put up for sale as surplus, they were flown to San Diego for open-air storage. Collectively, they had flown 8,300,000 miles on 3,650 ocean flights, averaging 2,270 miles per flight. In 1946, World Airways bought the *Pacific Clipper,* the *Dixie Clipper,* the *American Clipper* and the *Anzac Clipper.* The *Pacific Clipper* was later sold to Universal Airlines which broke it up for spare parts. All were scrapped by 1950.

The *Capetown Clipper* was sold to American International Airways in 1947. Renamed *The Bermuda Sky Queen* on 14 October 1947, on a flight from Poole to Baltimore with 62 passengers, it was forced down in mid-Atlantic by headwinds. Passengers and crew were rescued but the Clipper was smashed against the side of the Coast Guard rescue cutter USS *Bibb*. A danger to navigation, *The Bermuda Sky Queen* was sunk by shelling.

As to the man who had epitomized the Clipper Era, in 1946, President Harry Truman presented Juan Trippe with the Harmon Aviation Trophy in recognition of Pan American's contributions to the Allied victory. On 27 September 1946,

Trippe was also awarded the Medal for Merit, the highest civilian award in the United States at the time and a forerunner of the Medal of Freedom. Until he retired in 1968, Trippe would proudly display both citations in his office, habitually calling visitors' attention to them.

The unintentional obituary to the transatlantic flying boats appeared in the 28 January 1946 issue of *TIME* Magazine:

> Lumbering Pan American Airways clippers make the New York-to-Lisbon run in 24 flying hours with stops at Bermuda and the Azores. This week one of Pan Am's sleek new Constellations made the New York to Lisbon flight nonstop on a survey hop. Time: 9 hours, 58 minutes. Speed: 344 miles an hour.

J ohn Moore-Brabazon was one of the first to fly a powered aircraft in Britain. To prove that pigs could fly, in 1909, he would carry one aloft in a basket tied to a wing strut of his Short's-built Wright bi-plane. Forty years later, Moore (now First Baron Brabazon of Tara) and the British aviation industry would have recourse to remember that event.

One of the oft-repeated myths in aviation is that, during the Second World War, there was an agreement between Britain and the United States whereby the former would concentrate on building bombers and the latter transport aircraft. This was why, (so the myth went), in 1945 Pan American could inaugurate a Constellation service across the Atlantic while Britain emerged from the war without a commercially viable airliner. The real reason was that the country had never possessed the infrastructure to build its own DC-4 or Constellation. Contemporaries of the Boeing 307 and the Focke Wulf Condor were two British airliners that debuted in 1938 — the underpowered Armstrong Whitworth A.W. 27 Ensign and the De Havilland DH.91 which, while beautiful to look at, with its all-wood construction, was too delicate for operational use. In 1942 Churchill set up a committee to examine future requirements of civil aviation and, hopefully, leapfrog the Americans. Chaired by Brabazon, its first report recommended that, until the national industry caught up, civil versions of military aircraft would plug the postwar gap — the York and Lancastrian from the Lancaster, the Viking from the Wellington and the Sandringham and Solent from the Sunderland.

When the restrictions on commercial aviation were lifted in Britain on 1 January 1946, BOAC's senior management warned that the company "had now to face the problems of becoming a commercial airline and holding its own against rapidly growing international competition". On scheduled 5-day flights to Sydney, BOAC "made do" with Lancastrians joined later by Handley Page Haltons, a derivative of the Halifax bomber. With their 9-passenger capacity, both were money losers, but the prestige value of flights through a dwindling Empire made up for the monetary losses.

On the crucial Atlantic route, competition was fierce. The Avro Tudor, the intended replacement for the Boeing 314s, had been a disappointment, lethally so, killing not only Roy Chadwick, (the designer of the Avro Lancaster) but 80 occupants in the Fairflight crash on 12 March 1950 at Llandow, Wales, the highest loss of lives in aviation then. Nor could the Tudor operate south of Nairobi or east of Calcutta until the runways in those regions were lengthened. Cancelling the Tudor before it killed again put the emphasis on flying boats, except on the Atlantic.

Somehow, at a time when BOAC's initials were said to mean "Bring Over American Cash", the impoverished British government found the foreign exchange to buy three 049 Constellations, putting them on the London-Shannon-Gander-New York route on 1 July 1946. By the second half of 1947, while BOAC made 418 North Atlantic crossings with them, the U.S. airlines (American Overseas Airways, Pan American Airways and Trans World Airways) made 3,104 crossings, and European airlines (Air France, KLM, Scandinavian Airlines System and Sabena) flew a total of 1,012 crossings. As Sir Miles Thomas, a future chairman of BOAC remarked, "It was always a case of jam tomorrow."

British hopes (and resources) for a transatlantic airliner were focused on two gargantuan oddities, the Bristol Brabazon and the Saunders-Roe Princess — the mindset that had guided Imperial Airways in the 1930s — the philosophy of upper-class air travel where comfort and luxury for the few were more important than speed and payload for the many, having survived the war. The Bristol Brabazon made its first flight on 1 September 1949 (proving that pigs could fly?) but without interest from BOAC, would be broken up in 1953. The BOAC Chairman, Lord Knollys, who had toured India and Australia in 1944, stated in February 1946 what everyone knew, that, away from the Atlantic, flying boats would soldier on for "two or three years". The airline's war-weary *Hythe* class Sunderlands with their camouflage and bench-type seating, would not be missed. The shape of things to come was launched at Rochester in November 1945. To cater to the postwar commercial market, a Sunderland, G-AGKX, was modified with a faired nose and tail cone and as a Sandringham 1 was christened *Himalaya*. With seats instead of benches, it could accommodate 24-day and 16-night passengers. There would be seven marks of Sandringhams built. Beginning on 2 May 1947, BOAC would acquire nine in the *Plymouth* Class, all bearing names of British seaboard towns like *Portland, Pembroke, Poole* etc The Argentinian shipping owner, Alberto Dodero, who had made a fortune during the war, bought four Sandringhams fitted with Pratt & Whitney Twin Wasp engines. Five in a 37-passenger version were sold to DNL-Norwegian airlines for its Oslo-Tromso route above the Arctic Circle. On the way to Tromso, its passengers were able to see two wartime reminders — the now rebuilt town of Bodø and the upturned German battleship *Tirpitz*.

The other customers were Qantas which, took five from BOAC in 1950 for destinations in New Caledonia, New Hebrides, Fiji, New Guinea, and Lord Howe Island. Having been isolated during the war and now responsible for the Cook Islands and Western Samoa, New Zealand was a good customer for flying boats. Four Sandringhams were ordered by TEAL in 1946 and when the Solents arrived, two of them were sold to Qantas which later resold them to Ansett Flying Boat Services when it took over the Sydney-Lord Howe service.

The return of civil flying boats on the Empire routes began on 1 February 1946, when BOAC's *Hythe* made a route survey flight from Poole to Australia, New Zealand, Hong Kong, Shanghai, and Tokyo. On 12 May, the first joint BOAC/Qantas flying boat service from Britain to Australia began, taking five days. The "Dragon Service" to Hong Kong followed on 1 August (where the first air hostesses were employed on flying boats). On 30 September, flown by Capt. Dudley Travers, *Golden Hind* the remaining "G-class" S.26, inaugurated the service to Cairo via Augusta.

Alan McGregor was an aviation journalist and chose to fly on one of the last BOAC flying boats from Cairo To Southampton: "In mid-1946 I flew from London to Cairo aboard a twin-engine BOAC Dakota-class DC-3, a journey of almost 19 hours with refueling stops at Marignane (near Marseilles), Malta (with crew change) and El Adam. My return flight, however, was altogether more comfortable. In Cairo I met several people who praised BOAC'S flying boat service, and I learned that it would soon be discontinued. Not to miss my chance, I booked a 'flying boat' flight home, where a final rail connection would take me from Southampton Water to London.

"The Cairo check-in was for a civilized 0900 hours at the Air Booking Center, which lay across from the Egyptian Museum on Midan Ismailia (now Midan Tahrir). From there it was but a few minutes bus ride to Rod el Farag, below Bulak bridge on the Nile, where the Sunderland flying boat was moored close to the S.S. *Puritan*, a stern-wheeled Nile steamer that served as a 38-cabin floating hotel for transiting passengers traveling to and from points farther east. It was these passengers who were first to pass through customs, and to be conveyed by launch to the waiting flying boat. I could see that the crew was proceeding with pre-flight checks.

"On boarding through a low doorway, curved up at the top, the first impression was of relative spaciousness. Along a gently rising, carpeted corridor, the fuselage was divided into cabins, each seating four people facing each other, much like a European train compartment. There was ample breadth and leg room. I was shown to a cabin already occupied by three Burmese ladies who spoke almost perfect British English.

"One by one, the four supercharged Bristol Pegasus engines started up. As the craft gathered speed, the Burmese ladies startled me by suddenly and simultaneously drawing over their heads the outer layer of their copious garments. They remained thus as the aircraft surged forward under full take-off power, the high wave thrown up by its bows completely covering the cabin portholes. As a passenger remarked: 'The rise of a flying boat resembles all that (an amusement park) just fails to achieve.' Then we lifted clear of the water, and the three ladies, obviously seasoned travelers, immediately uncovered their heads and rearranged their dress.

"We followed the Nile, then turned northwest, crossed the coast, and headed out over the Mediterranean toward Crete. In late afternoon, we landed in the wide bay at Augusta, Sicily. A launch took us ashore, where a bus brought us to the BOAC rest-house — a former Italian naval barracks — a short distance along the coast. After dinner, I took a digestive stroll on the road by the rocky shore. Then to bed, lulled by the sound of the waves. I was awakened at 0700 hours by a steward's knock at the door; he also brought a cup of tea. There was time for an unhurried breakfast before the bus returned us to the harbor for embarkation. (On take-off the ladies from Burma repeated their head-covering maneuver.) A good tailwind made the refueling stop at Marignane unnecessary. We reached Southampton Water by mid-afternoon.

"The two-day trip, with regular meals, reading and sleep, wafted along at 311 kph (200 mph), was a real rest cure. Crammed nowadays into seat 56C or somewhere in the "serried rows" of 21st-century economy class, I remember it very fondly indeed."

The final transatlantic flight by a BOAC Boeing 314 took place on 7 March 1946. That it carried 55 passengers demonstrated its necessity. A thrice-weekly Bermuda to Baltimore service continued until January 1948 when *Bristol* made its last flight and the BOAC Darrell's Island base at Bermuda closed. In their six years, *Bangor, Berwick,* and *Bristol,* had flown a total of 4,258,876 miles, made 596 Atlantic crossings and carried 40,042 passengers without mishap. As with the Pan American Clippers, all three were bought by World Airways and scrapped. What had killed them off were the U.S. Navy's "See Bees" and

U.S. Army Corps of Engineers, the construction battalions that built thousands of hardened runways in the Pacific, South America, Europe, and Asia.

The country suffering severe food rationing and an Arctic winter in 1946-47, the original Empire flying boats went to their dismemberment without attention. They had dodged hippos on African rivers, hidden in funk holes from Zeroes and survived 'poor errors of judgement' on the part of their pilots — only to fall to the wrecking axes and oxyacetylene torches of R. J. Coley & Sons. All former Imperial Airways Empire flying boats were withdrawn from service at the end of 1946, to be recalled to Hythe and ignominiously cut up: *Cleopatra* with 10,513 hrs on the log on 4 November 1946, *Canopus* the first one launched (15,026 hrs) on 12 November 1946, *Cameronian* (15,652 hrs) on 13 January 1947, *Cambria* (13,892 hrs) on 15 January 1947, *Carpentaria* (14,989 hrs) on 19 January 1947, *Corsair* (13,262 hrs) on 20 January 1947, *Cooee* (10,628 hrs) on 2 February 1947, *Castor* (15,789 hrs) on 4 February 1947, *Cordelia* (11,665 hrs) on 5 February 1947, *Coorong* (12,472 hrs) on 10 February 1947, *Cathay* (6,683 hrs) on 9 March 1947 and *Champion* (12,013 hrs) on 16 March 1947.

The Horseshoe Route that had circumvented the Axis, lasted 6 years, 37 weeks and 5 days. It ended on 12 March 1947 when Capt. Peter Horne brought *Caledonia* from Durban to Southampton. Towed to Hythe, *Caledonia* (15,143 hrs) was scrapped on 23 March 1947. Still with QEA, *Coriolanus,* the aircraft that had begun author Alexander Frater's love for flying boats was withdrawn from service in December 1947 and scrapped at Rose Bay.

By continuing to fly for BOAC until 21 September, *Golden Hind* escaped Coley's axes, ending her days stored at Rochester where she had been built. Bought by Buchan Marine Services of Dorset, in October 1953, like Turner's *The Fighting Temeraire,* she was towed down the Thames, only to founder in a storm at Harty Ferry on the Swale Estuary in August 1954. As if completing the circle, *Golden Hind* went down not far from where the Short brothers, Horace,

Eustace, and Oswald first tested their aircraft and where Brabazon had airlifted a pig. Rather than being melted down to make cutlery, *Cathay* was offered to the Science Museum in London, for preservation as part of the National Aeronautical Collection. But as the Museum had lost a third of its display accommodation in the bombing during the war, it had no space available and the offer was declined.

The Empire flying boats had spanned a dozen years from Arthur Gouge's drawing board to the scrapping of the last in December 1947. The total distance flown by them during their service lives exceeded 33.26 million nautical miles. They had experienced events in places around the world, especially in the war years, that, in 1934 their designers on the Medway could never have dreamed of. Their role had been to keep the Empire together by communication and they had fulfilled it.

If there is any memorial to them, it is where some corner of a foreign field is forever Short's. *Caribou* and *Cabot* are at the bottom of Norwegian fiords, *Corinthian* buried somewhere in Darwin's harbor as is *Cygnus* at Brindisi's. The broken hulls of *Cassiopeia* and *Challenger* lie outside Sabang Harbor and Mozambique Island. What is left of *Corio* is at the mouth of the Noelmini river, near Koepang. Shot down with its crew of four and thirty passengers, *Circe* is somewhere between Tijlatjap and Broome. The mass graveyard of flying boats is Broome where *Centaurus* and *Corinna* lie. Pericles' funeral oration could have been written for them: "...in foreign lands there dwells an unwritten memorial of them, graven not on stone but in the hearts of men."

In 1901, Sam Saunders opened a workshop at Cowes in the derelict Columbine shipyard to build boats for wealthy sailing enthusiasts. His unique *Consuta* plywood hulls, sewn together by copper wire had, by 1912, attracted the attention of Thomas Sopwith for his flying boats. Aviation was a sideline for the company until the First World War when A. V. Roe contracted it to build Avro 514 trainers and Short 184 seaplanes. Postwar, boatbuilding was sent to Beaumaris, Anglesey and to attract orders from Imperial Airways, or the RAF, Saunders designed and built its own flying boats at Cowes. The *Consuta* wooden hulls were outdated by 1928, and to invest in it, Sir Alliot Verdon (A V) Roe took over the company. Renamed Saunders-Roe (or SARO) it began building metal-hulled flying boats. A party from Saunders-Roe toured the Dornier Do X when it arrived at Southampton Water in August 1930, and its size and solidity must have impressed them. The company built the Columbine hangar in 1936 for its A.27 London flying boat. It was bought by the RAF, but its next aircraft the A.36 Lerwick was so unstable in-flight that of the 21 built, 11 were lost in accidents.

Saunders-Roe's initial wartime contribution was building Supermarine Walruses and repairing Catalinas. It might have disappeared into British aviation history (like the Boulton Paul, Folland, Miles or Percival companies), had not Sir Arthur Gouge become Chief Executive and Vice-Chairman in 1943. Floatplane fighter aircraft had long been used by the Allies and the Axis alike, but they were slow, unwieldy, and stood awkwardly high off the water for the propeller. Henry Fowler, the chief designer at Saunders-Roe, and Gouge, would aim for the unconventional by designing the first jet-powered flying boat. Entirely of metal construction, the SR.A1 had a pressurized cockpit and one of the earliest Martin Baker ejection seats. Its two Metropolitan-Vickers F.2/4 Beryl turbojet engines were the byproduct of that company's collaboration on the Gloster Meteor. The world's first jet fighter flying boat was intended for operation from sheltered or inland waters, its jet engines giving it a low profile, allowing it to ambush the enemy. The engine's oval shaped intake had an extendable lip to overcome any water ingestion. At a time when American forces were suffering heavy casualties in the Pacific, dislodging the Japanese island by island, the SR.A/1 (called the "Squirt" by the workforce) was marketed as a "guerrilla fighter". With drop tanks, it would have excellent endurance, making it independent of aircraft carriers or land bases. Three of the snout nosed slab-sided seaplanes were built in parts at Beaumaris and assembled at Cowes. The war ended before the "guerrilla" idea could be pursued (although it was revisited in the Korean War), which was fortunate as early jet engines like the Metropolitan-Vickers F.2 proved unreliable in operation.

Geoffrey Tyson would have been Hollywood's (or Ealing Studios') idea of a test pilot. A former barnstormer, in August 1939 he had piloted the Harrow tanker that had refueled *Caribou* and *Cabot* for Cobham's in-flight refueling company. Although a civilian, he had been on bombing raids to see how well the Short Stirling worked. In 1945, Tyson succeeded Short's legendary John Lankester Parker as SARO's chief test pilot. He taxied TG263, the first SR.A/1 on July 16, 1947 and finding everything in order, took it off the water. He also demonstrated the flying boat jet at the Festival of Britain in June 1951, somehow landing and taking off from a crowded Thames at Woolwich Reach, from where it was towed to be displayed before the Festival Hall. Undoubtedly his greatest triumph (and typical of a barnstormer) would be at the 1951 SBAC Farnborough Airshow where he flew it — inverted! Of the other two SR.A/1s, one crashed at Felixstowe, killing its pilot and the other was lost when the test pilot Eric "Winkle" Brown hit a submerged log on landing. Tyson saw what happened and dived in the water to save Brown. The aircraft sank in the Medina and has never been found.

The Squirt was far ahead of its time — the Convair F2Y Sea Dart would not fly until 1953 — but Gouge's mind was on something closer to his heart. In 1944, the Air Ministry asked Short's and Saunders-Roe to collaborate on a replacement for the Sunderland. The resulting Short Shetland, later configured to a 70 seat commercial aircraft, was less than successful — only two were built but it led Gouge and Henry Fowler to consider designing an exceptionally large flying boat to cross the Atlantic.

Enter Reginald Fletcher, 1st Baron Winster, minister for civil aviation for all of 14 months, from 4 August 1945 to 4 October 1946. The recently elected Labour government was grappling with far reaching social programs and wanting to support British industry, Winster announced that there would

The Saunders-Roe SR.A/1 was a prototype flying boat fighter aircraft. It was the first jet-propelled water-based aircraft in the world.

be a great future for giant flying boats in the post-war world. In 1945, he was not alone in thinking this. In the United States, Howard Hughes had built the *Spruce Goose* and Glenn L. Martin had fulfilled his preoccupation for big flying boats with the Martin Mars family.

Science and technology were especially prominent in the Labour government's socialist programs. Britain might be losing its empire but, as a maritime nation, it still excelled in boats — flying boats. To pay for the SR.45s, the old justifications must have been dusted off, i.e. seventy percent of the Earth's surface is water and a flying boat could land anywhere if it was in trouble, the bigger the hull the better the payload and stability — and the former Imperial Airways bases were already in place. As Southampton was now thought to be too crowded for a giant flying boat, the Portsmouth City Council presented its prewar Langstone Harbor proposal for a futuristic seadrome. For a country crushed by austerity and gloom, the Brabazon, Princess and the Squirt must have been, to borrow the Festival's motto, "A Tonic for Britain."

In cooperation with the Ministry of Supply, on 12 April 1946, Winster placed a £2.8 million order for three SR.45s, (later called Princesses) on behalf of BOAC. The flying boats were for the transatlantic route, their passengers enjoying sleeping berths and lounge/bars, both in First Class and Tourist. Saunders-Roe, a relatively small company, was now committed to finding the space at its Columbine hangar, recruiting, and training enough personnel and — because of a lack of foreign exchange — making this an all-British project. That Capt. H. Alger, the veteran of Imperial Airways, was put in charge of BOAC's Princess unit gave Gouge encouragement. Whether as a reward or punishment, in October the prime minister sent Winster off to be Governor of Cyprus.

It was said of Isambard Kingdom Brunel that the *Great Eastern* the largest ship ever built until then, was both his crowning glory and ultimate downfall. So too, it was, for Sir Arthur Gouge and the SARO Princesses. As he had for his other creations at Rochester, Gouge meticulously built wooden models of the Princess, followed by a mock-up for wind tunnel testing, sending it to Farnborough. The biggest all-metal flying boat ever built was a forerunner of airliners to come. Pressurized, it had a rudimentary "fly-by-wire" control system and lightweight fiberglass in thermal and sound insulation. At a time when the Constellation crammed 62 passengers in serried seats, the Princess took 105 comfortably in two decks. Its low-drag hull bottom and retractable wingtip floats gave it a credible speed.

Ten Bristol turboprop engines would drive six sets of four-bladed propellers which were 16ft. 6 in. in diameter. The two outermost engines each drove a single propeller and were used for maneuvering the behemoth on water. The inboard eight called "Coupled Proteus", were mounted in pairs to drive four sets of contra-rotating propellers through a complex gearbox in opposite directions. The total power of the 10 engines was 30,000 hp and they were so complex that it required two flight engineers to monitor them.

Named for the Greek god Proteus who could change his shape to hide from his enemies, in later marks, the Bristol Proteus

The ten-engined Saunders-Roe SR.45 Princess was the largest
all-metal flying boat ever built.

engine would go on to power the Bristol Britannia and Donald Campbell's *Bluebird* racer but at this stage in its evolution, it was fraught with so many chronic problems that they delayed the Princess's first flight until BOAC and the aviation world had lost interest in it.

The political buzzword "optics" had not been invented yet but in the hard, grey years of austerity that Prime Minister

Saunders-Roe SR.45 Princess

Length: 148 ft.
Wingspan with floats down: 209 ft 6 in.
Wing area: 5,019 sq. ft.
Height 55: ft. 9 in.
All up weight: 330,000 lbs.
Speed: 360 mph at 34,500 ft altitude.
Range with 20,000 lbs. payload: 5,000 nautical miles.

Clement Attlee's government found itself in, the Brabazon and the Princesses were the wrong ones. Both projects had been bequeathed to them by the previous government which lost no opportunity to criticize while in opposition — Churchill's cheap jibe of Attlee as "a modest man with much to be modest about", was typical. As early as the autumn of 1947, the Labour government and BOAC began distancing themselves from both anomalies. Undaunted, even before the Princess flew, Henry Knowler would design the sweptwing Duchess, a jet-powered sweptwing flying boat with 6 DH Ghost jet engines and a 74-passenger capacity. Closer to science fiction than the realities of postwar Britain, it never got past the drawing board.

When Tyson did fly the Princess G-ALUN for the first time on 22 August 1952, BOAC's DH Comet G-ALYP had already inaugurated commercial jet service from London to Johannesburg on 2 May. The Jet Age was already four months old and the David Lean movie *Breaking the Sound Barrier* (with screenplay by Terrence Rattigan) had been released to celebrate the technological achievement. Movie audiences gasped at Nigel Patrick and Ann Todd flying a jet aircraft together (without refueling!) from London nonstop to Cairo. Sir Miles Thomas, who had been on the BOAC flight to Johannesburg, also witnessed the Princess taking off at Cowes. In his opinion, shared no doubt by the public, technically out of date, the giant flying boat had become a dinosaur.

The 1952 Farnborough Air Show is remembered more for the death of test pilot, John Derry, when, after breaking the sound barrier, his DH.110 crashed and killed 29 spectators, than by the flyby of the SARO Princess. Tyson took the Princess over the airfield, even doing a vertical bank with it that might have ended in disaster. It was later discovered that the flight control systems had jammed preventing him from rolling back upright. Although the Princess did a fly past once more at the 1953 Farnborough air show, it did not elicit any customers. It was offered to the RAF for trooping flights but with Britain closing bases, was turned down. Aquila Airways wanted to buy it on condition it be given access to some of BOAC's routes, but the government refused. The American Space program briefly considered buying the Princess to carry Saturn V rockets from Huntsville, Alabama, to Cape Canaveral, Florida. The U.S. Navy thought of having Convair re-power the boats with experimental nuclear reactors. Nothing came of these ideas. As happened to Brunel's *Great Eastern*, the SARO Princess had outlived its time.

Pirates had robbed ships for centuries, but the first aerial hijacking of a flying boat, indeed of any aircraft, was historic. The Bretton Woods Agreement prevented the British colony of Hong Kong from dealing in gold, but its neighbor Portuguese Macau, could. In 1948 Chiang Kai-Shek was fighting the Communists and to finance this, Chinese from all over the world were sending him gold. Cathay Pacific Airlines was just beginning and seized the opportunity to transport the bullion that came into Hong Kong to Macau. As Macau did not have an airport, at first the gold was dumped out of its DC-3 above the racetrack — which even the Portuguese authorities could not ignore. The airline then bought two PBY Catalinas from the United States Air Force Federal Liquidation Commission in Manila, in 1948, and chartered them to a dummy company called Macao Air Transport Company (MATCO). Twice daily a MATCO flying boat would leave Kai Tak for Macau with no questions asked about what was onboard. Everyone in the colony knew that its passengers were mainly local Chinese millionaires carrying gold on their persons to be laundered in Macau. The other MATCO Catalina flew for Macau's Banco Nacional Ultramarino taking the gold bullion to Saigon. Not for nothing were Cathay Pacific's original owners called "Syd's Pirates" named for its founder Syd de Kantzow who had flown for CNAC.

On the evening of July 16, *Miss Macao* the Catalina VR- HDT took off from Kai Tak. Dale Cramer was captain, Ken McDuff first officer and Delca da Costa the air hostess. There were 23 passengers onboard and 4 (it was later revealed) had fortunes in gold and dollars on their persons. When the aircraft did not arrive at Macau, the RAF sent its Sunderlands to search for it. The SS *Merry Moller*, a steamer on the Hong Kong to Macau run, found some wreckage the next day and a survivor, Wong Yu, washed up on the Macau shore. He would later confess that the plan had been for the three hijackers to hold up the plane, force it to land somewhere and rob the passengers. The millionaires could then be held on a remote island by relatives of the pirates and ransomed. Wong, the survivor, was a 24-year-old rice farmer who had been brought into the plot because of his detailed knowledge of the coastline where a hijacked Catalina might be hidden. One hijacker had even learned to fly Catalinas in Manila.

The four air pirates boarded *Miss Macao* with concealed handguns, two making sure they sat behind the pilots. Seven minutes after take-off they struck — one covered McDuff while the second demanded Cramer hand over the controls to him. Cramer, an ex-US Navy pilot, refused to move and McDuff hit one of the hijackers with a mooring flag. Then, according to

Wong, panic ensued in the confined space. The passengers intervened and tackled the hijackers. Cramer was shot in the head and slumped over the controls, sending the aircraft into an unrecoverable dive. With all that gold, the Catalina sank fast. All onboard were killed except Wong who managed to get out. Air piracy was so unknown then that there were no laws that covered it and neither the British nor Portuguese knew what to do with Wong. He was expediently put over the border to Communist China where the government detested planes being hijacked — too many of theirs had been lost that way — and it was rumored that he was executed in a contrived accident. *Miss Macao* would be the only flying boat ever hijacked.

By February 1949, BOAC had finally begun to shake off its wartime improvisations with the purchase of Boeing Stratocruisers and Canadair Argonauts. The Stratocruisers were put on the Atlantic run where, competing with so many other airlines, BOAC continued the tradition of catering to the wealthy. The premier Monarch service on them was extolled as "a roomy flying hotel with luxurious dressing rooms, comfortable armchairs, sleeper berths with breakfast in bed, and a spiral staircase leading down to the club-like atmosphere of a bar and lounge."

The Seaford, a modification of the Sunderland Mk.1V, had been designed for Far East service when the war ended. With the Seaford jigs available at Rochester, in what was a final attempt to interest the airlines, Shorts used them to build the Solent. The first was launched on 11 November 1946 and the last on 8 April 1948 — the last flying boat to be built at the historic Seaplane Works at Rochester. The Ministry of Civil Aviation ordered a dozen Solent 2s in 1949 for BOAC. Powered by four 1,690 hp Bristol Hercules engines, they were named for places (*Sark, Severn, Scapa, Somerset, Southampton* etc). Later, some would be renamed for British cities. (*London, Cardiff, Salisbury* etc.) Of the 12 Solents, the airline lost one on 1 February 1950 on Southampton Water when a gust caused it to lift on landing. There were no fatalities.

The BOAC Solents had three lower deck cabins each with six seats facing across tables and two seats on the starboard side. A promenade deck followed with steps to the starboard side entrance door. Then followed the two lavatories and the baggage and cargo hold. The cabins could be fitted for 24 passengers with day and night accommodation or 36-day passengers. There were rectangular windows except at the promenade area where they were vertical. A lounge and a 12-seat cabin were on the upper deck. The flight crew were two pilots, a navigator, a radio operator, and the flight engineer in a separate compartment (behind the flight deck opposite crew rest berths). There were two stewards to attend to the passengers. The airline advertised flying on its Solents as "On the Wings of Luxury". As flying boats and luxury ones at that, they symbolized a world which in 1949 was fast disappearing. Even Juan Trippe, who had brought Cunard comfort to aviation, was already planning low-cost transportation on a worldwide scale for Pan American. Flying had become democratized, with luxury travel the exception rather than the norm. The Age of Mass Mobility was about to dawn.

The New Zealand airline TEAL commissioned Shorts (Belfast) in 1949 to build four Solent 4s to replace its Sandringhams. These had a 2,540-gallon fuel capacity giving them a range of 3,000 miles compared with the BOAC's Solent's fuel capacity of 1,400 gallons which gave them 1,990 miles. The flagship *Aotearoa II* was christened by HRH. Princess Elizabeth at Belfast on the 26 May 1949. Its royal connection would continue in 1953 when Queen Elizabeth II and the Duke of Edinburgh would make Her Majesty's only flight in a flying boat aboard *Aotearoa II* on 19 December, boarding at Fiji. On 27 June 1954, the final trans-Tasman flying boat flight from Auckland to Sydney would take place, TEAL keeping the last Solent in service between Suva and Papeete. This too ended on 15 September 1960, closing an era of commercial flying boat operations in the South Pacific.

Waiting for its Handley Page Hermes and getting rid of the Yorks, BOAC put the Solents on the African route from Southampton

This Short S.45A Solent Mk 4, ZK-AMO, *Aranui*, is preserved at the
Museum of Transport and Technology, Auckland, New Zealand.

to The Vaal dam, (Johannesburg) on 4 May 1948. Called the
Springbok Route, it was Southampton-Augusta (Sicily)-Cairo-
Luxor-Khartoum-Port Bell-Victoria Falls-Vaal dam. This was
trialed on 2 December 1947 by G-AHIT *Severn* with Olive Marshall
as the stewardess. The flying boats now landed at Lake Vaaldam,
68 miles from Johannesburg and not Durban. The Vaal Dam was
chosen as a flying-boat station, according to a BOAC newsletter
from the time because: "With a useable area of approximately 90
square miles, and alighting areas varying from 11,000 to 20,000
feet in length, Vaaldam now makes an ideal flying boat station. It
is almost unheard of for flying conditions to be suspended owing
to severe weather." After taking off from the lake, the Solents
flew to Victoria Falls, a popular tourist attraction, landing on the
Zambezi. Station engineer, S. Kempson, described what it was
like seeing one of the flying boats coming in to land: "It circled
Victoria Falls at 14.08 hours and in a few moments was orbiting
the alighting area, four-and-a-half miles above the cataracts.
Approaching from low above Kandahar Island, the aircraft
lost height with superb grace, and scudding swiftly across

the waters of the Zambesi, completed a perfect touchdown. She taxied easily towards the mooring-buoy and tied up in seconds."

That the BOAC Solent flew over Nyasaland (now Malawi) played an important part in its last adventure. Sir Miles Thomas had been, until June 1949, the Chairman of the Colonial Development Office. There was little transport in the tiny mineral-poor, landlocked Nyasaland — no railroad link with Rhodesia and what roads there were washed out in rainy season. The only flying boat to land on Lake Malawi had been Alan Cobham's Short Singapore in 1928. The only airfield was at Monkey Bay and it was barely adequate for the East African Airways Corporation DH.89 Dominie — the luggage was weighed on the bathroom scales from the local hotel and stuffed into its rear.

After lobbying by Sir Geoffrey Colby, the Governor of Nyasaland, Thomas agreed to lend a Hythe flying boat (later replaced by a Solent) to "Operation Ploughshares", the moving of 117 tons of agricultural equipment from Lindi (now in Tanzania) to Nkhata Bay on Lake Malawi. The BOAC crews involved in the ferrying stayed at Cape MacLear which had been named by Dr. Livingstone in 1859 for his friend the Royal Astronomer Thomas Maclear. Once the tractor tires and rakes had been delivered, Thomas made Cape MacLear a regular if temporary stop on the route. The first Solent touched down at Cape MacLear on 7 October 1949 with 28 passengers, all of whom somehow managed to find overnight accommodation in the surrounding area. Suddenly, to be able to fly from Lake Malawi to England or South Africa was a boon to expatriates and locals alike. The Governor's ambition was for a scheduled flying boat service that would bring in tourists as a source of revenue and he arranged for a model of the flying boat to be placed in the window of the Nyasaland office in London.

All who made use of the BOAC Solent flights from Cape MacLear considered themselves fortunate to do so and when interviewed some fifty years later, their recollections of this unexpected bounty were clear. One remembered the flight in detail, especially the stop at Augusta where, if Stromboli was erupting, the captain would detour "circling round the belching volcano, then banking right over the top of it, so that passengers could see into the crater and watch the fountains of bright red lava being spewed up." Then they would fly along the North African coast to Alexandria for a lunch stop at Luxor, for the night, where they could tour the ruins, then Khartoum for lunch where, due to the intense heat, the flying boat was draped in red blankets. Port Bell, Entebbe followed for the night and Cape MacLear on the fourth day."

Another wrote: "The sheer thrill of take-off has left an effervescence with me that will always be associated with the Solent. It was the surging translation of the noise of the accelerating engines into the white spume on either side, right up to the sudden silence of the hill as the takeoff took place — the quiet after the crescendo. Unforgettable!"

"The landings and take-offs were quite thrilling actually" remembered one. "You couldn't see a thing but rushing water until the bows began to lift off. The take-offs and descents were spectacular — much more exciting than a landplane. You could watch the wing floats rising and finally leaving the water on take-off."

In July 1950, when Thomas accepted the second DH Comet prototype for BOAC crew training, the end of the airline's flying boat days was quick to come. The future was in speed with landplanes spanning whole continents and no longer stopping for leisurely lunches on the river. The last Solent called at Cape MacLear on 30 October and on 7 November the final one left Valdaam, overflying Cape MacLear, to arrive at Southampton on the 10th. The airline replaced the flying boats on the African routes with Handley Page Hermes and the Nyasaland passengers resigned themselves to once more being packed into the Dominie.

Former RAF Wing Commander Barry T. Aikman bought BOAC's Hythes in 1948, putting them on the lucrative Berlin Airlift, the genesis of many struggling British airlines. With the flight paths to Tempelhof and Gatow airports packed with endless lines of C-47s and C-54s, the flying boats were ideal to pick up supplies from the former Blohm and Voss yard at Finkenwereder on the River Elbe and land at Havel on the outskirts of the besieged city. When the airlift ended, with still more Hythes available at bargain prices, Aikman began Aquila Airways for charter flights. They took vacationers from Falmouth to the Scilly Isles and seamen from Hull to Aden. The longest flight undertaken by Aquila Airways was when the Falklands Island Company chartered G-AGJN *Hudson* for a survey trial run. The aircraft left Southampton on 21 April 1952 and with a full crew, including air hostess Veronica Mills, reached Port Stanley on 28 April 1952, via Lisbon-Madeira-Cape Verde-Natal-Rio de Janiero-Montevideo. It brought the first airmail to the islands. In 1978, a commemorative stamp was issued depicting the *Hudson* moored at Port Stanley. After that, floatplane flights to Port Stanley from Comodoro Rivadavia, Argentina would begin.

Aikman then replace the Hythes with Solents from BOAC and TEAL, for charters to Funchal, Madeira Island and Las Palmas, in the Canary Islands. Madeira was popular with British tourists who stayed at Reid's Hotel and Aquila Airways was the island's only air connection — an airport would not be built here until 1964. For Aquila Airways, these were its golden years with two weekly shuttle flights begun. The airline's offices opened at No. 1 Great Cumberland Place, London W1 and maintenance was set up at Hamble. Once more passengers were brought by train from Waterloo — where they were weighed (the limits were 75 kilos for males and 65 kilos for females) and visas added to their passports. For those who drove, arrangements were made to garage their cars either in London or Southampton. As the flying boat left Southampton at 8 pm, and later, local airline staff had all day to prepare, including picking up the bonded alcohol from Hamble and the latest newspapers from W. H. Smith's. There were some benefits to being the only flying boat airline now, as Aquila Airways got to use the former BOAC Marine Air Terminal at Berth 50. When Lisbon was added to the itinerary, Aquila Airways was the sole beneficiary of its new Marine Terminal at Cabo Ruivo where the jetty remains today for oil tankers. Released from its pontoon at Berth 50, the departing Solent would follow the "control-tower" launch, on a long taxi down Southampton Water, past the ocean liners blazing with lights to Netley where the temporary runway lights had been set up. With the flying boat pitching and rolling at such a low speed, the passengers would experience the first signs of seasickness. An old Aquila Airways skipper used to quip that a flying boat was, "the only place on earth where you could be airsick, seasick and homesick at the same time." The Solent would alight on the Tagus at dawn at Lisbon and the bleary-eyed, deafened passengers were taken ashore for a hearty breakfast — there still being food rationing in Britain.

Churchill was a passenger on Aquila Airways (as were Dennis and Margaret Thatcher on their honeymoon), visiting Madeira to rest, write and paint at Cape Funchal. While he was there, Attlee called a snap election in early 1950 and he returned home to fight it. He and his party boarded the Hythe *Hampshire* on 12 January with Capt. Andrew Evans in command for the nine-hour flight home. The crew reported that the former prime minister (now a national treasure) ate a hearty breakfast, had lunch, enjoyed his cigars, and slept. Thick fog over Southampton cleared just in time to prevent them diverting to the RAF base at Pembroke Dock. Churchill arrived at Berth 50, looking very refreshed. Unfortunately, he lost the General Election to Attlee once more — but this time with a greatly reduced margin.

The actor Brian Rix needed a holiday in 1952 and choosing Madeira, discovered he would have to take an Aquila Airways flying boat from Southampton to get there. "After several abortive starts" he wrote, "because icing on the wings prevented the plane from taking off, the journey began seven hours late, by which time the passengers were beginning to wonder why they had come. The Sunderland (sic) lumbered through the skies at about two hundred knots and at an altitude of seven thousand feet. Not exactly speedy and not exactly comfortable to the old ears. Further, the flight to Madeira took eight hours, so one had to suffer the discomfort for a long time. All right I suppose, if you were warmly clad in flying boots and jacket, with the adrenaline pumping as you chased Nazi submarines, but not so good for peacetime passengers." Rix concluded with understandable pride, that he was the only one not to need the sick bags "so thoughtfully provided by the airline."

The airline took several celebrities to Madeira and once the complete cast and film crew of a movie. When John Huston directed the movie *Moby Dick* in 1956, the islands were chosen because there were still whalers living there who could train the actors Gregory Peck, Richard Basehart and Orson Welles to harpoon whales. The flying boat also brought in a rubber whale made by Dunlop and buoyed with compressed air, it filled in for the actual White Whale.

In August 1956, when Egyptian President Nasser nationalized the Suez Canal, Britain evacuated all British subjects working or living along the Canal. There was a former British Armed Forces Club on the Great Bitter Lakes called "The Vic Lido" with a jetty that went out to an old shipwreck. The Egyptian government allowed the women and children to leave and on 14 August, in what would be known as "Operation Nursery", Aquila Airlines' Solent flying boats came alongside the jetty to fly them to Malta and later to Southampton. The men (471 of them) were taken to the civilian jail in Cairo where, when the British and French forces landed, they were traded for 471 Egyptians. The following month, on 26 September 1956 one of the Aquila Airways Solents G-ANAJ used in the operation was destroyed in a violent storm at the Italian resort of Santa Margherita.

But with more landplanes and airports available and the lack of spare parts for its flying boats, Aquila Airways was teetering towards bankruptcy. What occurred on 15 November 1957 would put it out of its misery. The Solent G-AKNU with a crew of 8 and 50 passengers took off from Southampton at about 10.46 pm for Las Palmas. Soon after takeoff, No. 4 engine stopped to be followed by No. 3. The captain radioed that he was going to return but with the loss of two engines. The flying boat banked out of control over the Isle of Wight and hit the face of a disused chalk pit near Chessell. Forty-three passengers and crew died in the crash and two later in hospital. Among them were three honeymoon couples and an eight-year-old girl. Soldiers from nearby Golden Hill Fort were on a night map reading exercise that night and assisted the overwhelmed local rescue services that had rushed to the scene. Together they saved 14 people. Three of the military were later decorated for repeatedly entering the burning wreckage to rescue survivors. The author J B Priestley was among those who came to the crash site. The enquiry by the Accident Investigationboard suggested that an attempt to deal with the failure of No. 4 engine may have led to a possible error by the crew and the turning off of a cut-off actuator, thus causing the No. 3 engine to also fail. However, before 'black boxes' there was no real evidence to support this and the Board's conclusion was "cause unknown."

Commercial operations by flying boat in Britain ended on 30 September 1958 when Aquila Airlines closed down. Two of the Solents were sold to Artop in Portugal, but they sat abandoned on the shores of the Tagus for years until scrapped.

Sir Arthur Gouge's dream — the SARO Princess, would make its last flight on 27 May 1954, to be brought ashore later for cocooning at West Cowes, like an unwanted Christmas present. The two unfinished airframes were cocooned at the old RAF base at Calshot. When Saunders-Roe began building helicopters in 1959, Gouge retired. His Princesses would outlive him, but only just. In 1967, G-ALUN, the only Princess to fly, would be towed to Southampton to be scrapped, the other two having done so three years before, all three generating a sad total of £18,000 in scrap value.

The only aim of air transport from now on was to get the traveler to his destination quickly and safely. When compared with a flying boat, modern aircraft, (all composite plastic and computer terabytes), are underwhelming. One cannot imagine, at an airport today, Postmaster Jim Farley announcing, "Captain Musick, you have your sailing orders. Cast off and depart for Manila in accordance therewith." No longer is the traveler gradually infiltrated into another continent as on a train but, like an astronaut, injected into it. High altitudes, pressurized cabins and PEDs (personal entertainment devices) make promenade decks superfluous — as are the captain's detours to look at elephant herds or basking sharks below. Travel by an unpressurised flying boat was long, slow, and deafening — but never boring. Travel has become as Paul Theroux wrote, only glamorous in retrospect.

Invented by Curtiss, flying boats, whether wood or metal, were a formidable achievement in aviation history, especially between the wars when landplanes did not have the range to cross oceans. The men who designed, built and bought these half-boat, half-planes — Curtiss, Dornier, Lindbergh, Trippe, Sikorsky, Gouge — had been born in the Edwardian era of steam locomotives and great ships — and their actions (obsessions?) for better or worse reflected that. Perhaps, like Othello, they loved not wisely, but too well. If, since Icarus, man's ambition was to fly like a bird, flying boats allowed him even greater freedom — to fly like geese, at home in both mediums, the sky and water.

In our present world, filled with hazard, especially for travel, flying boats have entered the realms of romantic aviation legend. We are fascinated because we will never experience a flying boat racing forward thunderously to break the suction, or the foaming green water cover the windows on take-off. Or that somewhere over the Pacific, a steward will serve us, all well-dressed diners, *filet mignon* with buttered peas and new potatoes from the steam table. The Qantas chief, Hudson Fysh, penned perhaps the best description of travel by flying boat: "Getting up out of his chair, a passenger could walk about and, if his seat was in the main cabin, stroll along to the smoking cabin for a smoke, stopping on the way at the promenade deck, with its high handrail and windows at eye level, to gaze at the world of cloud and sky outside, and at countryside or sea slipping away below at a steady 150 miles an hour. On the promenade deck there was also a practical, useable space where quoits or clock golf were played."

Would that be possible now?

Also by Peter Pigott

Brace for Impact: Air Crashes and Aviation Safety (2016)

Air Canada: The History (2014)

From Far and Wide: A Complete History of Canada's Arctic Sovereignty (2011)

Sailing Seven Seas: A History of the Canadian Pacific Line (2010)

Canada in Sudan: War Without Borders (2009)

Canada in Afghanistan: The War So Far (2007)

Royal Transport: An Inside Look at the History of British Royal Travel (2005)

On Canadian Wings: A Century of Flight (2004)

Wingwalkers: The Rise and Fall of Canada's Other Airline (2003)

Taming the Skies: A Celebration of Canadian Flight (2003)

Wings Across Canada: An Illustrated History of Canadian Aviation (2002)

National Treasure: The History of Trans Canada Airlines (2001)

Flying Canucks III: Famous Canadian Aviators (2000)

Wingwalkers: The Story of Canadian Airlines International (1998)

Flying Canucks II: Pioneers of Canadian Aviation (1997)

Flying Colours: A History of Commercial Aviation in Canada (1997)

Gateways: Airports of Canada (1996)

Hong Kong Rising: The History of a Remarkable Place (1995)

Flying Canucks: Famous Canadian Aviators (1994)

Kai Tak: The History of Aviation in Hong Kong (1988)

BIBLIOGRAPHY

BOOKS

Bender, Marilyn and Selig Altshul. *THE CHOSEN INSTRUMENT. Pan Am/ Juan Trippe. The Rise and Fall of an American Entrepreneur.* New York. Simon & Schuster, 1982.

Bercuson, David & Holger Herwig. *One Christmas in Washington.* Toronto. McArthur & Co. 2005.

Cassidy, Brian. *Flying Empires. Short 'C' class Empire flying boats.* Bath. Queens Parade Press, 2004.

Coster, Graham. *Corsairville. The Lost Domain of The Flying Boat.* Harmondsworth. The Penguin Group, 2000.

Davies, R.E.G & Robert Gand. *Skygods. The Fall of Pan Am.* Paladwr Press, 2000

Davies, *R.E.G. British Airways. An Airline and its Aircraft Vol 1. 1919-1939 The Imperial Years.* Paladwr Press, 2005.

Daley, Robert. *An American Saga. Juan Trippe and His Pan Am Empire.* Riviera Productions, 1980.

Dawson, Leslie. *Fabulous Flying Boats. A History of the World's Passenger Flying Boats.* Pen and Sword, Illustrated edition Sept. 19, 2013.

Follett, Ken. *Night over Water.* Penguin Books; Reprint edition, April 6, 2004.

Frater, Alexander. *Beyond the Blue Horizon.* Penguin Books, 1987

Gandt, Robert. *China Clipper. The Age of the Great Flying Boats.* Naval Institute Press, 2013

Hudson, Kenneth & Julian Pettifer. *Diamonds in The Sky. A Social History of Air Travel.* The Bodley Head, 1979

Knot, R. *The American Flying Boat. An Illustrated History.* Naval Institute Press, 1979

Serling, Robert J. Legend & Legacy. *The Story of Boeing and Its People.* New York. St. Martin's Press, 1992

Sims, Phillip E. *Adventurous Empires. The Story of the Short Empire Flying-boats.* Airlife England, 2000

Taylor, Michael J.H. *The Aerospace Chronology.* London, Tri-Service Press, 1989

Trautman, James. *Pan American Clippers. The Golden Age of Flying Boats.* Boston Mills Press, 2011.

Watson, Max. *The Man Who Made Pan Am.* CreateSpace Independent Publishing Platform, 2017

Wildenberg, Thomas & R.E.G. Davies. *Howard Hughes. An Airman, His Aircraft, and His Great Flights.* Paladwr Press, 2006

Wright, Carol. *Tables In The Sky.* London. W.H. Allen & Co. 1985,

Yenne, Bill. *The Story of the Boeing Company.* An AGS Works Book, Seattle, WA.

ARTICLES & WEBSITES

Susan Bolotin, New York Times, July 29, 1982.

Botwood Flying Boat Museum (Museum Association of Newfoundland)

John Borger. *When We Built the Transpacific Air Route* (Originally printed in the PAH F Clipper Newsletter), Spring 1995

Crash of a Boeing 314A Clipper off Lisbon. 24 killed. www.baaa-acro.com.

Grace Crile, Skyways to a Jungle Laboratory. An African Adventure New York. W.W. Norton, 1936.

https://www. evergreenmuseum. org/general-aviation - publicity@sprucegoose.org

Foynes Flying Boat and Aviation Museum. https://www.flyingboatmuseum.com/

Peter G. Masefield, Some Economic Factors in Air Transport Operation, Journal of the Institute of Transport, March 1951.

Wings versus The Trident. Famous Authority Says Britain's Future Greatness Lies In the Air. MacLean's Magazine, Sept 1,1925. p.12

Safety and Accommodation in European Passenger Planes, No. 3, New York, Daniel Guggenheim Fund for the Promotion of Aeronautics Inc., 1928, P. 29-30.

Alan McGregor. *Flying the Furrow.* Saudi Aramco World, March/April 2001, Pg. 24–31

Feature article #3 / Heritage Week 2009,11 February 2009, Govt. New Brunswick Home.

Lawrence Mahoney. *All He Wanted To Do Was Fly.* South Florida Sun Sentinel Oct. 25, 1987.

Adapted from H. Hobson, Eric Brazil From Above Expedition Magazine 60.3 (2018). Expedition Magazine. Penn Museum, 2018 .

M. Hindley. *Glamorous Crossing How Pan*

American Airways Dominated International Travel in the 1930s. Longreads, February, 2015.

Gordon Pirie. *Incidental tourism. British Imperial air travel in the 1930s.* Journal of Tourism History, 2009, 49-66.

Dieter Scholz. *Pan Am's Historic Contributions to Aircraft Cabin.* Hamburg University of Applied Sciences, German Aerospace Society, Hamburg Branch. Hamburg Aerospace Lecture Series 2017.

Gregory Votolato. *Transport Design. A Travel History.* Trowbridge. Cromwell Press, 2007. P. 180.

Vaughan Yarwood. *Wings Of Desire.* New Zealand Geographic, October–December 1998.

Stephan Wilkinson. *Flight of The River.* Phoenix Aviation History, March 2013,

Antonio Finns. *Sky Kings.* Sun Sentinel, Sept. 24, 2000

New Horizons, September 1941. Written by W.B. (Shorty) Greenough-Pan American Airways Chief Mechanic-Hong Kong

Voices of My Peers, a collection of experiences contributed by Pan American personnel, compiled by Eugene J.

Dunning, Clipper Press, 1996.

John A. Marshall. The Round The World Saga of the Pacific Clipper. https://www.panam.org/pan-am-inspirations/634-saga-of-the-pacific-clipper

M.McCarthy, J. Green, S. Jung and C. Souter. The Broome Flying Boats Report — Department of Maritime Archaeology, Western Australian Maritime Museum. No. 170. 2002

Alan McGregor. *By Flying Boat from Cairo To Southampton.* March–April 2001 Saudi Aramco World.

Brian Rix. *My Farce From My Elbow.* Secker & Warburg; 1975

John Stroud, Postwar Prop Liners Aeroplane Monthly, April 1993.

WHAT WAS IT LIKE TO FLY? Smithsonian National Air and Space Museum, https://airandspace.si.edu/exhibitions/hawaii-by-air/online/

Peter M. Bowers, Individual Boeing Clipper histories www.svsu.edu.archives.

Sam Weigel, Pan Am Clippers in Ireland. The glamorous era of the original transatlantic flights. flyingmag.com. November 19, 2019.